TRUE SCIENTISTS,
TRUE FAITH

TRUE SCIENTISTS, TRUE FAITH

Some of the world's leading scientists reveal the
harmony between their science and their faith

Edited by
R. J. Berry

MONARCH
BOOKS
Oxford, UK & Grand Rapids, Michigan, USA

Published by Monarch Books
an imprint of
Lion Hudson plc
Wilkinson House, Jordan Hill Road,
Oxford OX2 8DR, England
Email: monarch@lionhudson.com
www.lionhudson.com/monarch

ISBN 978 0 85721 540 6
e-ISBN 978 0 85721 541 3

First edition 2014

Acknowledgments

Scripture quotations, unless otherwise
stated, are taken from the *Holy Bible,
New International Version*, copyright
© 1973, 1978, 1984 International Bible
Society. Used by permission of Hodder
& Stoughton, a member of the Hodder
Headline Group. All rights reserved.
'NIV' is a trademark of International Bible
Society. UK trademark number 1448790.
Scripture quotations marked ESV are
from The Holy Bible, English Standard
Version® (ESV®) copyright © 2001 by
Crossway, a publishing ministry of Good
News Publishers. All rights reserved.
Scripture quotations marked KJV are
taken from The Authorized (King James)
Version. Rights in the Authorized Version
are vested in the Crown. Reproduced
by permission of the Crown's patentee,
Cambridge University Press.
Scripture quotations marked NASB are
taken from the New American Standard
Bible®, Copyright © 1960, 1962, 1963,
1968, 1971, 1972, 1973, 1975, 1977, 1995
by The Lockman Foundation. Used by
permission.
Scripture quotations marked REB are
taken from the Revised English Bible ©
Oxford University Press and Cambridge
University Press 1989.
Scripture quotations marked RSV are
from The Revised Standard Version of the
Bible copyright © 1346, 1952 and 1971 by
the Division of Christian Education of the
National Council of Churches in the USA.
Used by permission. All Rights Reserved.
pp. 114, 120–21: Extract from *Mere
Christianity* by C. S. Lewis copyright © C.
S. Lewis Pte. Ltd. 1942, 1943, 1944, 1952.
Reprinted by permission of The C. S.
Lewis Company.
pp. 9, 17, 184, 185: Extract from *The
Limits of Science* by Peter Medawar
copyright © 1988, Peter Medawar.
Reprinted by permission of Oxford
University Press.
p. 19: Extract from *The Selfish Gene*
by Richard Dawkins copyright ©
2006, Richard Dawkins. Reprinted by
permission of Oxford University Press.
p. 23: Extract from *Models and Mystery*
by Ian T. Ramsey copyright © 1964 Ian
T. Ramsey. Reprinted by permission of
Oxford University Press.
p. 150: Quotation from Richard Holloway
reprinted by permission of United Agents.

A catalogue record for this book is
available from the British Library

Printed and bound in the UK, September
2014, LH26

This book is dedicated to the memory of

OLIVER BARCLAY (1919-2013)

Zoologist and Christian

Founder and Long-time Secretary of Christians in Science

Founding Editor of the Journal *Science & Christian Belief*

The life and contributions of Oliver Barclay are described in *Science & Christian Belief*, **26**: 83-88, 2014

RIEKE

Contents

Foreword		9
1.	*Alister McGrath:* Science, Faith, and Making Sense of Things	12
2.	*John Houghton:* A God Big Enough	28
3.	*Andrew Briggs:* And Information Became Physical	39
4.	*Chris Done:* From Spock to the Supernatural	54
5.	*Colin Humphreys:* Can Science and Christianity Both Be True?	64
6.	*Simon Stuart:* Reflections of a Christian Working in Science and Conservation	86
7.	*Francis Collins:* What Do *You* Believe, Doctor?	104
8.	*Ghillean Prance:* A Talent for Science	136
9.	*Monty Barker:* Man – Dust with a Destiny	148
10.	*John Wood:* From Nanotechnology to Macro-Organizations – Engineering Atoms and More	162
11.	*Andy Gosler:* Surprise and the Value of Life	176
12.	*Jennifer Wiseman:* Inspired by the Heavens	196
13.	*Sam Berry:* Genes, Genesis and Greens	210
14.	*John Wyatt:* No Easy Answers	225
15.	*Bob White:* Earthquakes, Volcanoes, and Other Catastrophes	239
16.	*Simon Conway Morris:* One Impossible Thing Before Breakfast: Evolution and Christianity	255
17.	*David Raffaelli:* Inconvenient Truths	276
18.	*Denis Alexander:* A Different Drum-beat	288

19. *Rosalind Picard:* Building Technology with Emotion   308

20. *Donald MacKay:* Science and Christian Faith Today   322

Suggestions for Further Reading   344

Index of Bible References   347

Index of Bible References   348

Foreword

There is a widespread assumption that science has somehow "disproved" the truth of religion; that belief in God is no more than an insurance policy for people wanting some sort of existence after their present life. A band of "new atheists" trumpets that there is no God and those who claim there is one are intellectually delusional. Darwin's friend, Thomas Huxley, proclaimed: "Extinguished theologians lie about the cradle of every science as the strangled snakes beside that of Hercules; and history records that whenever science and orthodoxy have been fairly opposed, the latter has been forced to retire from the lists, bleeding and crushed if not annihilated; scotched, if not slain."

Unhappily for those who propagate such ideas, the evidence is firmly against them. As Nobel Prize winner Peter Medawar (a non-believer) said, "there is no limit upon the power of science to answer questions of the kind that science *can* answer", *but that science has "limits is shown by the existence of questions that science cannot answer and that no conceivable advances of science would empower it to answer… it is not possible to derive from the axioms and postulates of Euclid a theorem to do with how to cook an omelette or bake a cake." He concluded: "science should not be expected to provide solutions to problems such as the purpose of life or the existence of God" (*The Limits of Science*, Oxford University Press, 1984).

A compelling response to doubters about the compatibility of science and belief is the existence of many scientists who accept and witness to an orthodox religious faith. This book is direct evidence from such people. It contains the testimonies of twenty leading scientists, all of national and some of international renown. Fifteen of them have been lightly revised from their previous publication in *Real Science, Real Faith* (1991) or *Real Scientists, Real Faith* (2009), but both books are out of print and feedback of their impact has suggested it is worth making them available again. Five chapters (by Chris Done, Rosalind Picard, Jennifer Wiseman, David Raffaelli and John Wood) are new in this volume.

In a Foreword to *Real Science, Real Faith*, Philip Hacking (then Chairman of the Keswick Convention) wrote: "This book will be a tremendous help and encouragement to scientists who may be going through a struggle in their pilgrimage. It will confirm faith in a totally honest way. It is equally prescribed reading for non-scientists who need to understand the tensions that can arise and the process through which faith is strengthened in the mind and life of Christians."

This commendation applies just as much to this enlarged edition. There is a tradition that God wrote a Book of Words (the Bible), but also a Book of Works (Creation); the Books have the same author, but are written in very different languages. Science is the study of creation; to understand God's purposes fully we need to read both his books.

The only essay in this collection which is not a personal story is the last, by Donald MacKay, engineer turned brain investigator. He was one of the most incisive science–faith thinkers of recent generations. He emphasized that scientific and divine (or metaphysical) accounts may be complementary: knowing the physical "cause" of any event does not mean that we know all there is to know about it. The "cause" of water boiling in a kettle is due to the motion of the water molecules, but another cause could well be my desire for a hot drink. There is no conflict between the two "causes". In the same way, a scientist studying creation – whether at the nano, the molecular, the organismal or the ecosystem level – can rejoice in that he or she may also be discovering something about God's work, or in Johannes

Kepler's well-known phrase, "thinking God's thoughts after him". It is "by faith we understand that the universe was formed at God's command" (Hebrews 11:3), but that does not mean we cannot discover something about the methods he used. It is the responsibility of scientists who are Christians to demonstrate the shallowness of those who ignore the multifaceted nature of causation. Properly understood, science is an encouragement to faith, not a barrier.

Chapter 1

Science, Faith, and Making Sense of Things

Alister McGrath was born in Belfast and was a convinced atheist until going to university. He read Chemistry at the University of Oxford and earned a DPhil in Biochemistry before switching to Theology and subsequently being awarded a Doctorate in Divinity and a Doctorate of Letters. He served as Oxford University's Professor of Historical Theology from 1999 to 2008, before moving to King's College London as Professor of Theology, Ministry, and Education until 2014. He is presently Andreas Idreos Professor of Science and Religion at Oxford. He has written widely on the relationship between science and the Christian faith, including two widely read critiques of the ideas of Richard Dawkins – *Dawkins' God* (2004) and *The Dawkins Delusion* (2007). His most recent book is *Emil Brunner: An Appraisal* (2014).

Real scientists do not believe in God! This sound bite will be depressingly familiar to those who have struggled through the endless digressions, exaggerations and misunderstandings found in Richard Dawkins' *God Delusion* (2006). It is a viewpoint that can only be sustained by the relentless use of selective attention and turbo-charged shock-and-awe rhetoric, rather than evidence-based argument. Yet it is a view that many in Western culture seem prepared to accept as the wisdom of our age. As Karl Marx once pointed out, the constant repetition of something that is fundamentally untrue creates the impression that it is trustworthy and reliable.

Dawkins seems to regard the intrinsic atheism of the natural sciences as self-evidently true to all except those who are congenital idiots, or whose minds have been warped and infested by the debilitating notion that there exists a God who might be interested in us and our wellbeing. Perhaps this may help us understand his anger, intolerance and arrogance at the persistence – some would say resurgence – of belief in God, when the secularizing prophets of the late 1960s and early 1970s foretold its inevitable death.

Dawkins is modest in the provision of autobiographical detail. However, if I have understood his account of his own conversion to atheism, the pivotal element of the process was a growing belief that Darwinism offered a far superior account of the nature of the world than anything based on an appeal to God. Dawkins' discovery of Darwinism began during his time as a student at Oundle School, and was consolidated during his study of zoology at Oxford University. The natural sciences thus acted as a catalyst for his deconversion from what appears to have been a somewhat anaemic form of nominal Anglicanism.

Now, all of us are prone to see our own personal histories as somehow disclosing a broader pattern of things, or the deep structure of reality. Beliefs that we personally find to be compelling must be so for all. Unsurprisingly, those who don't fit the pattern are seen as dangerous. They tend to get dismissed as oddballs, idiots, or psychotics. Why? Precisely because they are a threat to the credibility of the simplistic creed they refuse to accept. For what Dawkins regards as a universal, normative pattern is nothing more than one possible intellectual option among several, each of which have found their supporters over the years. In this essay, I shall tell my own story, and leave it for my readers to decide whether it has wider significance.

My love affair with the natural sciences began when I was nine or ten. I was overwhelmed with the beauty of the night sky, and longed to explore it further. I ransacked my school library for books on astronomy, and even managed to build myself a small telescope to enable me to observe the moons of Jupiter. Around the same time, a great-uncle who had headed up the pathology department at the Royal Victoria Hospital, Belfast, gave me an old German microscope, which allowed me to explore another new world. It still sits on my study desk, a reminder of the power of nature to enthral, intrigue, and provoke questions.

One of those questions troubled me greatly. While in my teens, I had absorbed an uncritical atheism from writers such as Bertrand Russell. Atheism was, I believed, the natural resting place for a scientifically informed person, such as myself. The natural sciences had expanded to inhabit the intellectual space once occupied by the derelict idea of God. There was no need to propose, let alone take seriously, such an outmoded idea. God was a baleful relic of the past, revealed as a delusion by scientific advance.

So what was life all about? What was its meaning? As I reflected on the scope and power of the sciences, I gradually came to the view that there was no meaning to life. I was the accidental by-product of blind cosmic forces, the inhabitant of a universe in which one could speak only of direction but not purpose. It was not a particularly appealing idea, but I found solace in the idea that its bleakness and austerity were certain indications of its truth. It was so unattractive that it just had to be right. I must confess to a certain degree of smugness at this point, and a feeling of intellectual superiority over those who found solace and satisfaction in their belief in God.

Yet questions remained. As I continued to examine the night sky, I found its silence disturbing. I used to enjoy looking through my small telescope at M31, a famous nebula in the constellation of Andromeda which is bright enough to be seen by the naked eye. I knew that it was so distant that the light now leaving the nebula would take 2 million years to reach earth. By that time, I would have died. The night sky thus became a sombre symbol of the troubling brevity of human life. What was the point of it? Tennyson's lines from "The Brook" seemed to sum up the human situation:

For men may come and men may go,
But I go on for ever.

However, I remained obstinately convinced that the severity and dreariness of this position were confirmations of its truth. It was axiomatic that science demanded atheism, and I was willing to be led wherever science took me.

And so I continued working at mathematics, physics and chemistry, eventually winning a scholarship to Oxford University to study chemistry. At that stage, most people gained admission to Oxford in the seventh term of the sixth form. I learned that I had won a scholarship to Oxford in December 1970, but was not due to begin my studies until October 1971. What was I to do in between? Most of my friends left school in order to travel or earn some money. I decided to stay on, and use the time to learn German and Russian, both of which would be useful for my scientific studies. Having specialized in the physical sciences, I was also aware of the need to deepen my knowledge of biology. I therefore settled down to begin an extended period of reading and reflection.

After a month or so of intensive reading in the school science library, having exhausted the works on biology, I came across a section that I had never noticed before. It was labelled "The History and Philosophy of Science", and was heavy with dust. I had little time for this sort of stuff, tending to regard it as uninformed criticism of the certainties and simplicities of the natural sciences by those who felt threatened by them. Philosophy, like theology, was just pointless speculation about issues that could be solved through a few decent experiments. What was the point? Yet by the time I had finished reading the somewhat meagre holdings of the school in this field, I realized that I needed to do some very serious rethinking. Far from being half-witted obscurantism that placed unnecessary obstacles in the relentless path of scientific advance, the history and philosophy of science asked all the right questions about the reliability and limits of scientific knowledge. And they were questions that I had not faced thus far. Issues such as the under-determination of theory by data, radical theory change in the history of science, the difficulties in devising a "crucial experiment", and the enormously complex issues associated with devising what was the "best explanation" of a given set of observations crowded in on me, muddying what I had taken to be the clear, still, and above all *simple* waters of scientific truth.

Things turned out to be rather more complicated than I had realized. My eyes had been opened, and I knew there was no going back to the simplistic take on the sciences I had once known and enjoyed. I had enjoyed the beauty and innocence of a childlike attitude to the sciences, and secretly wished to remain in that secure place. Indeed, I think that part of me deeply wished that I had never picked up that book, never asked those awkward questions, and never questioned the simplicities of my scientific youth. But there was no going back. I had stepped through a door, and could not escape the new world I now inhabited.

By the time I arrived in Oxford in October 1971, I had realized that I had a lot of rethinking to do. Up to that point, I had assumed that, when science could not answer a question, there was no answer to be had. I now began to realize that there might be limits to the scientific method, and that vast expanses of intellectual, aesthetic and moral territory might lie beyond its compass. I would later find this idea expressed by Peter Medawar, in his excellent *The Limits of Science* (1984). Emphasizing that "science is incomparably the most successful enterprise human beings have ever engaged upon", Medawar distinguished between what he termed "transcendent" questions, which are better left to religion and metaphysics, and scientific questions about the organization and structure of the material universe. With regard to these latter, he argued, there are no limits to the possibilities of scientific achievement. So what about the question of God? Or of whether there is purpose within the universe? Medwar was clear: science cannot answer such questions, even thought there may be answers to be found:

> *That there is indeed a limit upon science is made very likely by the existence of questions that science cannot answer, and that no conceivable advance of science would empower it to answer... I have in mind such questions as:*
>> *How did everything begin?*
>> *What are we all here for?*
>> *What is the point of living?*

I could no longer hold on to what I now realize was a somewhat naïve scientific positivism; it became clear to me that a whole series of questions that I had dismissed as meaningless or pointless had to be examined again – including the God-question.

Having set to one side my rather dogmatic belief that science necessarily entailed atheism, I began to realize that the natural world is conceptually malleable. Nature can be interpreted, without any loss of intellectual integrity, in a number of different ways. Some "read" or "interpret" nature in an atheistic way. Others "read" it in a deistic way, seeing it as pointing to a creator-divinity, who is no longer involved in its affairs. God winds up the clock, then leaves it to work on its own. Others take a more specifically Christian view, believing in a God who both creates and sustains. One can be a "real" scientist without being committed to any specific religious, spiritual or anti-religious view of the world. This, I may add, is the view of most scientists I speak to, including those who self-define as atheists. Unlike their more dogmatic atheist colleagues, they can understand perfectly well why some of their colleagues adopt a Christian view of the world. They may not agree with that approach, but they're prepared to respect it.

Stephen Jay Gould, whose sad death from cancer in 2002 robbed Harvard University of one of its most stimulating teachers, and a popular scientific readership of one of its most accessible writers, was absolutely clear on this point.[1] The natural sciences – including evolutionary theory – were consistent with both atheism and conventional religious belief. Unless half his scientific colleagues were total fools – a presumption that Gould rightly dismissed as nonsense, whichever half it is applied to – there could be no other responsible way of making sense of the varied responses to reality on the part of the intelligent, informed, people that he knew.

The real problem is that, since the scientific method clearly does not entail atheism, those who wish to use science in defence of atheism are obliged to smuggle in a series of non-empirical metaphysical ideas to their accounts of science, and hope that nobody notices this intellectual sleight of hand. Dawkins is a master of this art. In his superb recent study *The Music of Life*,[2] the Oxford systems biologist Denis Noble took a passage from Dawkins's *The Selfish Gene*,[3] and rewrote it, retaining what was empirically verifiable, and inverting Dawkins' somewhat questionable metaphysical assumptions. The result dramatically illustrates the ease with which non-empirical assumptions can be imported into scientific thinking.

First, consider Dawkins' original passage, which sets out a gene-centred approach to evolutionary biology, which was then gaining the ascendancy. Note how agency is attributed to genes, which are portrayed as actively controlling their destiny. I have emphasized what is empirically verifiable:

> *[Genes] swarm in huge colonies, safe inside gigantic lumbering robots, sealed off from the outside world, communicating with it by tortuous indirect routes, manipulating it by remote control. **They are in you and me**; they created us, body and mind; and their preservation is the ultimate rationale for our existence.*

In rewriting this, Noble moves away from any idea that genes can be thought of as active agents. Once more, I have emphasized what is empirically verifiable:

> *[Genes] are trapped in huge colonies, locked inside highly intelligent beings, moulded by the outside world, communicating with it by complex processes, through which, blindly, as if by magic, function emerges. **They are in you and me**; we are the system that allows their code to be read; and their preservation is totally dependent on the joy that we experience in reproducing ourselves. We are the ultimate rationale for their existence.*

Dawkins and Noble see things in completely different ways. (I recommend reading both statements slowly and carefully to appreciate their differences.) They both cannot be right. Both smuggle in a series of quite different values and beliefs. Yet their statements are "empirically equivalent". In other words, they both have equally good grounding in observation and experimental evidence. So which is right? Which is the more scientific? How could we decide which is to be preferred on scientific grounds? As Noble observes – and Dawkins concurs – "no-one seems to be able to think of an experiment that would detect an empirical difference between them."

Let me return to explaining my own change of mind on the relation of science and faith. Having realized that a love of science allowed much greater freedom of interpretation of reality than I had been led to believe, I began to explore alternative ways of looking at it. While I had been severely critical of Christianity as a young man, I had never extended that same critical evaluation to atheism, tending to assume that it was self-evidently correct, and was hence exempt from being assessed in this way. During October and November 1971, I began to discover that the intellectual case for atheism was rather less substantial than I had supposed. Far from being self-evidently true, it seemed to rest on rather shaky foundations. Christianity, on the other hand, turned out to be far more robust intellectually than I had supposed.

My doubts about the intellectual foundations of atheism began to coalesce into a realization that atheism was actually a belief system, where I had somewhat naïvely and uncritically assumed that it was a factual statement about reality. I also discovered that I knew far less about Christianity than I had assumed. It gradually became clear to me that I had rejected a religious stereotype. I had some major rethinking to do. By the end of November 1971, I had made my decision: I turned my back on one faith, and embraced another.

It did not take me long to begin to appreciate the intellectual capaciousness of the Christian faith. Not merely was it well grounded; it was also intellectually enabling and enriching. Here was a lens, which enabled reality to be brought into sharp focus. The Christian faith both made sense in itself, and made sense of things as a whole. "I believe in Christianity as I believe that the sun has risen, not only because I see it, but because by it I see everything else" (C. S. Lewis). I suddenly found that the entire scientific enterprise made a lot more sense than I had ever appreciated. It was as if an intellectual sun had risen and illuminated the scientific landscape, allowing me to see details and interconnections that I would otherwise have missed altogether.

In September 1974, I joined the research group of Professor Sir George Radda, based in Oxford University's Department of Biochemistry. Radda was then developing a series of physical methods for investigating complex biological systems, including magnetic resonance approaches. My particular interest was developing innovative physical methods for studying the behaviour of biological membranes, which eventually extended to include techniques as different as the use of fluorescent probes and antimatter decay to study temperature-dependent transitions in biological systems.

But my real interest was shifting elsewhere. I never lost my fascination with the natural world. I just found something else rising, initially to rival it, and then to complement it. What I had once assumed to be the open warfare of science and religion increasingly seemed to me to represent a critical yet constructive synergy, with immense potential for intellectual enrichment. How, I found myself wondering, might the working methods and assumptions of the natural sciences be used to develop an intellectually robust Christian theology? And what should I do to explore this possibility properly?

In the event, I decided that I could best achieve this goal by ceasing active scientific research, and becoming a theologian. I was, however, determined that I would be a theologian who was up to date in his reading of the scientific literature, especially in the field of evolutionary biology, and who actively sought to relate my science and my faith. I had no time for the "God of the Gaps" approach, which sought to defend the existence of God by an appeal to gaps in scientific explanation. While an undergraduate at Wadham, I had come to know Charles Coulson (1910–74), Oxford University's first professor of theoretical chemistry, who was a vigorous critic of this approach. For Coulson, reality as a whole demanded explanation. "Either God is in the whole of Nature, with no gaps, or He's not there at all."

I increasingly came to the view that the explicability of nature was itself astonishing, and required explanation. As Albert Einstein pointed out in 1936, "the eternal mystery of the world is its comprehensibility." For Einstein, explicability itself clearly requires explanation. The most incomprehensible thing about the universe is that it is comprehensible. The intelligibility of the natural world, demonstrated by the natural sciences, raises the fundamental question as to why there is such a fundamental resonance between human minds and the structures of the universe.

As I reflected on the cognitive implications of the Christian faith, I came to see that it offered a "big picture" account of things, which allowed us to make sense of what we observed in everyday life, and especially in scientific explanation. "Religious faith", wrote William James (1842–1910) with his characteristic insight, is basically "faith in the existence of an unseen order of some kind in which the riddles of the natural order may be found and explained." Human beings long to make sense of things – to identify patterns in the rich fabric of nature, to offer explanations for what happens around them, and to reflect on the meaning of their lives. It is as if our intellectual antennae are tuned to discern clues to purpose and meaning around us, built into the structure of the world. "The pursuit of discovery," the chemist-turned-philosopher Michael Polanyi (1891–1976) noted, is "guided by sensing the presence of a hidden reality toward which our clues are pointing."

This led me to take a second step, moving away from the idea that one can "prove" the existence of God from the natural world. Rather, I came to see that the key point is that there is a high degree of intellectual resonance between the Christian vision of reality and what we actually observe. The Christian faith offers an "empirical fit" with the real world. This notion of "empirical fit" was explored theologically by the Oxford mathematician and philosopher of religion Ian T. Ramsey (1915–72), who stated it as follows:

> The theological model works more like the fitting of a boot or a shoe than like the "yes" or "no" of a roll call. In other words, we have a particular doctrine which, like a preferred and selected shoe, starts by appearing to meet our empirical needs. But on closer fitting to the phenomena the shoe may pinch. When tested against future slush and rain it may be proven to be not altogether water-tight or it may be comfortable – yet it must not be too comfortable. In this way, the test of a shoe is measured by its ability to match a wide range of phenomena, by its overall success in meeting a variety of needs. Here is what I might call the method of empirical fit which is displayed by theological theorizing.

This is a fundamentally empirical notion, originating within the natural sciences, which Ramsey believed – rightly, in my view – had considerable theological potential.

This led me to consider the apologetic possibilities of the natural sciences. I became interested in the field of natural theology, which I understood, not as an attempt to deduce the existence of God from a cold, detached observation of nature, but rather as the enterprise of seeing nature from the standpoint of faith, so that it is viewed, interpreted and appreciated with

Christian spectacles. Events and entities within nature are thus not held to "prove", but to be consonant with, the existence of God. What is observed within the natural order resonates with the core themes of the Christian vision of God.

An example is provided by the doctrine of creation set out in the writings of Augustine of Hippo (354–430), unquestionably the most respected and widely cited theologian in Western Christianity. Augustine does not translate his theological principles into explicit scientific statements, even though at times his statements reflect the prevailing consensus of his era. Rather, Augustine bequeathed to his successors a set of theological principles concerning the Christian doctrine of creation that are capable of provisional correlation with the scientific worldview of our own day.

Augustine interweaves biblical interpretation, an appeal to "right reason", and a knowledge of contemporary science in his theological reflections concerning creation, which can be summarized as follows:

1. God brought everything into being at a specific moment.

2. Part of that created order takes the form of embedded causalities which emerge or evolve at a later stage.

3. This process of development takes place within the context of God's providential direction, which is integrally connected to a right understanding of the concept of creation.

4. The image of a dormant seed is an appropriate, but not exact, analogy for these embedded causalities.

5. The process of generation of these dormant seeds results in the fixity of biological forms.

The first of these points is significant. God, Augustine insists, could not be considered to have brought the creation into being at a certain definite moment in time, as if "time" itself existed prior to creation, or as if creation took place at a definite moment in a chronological continuum. For Augustine, time itself must be seen as an aspect of the created order, to be contrasted with the timelessness which he held to be the essential feature of eternity. Augustine thus speaks of the creation of time (or "creation *with* time"), rather than envisaging the act of creation as taking place in time. Time is a constituent characteristic of the domain of the created, which remains dependent upon its creator. "We speak of 'before' and 'after' in the relationship of creatures, although everything in the creative act of God is simultaneous." There is no concept of a period intervening before creation, nor an infinitely extended period which corresponds to "eternity". Eternity is timeless; time is an aspect of the created order. This fits remarkably well with contemporary cosmological theory, which insists that time and space both came into being in the primordial cosmic event usually referred to as the "big bang".

The first four of these points are all derived from Augustine's reading of Scripture; the fifth is what seemed to be a self-evident truth to Augustine, in the light of his personal experience and the contemporary scientific consensus. Augustine's espousal of the fixity of species is best seen as a provisional judgment of experience, not a fixed statement of theological interpretation. As Augustine himself constantly and consistently emphasized, there is a danger of making biblical interpretation dependent on contemporary scientific opinion, leaving its outcome vulnerable when today's consensus is replaced with tomorrow's.

My point is that, rather than suggesting that God offers an explanation of what the natural sciences are currently unable to explain, we ought to emphasize the importance of belief in God in explaining the "big picture" – that is to say, the overall patterns of ordering which are discerned within the universe.

The British philosopher of religion Richard Swinburne insists that the explanatory aspects of theism are not limited to the fine details of reality, but extend far beyond these to embrace the great questions of life – those things that are either "too big" or "too odd" for science to explain. The reliability of such explanations is, of course, open to challenge; there is, however, no doubt that such explanations are being offered, and are seen as important.

An obvious example of "big" and "odd" things about the universe that seem to demand an explanation are what are now widely described as "phenomena". The language of "fine-tuning" has increasingly been found appropriate to express the idea that the universe appears to have possessed certain qualities from the moment of its inception for the production of intelligent life on Earth at this point in cosmic history, capable of reflecting on the implications of its existence. Nature's fundamental constants turn out to possess reassuringly life-friendly values. The existence of carbon-based life on Earth depends upon a delicate balance of physical and cosmological forces and parameters, which are such that were any one of these quantities to be slightly altered, the balance would be destroyed and life would not exist. While these phenomena do not represent a "proof" of the existence of a creator God, they are clearly consistent with the view of God encountered and practised within the Christian faith. The observation of anthropic phenomena thus resonates with the core themes of the Christian vision of reality.

Yet my deepest intuition about the relation of science and faith is that theology has much to learn from the working methods and assumptions of the natural sciences. In a major three-volumed work entitled *A Scientific Theology* (2001–3), I set out a vision of how Christian theology could benefit from the intellectual rigour of the sciences. Throughout the centuries, Christian theology has engaged with a series of conversation partners, ranging from Platonism to existentialism. The slightly condescending phrase *ancilla theologiae* ("handmaid of theology") is sometimes used to refer to this process of intellectual engagement and enrichment. In my view, the natural sciences have a key role to play in catalysing the development of Christian theology, and I hope to be able to play a small part in encouraging this development.

I myself owe an enormous amount to scientists who, like Charles Coulson, set out to integrate their faith and work. There is huge potential for intellectual synergy. It is my hope that many active scientists will catch something of this vision, and come to appreciate the importance of their faith for informing and energizing their work – and passing on this vision to their students and colleagues.

Notes

1. Gould, S. J. (1999), *Rocks of Ages*, Ballantine.
2. Noble, D. (2006), *The Music of Life*, Oxford University Press.
3. Dawkins, R. (1976), *The Selfish Gene*, Oxford University Press.

Chapter 2
A God Big Enough

Sir John T. Houghton, CBE, DPhil, FRS. Educated at Rhyl Grammar School and Jesus College, Oxford. Professor of Atmospheric Physics, Oxford University, 1976–83. Director-General (later Chief Executive) of the Meteorological Office, 1983–91. President of the Royal Meteorological Society, 1976–78. Chairman of the Scientific Assessment of Intergovernmental Panel on Climate Change (awarded the Nobel Peace Prize, 2007), 1988–2002, and of the Royal Commission on Environmental Pollution, 1992–98. Awarded Japan Prize, 2006. Author of *Does God Play Dice?* (1988), *Global Warming* (4th ed., 2009), *The Search for God: Can Science Help?* (1995), and an autobiography, *In the Eye of the Storm* (2013).

When people discover that I am involved with weather forecasting and also that I am a Christian, I am often asked if I believe that there is any point in praying about the weather – praying for rain, for instance, when it is badly needed. I reply that I believe it is entirely sensible and meaningful to pray about the weather as, indeed, it is to pray about other things. But I also say that my belief in the meaningfulness of prayer in no way alters my determination as a scientist to develop the very best means of weather forecasting, nor does it cause me to doubt that the behaviour of weather systems follows deterministic scientific laws.

One of the outstanding successes of science over the last thirty years has been that of weather prediction through the use of computer models of the atmospheric circulation. Let me explain how these models are employed in what is called numerical weather prediction. First of all, observations of the state of the atmosphere over the globe are received from orbiting satellites, from balloons, from ships, from automatic recording stations and from conventional land stations. These are brought together every twelve hours to make the best description possible of the atmosphere's state at that time. Starting from the initial state, the computer solves the appropriate equations of motion and produces a forecast for the whole globe for ten or more days ahead; for this task the largest and fastest computer available is required.

Meteorologists have no doubt that the atmosphere is basically a deterministic system; in other words, that the atmosphere's future behaviour is determined by its present state and by the laws of physics. This does not mean that weather prediction can ever become an exact science. One of the main reasons for this is that the atmosphere is what is known as a chaotic system – a technical term for a system in which developments occur which are extremely sensitive to the initial conditions.

For the atmosphere, the implications of "chaos" are such that, as Edward Lorenz, one of the world's leading meteorologists, has explained,[1] the flapping of a butterfly's wings somewhere in the atmosphere can have a noticeable effect on weather developments thousands of miles away. No conceivable observing system could record the atmosphere in that sort of detail. Not only are there practical limits to our ability to measure and observe, there are also fundamental limits. Meteorologists have a great deal to learn about the science of "chaos" and its implications for predictability. Our current expectation is that we have a good chance of predicting the general pattern of climate change which might occur over the next hundred years or so due to man's activities – for instance, through the burning of fossil fuels – but that our ability to forecast detailed weather cannot extend to more than perhaps two weeks.

My belief, on the one hand, in the reality of prayer and, on the other, in the scientific study of the material world as a deterministic system may seem at first to be contradictory. At best, it may seem that my life as a scientist and my religious life are in separate compartments. This, however, is not the case. It is very important to me that the two strands of my life, as a scientist and as a Christian, are brought together side by side and, so far as it is possible, intertwined. How, therefore, can the idea, on the one hand, that God is active in the world and, on the other, that events are governed by scientific laws be reconciled? The clue, I believe, is in making God big enough. To do that it is necessary to really stretch our ideas and imagination. I believe science can help in this.

Think, for instance, about the universe and its utterly fantastic size and complexity. Planet earth is one of the smaller planets orbiting around a modest-sized star we call the sun. The sun is just one of 100 billion (10^{11}) stars in the galaxy to which it belongs; some of the brightest of these stars we see in the Milky Way. Within the whole universe there are upwards of a billion (10^9) galaxies. To travel to our sun 150 million kilometres away would take just 8 minutes if travelling at the speed of light. To reach the edge of the galaxy would take 100,000 years, and to reach the edge of the universe, if that were possible, about 10 billion (10^{10}) years. These are completely mind-boggling numbers.

As astronomers have probed the universe with their telescopes – optical and radio telescopes on the ground, X-ray, ultra-violet and infra-red telescopes out in space – they have been able to discover a great deal about the processes going on in the stars, the galaxies and the space in between. Many new objects have been identified: quasars, pulsars and black holes. One of the remarkable features of this story of discovery is that the physical laws which govern what is going on in widely different parts of the universe are the same physical laws which describe events here on earth. In fact, a major achievement of modern science has been the way in which it has been possible to apply the physics of the very smallest components of matter (which are as many orders of magnitude smaller than us as the universe is larger) to reach some understanding of what is known as the Big Bang – that singular event over 10 billion years ago from which the expansion of the universe began.

A similar and perhaps even more remarkable story can be told about the structure of life, with the many complex and interdependent molecules that make up even the simplest living cell. Although there remains a tremendous amount to learn about many parts of these scientific stories, all of us, scientists and laymen alike, cannot fail to be impressed with the vastness, the complexity, the intricacy and the order of it all.

We all know what it means to create something – a painting, a three-course meal, a computer programme – we are creating all the time. Just try to imagine the skill and power of the One who has conceived and created the universe and who continues to maintain it in being. He is the God we are trying to think about. The size, the complexity, the beauty and the order we find in the universe are expressions of the greatness, the beauty and the orderliness of the Creator.

How does all this tie up with the scientific description of the world and the laws which we deduce from the description? The conflict which is often thought to be present between the scientific description and the description of God as Creator arises, I believe, from a misunderstanding of what both descriptions are about. Rather than a conflict, there is a close connection; the order and consistency we find in our science can be seen as reflecting orderliness and consistency in the character of God himself.

Created along with the universe is its framework of space and time. This means that when we think of the Creator we think of him as being outside the space and time dimensions of our world and our experience. That does not mean, as some suggest, that God is not present and active in the world; but it does mean that he is not confined by it. Because God's activity continually pervades the world, I do not like to talk about God intervening in our world. Although he may seem to be in some events more than others, he is in a real sense present with us all the time.

In the Gospels we find Jesus emphasizing God's control over the world and God's concern for even the smallest events. A sparrow cannot fall to the ground without our heavenly Father's knowledge (Matthew 10:29). Jesus encouraged his followers to look at events and circumstances in terms of God's activity. He chided the Pharisees, the religious leaders of the day, for their blindness. When they wanted to forecast the weather, their interpretation of the sky was quite good, he told them, but their interpretation of the events of the times was seriously lacking (Matthew 16:3). In other words, their meteorological science was effective, but they were blind towards any appreciation of God's activity in the world.

As a Christian believer, therefore, I am looking for more than scientific order and consistency in the world and the events that surround me. Because I believe that God is also a Person who is concerned about the people he has created and is therefore concerned even about me and my small world, I am looking for evidence of God's activity in these events and circumstances. I am also looking for answers to my prayers. As I have argued in more detail elsewhere,[2] I believe that God is big enough to provide this double order and consistency. On the one hand, we can look for order and consistency in the scientific description of events, and on the other hand, for order and consistency in a description of those events in terms of God's activity.

It is on the subject of answers to prayer that the sceptic can be at his most critical. Christians seem to argue that God always answers their prayers even if such argument flies in the face of the facts. They pray for healing, for instance. If recovery occurs, that is a positive answer. If it does not, God still answers; he knows, they say, what is best. How, in the face of such blind faith, the sceptic will exclaim, is it possible to establish objective facts in a scientific manner? Is not the Christian indulging in a heavy dose of wishful thinking?

To question in this manner, however, is to misunderstand the nature of prayer. Prayer is not going to God with a shopping list. It is not looking for magic, rubbing the lamp and making wishes. God is not a great impersonal potentate, nor a grand Santa Claus, but he is a Person with whom we human beings can form a relationship. The exercise of prayer is the means whereby that relationship is developed. A model which Christians find helpful for that relationship is that of us as God's children communicating with him as our Father. A child is constantly asking for things. Because the child does not understand enough of his needs to know what is good for him, his father will grant some of his requests and not grant others. We can expect and want God to treat our prayers in a similar way.

Prayer is not something I find easy; I sometimes envy those much more pious in disposition than I to whom it seems to be second nature. But it is an activity which, like many things we do, becomes more real and meaningful with practice. The practice of prayer has various forms. Let me divide them into the formal and the informal. Formal prayer is presented by groups of Christians meeting together for worship in church or elsewhere. I also engage in more or less formal prayer when my wife and I each day have a short prayer time when we commit to God particular problems or the needs of particular people. I also attempt to practise more or less formal prayer on my own, although that is a discipline I cannot say I have mastered. Informal prayer I define as the bringing to God, often very briefly and without it being in any way obvious to others who may be around, a particular need, a problem of the moment or a special expression of gratitude or thanks. That sort of prayer is very important to me, not only because I find it a source of strength in the stress and tumble of everyday living, but also because it is an important way in which my faith is integrated with and woven into the rest of my life. It is probably the sort of prayer to which the apostle Paul was referring when he urged the readers of the Epistle to the Thessalonians to pray without ceasing (1 Thessalonians 5:17).

Those who are engaged in full-time Christian work often speak of answers to prayer which have come through unusual events. Over a number of years I was closely involved with the setting up of a residential centre in Oxford for students from overseas. To those of us involved it seemed a very Christian enterprise for which it was entirely appropriate to ask for God's help. And help came. Money came in from unexpected sources just when it was needed. A surprising property for which we had been negotiating but which we thought had been lost to us. The coupling of our prayers with these circumstances encouraged us to believe that we were partners with God in what we were trying to do; not that we should look for God only in the unusual events which may occur from time to time and which may provide a particular stimulus of faith. God is also there in the usual – I feel that it is important to attempt to look at all the circumstances that surround me from the standpoint of my relationship with God. There have, for instance, been occasions when I have prayed about particular problems or events in my scientific work. And I believe these prayers have been answered. Although in the very nature of things these answers are of a personal kind and not easy to describe to others in an objective way, they are nevertheless real.

God's work in the world is more often that not through people; that is certainly true of God's work in my own life. This means that as people we have a great responsibility – we need to be sensitive to what God wants from us. For those of us who are scientists it means that we need to face up to the question of what is the value of our scientific work and to try, as far as we are able, to ensure that the science for which we have some responsibility is properly used.

Very early in the Bible (Genesis 1:27–28) we are told that man has been made in the image of God and that he has been placed on the earth to be its steward. We should not, therefore, be afraid to grasp the resources and capabilities we have been given, using them, first, to express worship for the Creator, and second, to care for the world and the human beings within it in ways which are consistent with the declared wishes and purpose of the One for whom we are acting as stewards. A big challenge currently faced by scientists – especially by those of us who are involved with the science of the environment – is the concern about the climate change which will occur next century largely because of our increased burning of fossil fuels. We first need to understand what change in climate may take place. But our responsibility as scientists does not stop there; we also need to be thoroughly involved in the debate regarding what action can be taken to limit the amount of change, to alleviate the problems arising from change and to assist those who will have to cope with substantial change.

When thinking about God's work in the world, a particularly perplexing problem is the problem of suffering. I do not think I am unusual in finding it a real difficulty. My first wife, Margaret, fought cancer for ten years; eventually she died from it at the age of fifty-four. We prayed a lot for healing, as did many of our friends. Were those prayers answered or not? I believe they were, in two ways.

First, there were the times of particular crisis when the right medical treatment was needed and needed urgently. On many of these occasions, from the various possibilities available it was not obvious what should be done for the best. Advice came at different times from different people and different quarters, but each time we felt content that the medical course being taken was right and indeed the best available. After all, the practice of medicine is a direct use of the material resources which God has provided for us in his creation. Healing through medical means is just as much God's work as healing by any other means, natural or supernatural. The combination of medicine and prayer is therefore entirely appropriate when tackling disease.

The second way in which we felt our prayers were answered was that God provided strength to face the battle – physical, mental and spiritual – involved in coping with cancer. This was particularly the case towards the end when we had to face the fact that the cancer was winning. The quality of Margaret's faith and trust in God was truly remarkable and an inspiration to all who met her during that period. We were very conscious of the power of God through prayer to transform our circumstances and suffering into some lasting good.

After Margaret died I questioned my belief in resurrection and the afterlife. Looking at her cold, lifeless body, it seemed impossible that she could live on; but then it also seemed impossible that her strong faith and radiant spirit could just fade away into nothingness. I realized the key to my belief was the resurrection of Jesus. The historical evidence alone is not the basis of that belief. As a scientist, however strong that evidence seems to be, it cannot on its own compensate for the scepticism I am bound to feel about dead bodies coming to life. But there is other evidence too. There is the testimony of millions of Christians over the centuries, from the first disciples who carefully recorded their experiences in the books of the New Testament, to that of Margaret, still very vivid in my memory. And there is the personal experience I have of Jesus as One who is alive in my experience today. The Jesus I meet in the pages of the Gospels is the One I meet as I attempt to communicate with God in prayer and the One I meet through the lives and conversations of others in the Christian community.

When thinking about resurrection, an analogy I find helpful is one based on the computer.[3] Computer hardware consists of the silicon chips, the wires, the disc stores, the keyboards and tape desks with which the input can be introduced, and the screens and printers which display the output. The software consists of the programmes which manipulate (and in sophisticated computers, learn from) the input data and provide the means to organize the output and the contents of the store. The software is no use by itself; it needs hardware on which to act and through which to be expressed. The hardware has a limited life; in time it wears out. The software is not so perishable – it can be transferred to new hardware, although it will still bear characteristics of the hardware for which it was originally written. New, more advanced hardware can provide more scope for the software, enabling not only larger calculations to be carried out but perhaps providing new capabilities. Our bodies are like the hardware providing input devices (our senses) and output devices (our limbs, speech etc.), and processor and storage (our brains). Some of the software is built in from the start; it is genetically determined. Other software is continuously generated throughout our lives from interaction with our environment and with other people, from our thought processes and our choices and from interaction with the hardware. In resurrection, the Christian hope is for a new body which will have sufficient continuity with the old to take on the old software and which will give us new means of expression.

This computer analogy illustrated a way in which scientific thinking and thinking about faith can be brought together. I have tried to pursue elsewhere other, not dissimilar, analogies.[4] An important characteristic of faith is that it brings together and gives meaning to seemingly very different parts of life and experience. There are two ways in which we can learn about and relate to God. He has revealed himself in the world around us with all its order, intricacy and fascination. He has also revealed himself in the Person of Jesus. Think for a moment about the appreciation of depth which is contained in a scene viewed with both eyes rather than with one eye, or the depth which stands out in pairs of pictures viewed through a stereoscope. Objects appear solid; estimates of distance can be made. Putting the two revelations of God together is like having binocular vision. A new depth and reality are created in our appreciation of the world around us and of God himself. We also appreciate how much more there is to explore, both in the world and in God.

Notes

1. Gleick, James (1987), *Chaos*, Heinemann.
2. Houghton, John T. (1988), *Does God Play Dice?*, IVP.
3. Houghton, John T. (1988), *op. cit.*, p. 127.
4. Houghton, John T. (1988), *op. cit.*

Chapter 3

And Information Became Physical

Andrew Briggs is Professor of Nanomaterials at the University of Oxford. From 2002 to 2009 he was Director of the UK national interdisciplinary research collaboration in Quantum Information Processing. He is a Fellow of St Anne's and Wolfson Colleges, Oxford, of the Institute of Physics, and an Honorary Fellow of the Royal Microscopical Society. He is a Liveryman of the Clothworkers' Company, and a Member of the International Society for Science and Religion and of Academia Europaea. He has a degree in theology and a private pilot licence. For a further discussion of the issues in this chapter see Andrew Briggs' and Roger Wagner's (forthcoming) *The Penultimate Curiosity*.

In 1972 the Cavendish Laboratory [Physics Department] of the University of Cambridge moved to a new set of buildings. It had previously been located in the centre of the city, with its main entrance in Free School Lane. The original laboratory was opened in June 1874. On the doors had been carved, almost certainly at the instigation of the first Cavendish Professor, James Clerk Maxwell, a verse from Psalm 111: *Magna opera Domini exquisita in omnes voluntates ejus.* The Cavendish Professor at the time of the move, Sir Brian Pippard, has written:

> *Shortly after the move to the new buildings in 1973 a devout research student suggested to me that the same text should be displayed, in English, at the entrance. I undertook to put the proposal to the Policy Committee,*

> *confident that they would veto it; to my surprise,*
> *however, they heartily agreed both to the idea and to*
> *the choice of Coverdale's translation.*

It was carved on mahogany by Will Carter, and placed over the new entrance. It reads:

> *The works of the Lord are great,*
> *sought out of all them that have pleasure therein.*

I was that research student. I love this text, because it says that what we scientists are doing is studying how God makes the world work.[1] I find that many of the challenges in relating science and faith spring from an inadequate appreciation of what this means. Conversely, just as there is an added dimension of pleasure in enjoying the creative work of someone you know, so there is an added pleasure in studying the world if you know the Creator.

I grew up in Cambridge, with the reputation of the Cavendish Laboratory part of the local folklore. I remember my mother telling me that this was where Rutherford had split the atom. As an undergraduate I studied physics at Oxford, returning to Cambridge for my graduate studies. After my PhD I planned to be ordained in the Church of England, and I took the Cambridge Theology Tripos. But the call of science was too strong for me, and after a short period of post-doctoral research in the Cambridge University Engineering Department, I moved to Oxford to join Sir Peter Hirsch at what was then the Department of Metallurgy and Science of Materials. I became obsessed with microscopy, and the ability to study materials on an ever smaller scale. This was the beginning for me of what is now known as nanotechnology. In due course the University of Oxford created a Chair in Nanomaterials, and I was appointed as the first Professor of Nanomaterials.

Nanotechnology and quantum computing

As you make things smaller and smaller, you can ask the question, "How is small different from big?" The answer may take many forms. The surface increasingly dominates the bulk, so that adhesion becomes more important than inertia, with consequences for nano-electro-mechanical systems. A higher proportion of the atoms are at the surface, with consequences for chemical reactivity and catalysis. As you make things very small, so discrete quantum states emerge, and these can be studied and manipulated. This has led to the emerging discipline of quantum nanoscience.

In 1997 I spent a sabbatical year at the Hewlett-Packard Laboratories in California. I had become interested in the growth and properties of quantum dots which can form during the growth of semiconductor wafers. Germanium atoms are slightly larger than silicon atoms, so if you try to grow germanium on a silicon wafer, the germanium atoms get squashed sideways like people in an overcrowded train. The germanium can grow like this for a few layers, but then the strain becomes too great, and tiny islands of germanium spontaneously form. These grow into quantum dots. At Hewlett-Packard we studied such materials systems with atomic resolution, and tried to account for the resulting distributions of shapes and sizes of the resulting dots. While I was there I learned about quantum computing. At the time I could not think of any experiments which I could do that would contribute to building a quantum computer, but I found the subject deeply fascinating and I determined to find out more.

The discipline of quantum information processing owes much to the insight that information can be described physically. In the 1940s, Claude Shannon had perceived how information could be described mathematically. He found that equations describing information – for example, how it could propagate in an imperfect channel – had the same form as equations which had been developed in the nineteenth century to describe the thermodynamics of particles. This is why terms such as entropy are often used to describe information. At about the same time that Shannon was developing his insights about the mathematical nature of information, Alan Turing in Cambridge was developing ideas about a universal machine for computing.[2] Half a century later, David Deutsch at Oxford published a paper which in many ways has served as a manifesto for quantum computation.[3] He built on Turing's insight:

> *Every "function which would naturally be regarded as computable" can be computed by the universal Turing machine.*

David Deutsch observed that although Turing was writing about a machine for computation, he did so in an abstract way: "The conventional, non-physical view interprets it as the quasi-mathematical conjecture that all possible formalizations of the intuitive mathematical notion of 'algorithm' or 'computation' are equivalent to each other." He criticized formulations such as Turing's as being vague, for example in speaking of "what would naturally be regarded". He re-expressed Turing's formulation as a physical statement:

> *Every finitely realizable physical system can be perfectly simulated by a universal model computing machine operating by finite means.*

Deutsch preferred this as both better defined and more physical, because it used objective concepts such as "measurement", "preparation" and "physical system", which were already known in measurement theory.

This may sound like philosophical nit-picking, but it turns out to have practical consequences. If information is to be computed in a physical system, then it had better be regarded as quantum, because at the relevant level physical systems are quantum. And if it is quantum, then whatever you can do with a quantum object you can do with information. Quantum information processing rests on this fundamental understanding. It was further articulated by Rolf Landauer of IBM in a paper on "The physical nature of information".[4] The opening paragraph is headed "Information is physical":

> *Information is not a disembodied abstract entity;*
> *it is always tied to a physical representation. It is*
> *represented by engraving on a stone tablet, a spin, a*
> *charge, a hole in a punched card, a mark on paper,*
> *or some other equivalent. This ties the handling of*
> *information to all the possibilities and restrictions*
> *of our real physical world, its laws of physics and its*
> *storehouses of available parts.*

Landauer was initially sceptical about the feasibility of quantum computing, because quantum superposition states are so delicate that it seemed that it would be impossible to preserve them for long enough to do sustained calculations. He changed his mind when he learned about methods for fault-tolerant error correction in quantum computing, one of them invented at Oxford by my colleague Andrew Steane.[5]

The physical description of information should not be taken as reductionist, as if by reducing it to that level of explanation that would be all that there is to be said. The mathematical description is no less valid in the presence of the physical description, and neither the physical nor the mathematical description obviates what may be the meaning of the information, which could range from technical to personal. So far from diminishing our understanding of information, the insight that it is physical enriches what we can do. Quantum bits of information, known as *qubits*, exhibit properties that are denied to their classical counterparts. Whereas classical bits are each either zero or one at any given moment, a *qubit* can be both a zero and a one at the same time. This is known as superposition. It makes possible an operation which is halfway to the inverting operation in classical logic. Even more remarkable, two *qubits* can experience a phenomenon known as entanglement, whereby even without any apparent connection between them they appear to be correlated in a remarkable way. This makes possible an operation which is halfway to a swapping operation that can be done in classical logic. These two phenomena of superposition and entanglement are unique to quantum information, and together they provide the spectacular potential of quantum computing.

During the year following my return from California, I began to think more and more about how you might use quantum properties of materials to build a quantum computer. At the time I was a visiting professor at the Ecole Polytechnique Fédérale de Lausanne, and we were engaged in some experiments to measure the mechanical properties of carbon nanotubes.[6] These consist of sheets of carbon atoms rolled up to make tubes that are so tiny that if you put 50,000 of them side by side, that would be about the width of a human hair. I thought about how you might put *qubits* inside a carbon nanotube to create an array for a quantum processor. The ideas grew, and there is now a sizable community of us at Oxford and beyond studying the properties of carbon nanomaterials for quantum technologies.[7] One of the most remarkable molecules for this purpose is a cage of sixty carbon atoms, arranged like the vertices on a soccer ball, inside which we can place a single nitrogen atom. The nitrogen atom behaves as though it were almost perfectly isolated, so that we can manipulate the quantum states of its electrons and its nucleus with exquisite precision. The accuracy with which we can do this, and the time over which the quantum information can be retained, are sufficient for this to be used as a component for a solid state quantum computer.

God, creation and history

Quantum computing is not the only field of science where what might previously have been described by an abstract noun is now seen to have a physical embodiment. There is a growing amount of experimental data showing how behavioural attributes, such as personality and character, correspond to physical states and processes in the brain.[8] Such advances in neuroscience prompt afresh questions of human freedom and responsibility in the light of the mechanisms of the brain. Can the new understanding of the physical nature of information similarly stimulate fresh insights about the nature of God's involvement in the world?

There is a seamless continuity between God's activity in creation and his subsequent activity in history. Although these two can be distinguished they cannot usefully be separated. At least four different belief paradigms can be identified, using Oxford English Dictionary definitions:

- *Atheism.* Disbelief in, or denial of, the existence of a God. "A little superficial knowledge of philosophy may incline the mind of man to atheism" (Francis Bacon, 1561–1626).

- *Deism.* Belief in the existence of a God, with rejection of revelation: "natural religion". "Deism being the very same with old Philosophical Paganism" (Richard Bentley, 1662–1742).

- *Agnosticism.* Holding that the existence of anything beyond material phenomena cannot be known (Thomas Henry Huxley, 1825–95).

- *Theism.* Belief in a deity or deities, as opposed to *atheism*. Belief in one God as creator and supreme ruler of the universe, without denial of revelation; in this use distinct from *deism*.

Since atheism denies the existence of God, an atheist believes neither that God created the world nor that he subsequently sustains it, there is little more to be said. Deism asserts that God created the world, but that he subsequently left it to itself and has no further interaction with it. A consequence is that there is no revelation from God to man. Knowledge of God comes instead through so-called natural theology, whereby man is able to deduce through the exercise of his reason what God is like. The sciences play a special role in this, since they provide the empirical evidence to which reason is applied. Robert Boyle may have unwittingly contributed to the rise of Deism through likening the universe to a famous clock at Strasbourg whose mechanism can be studied. Boyle meant this to convey the sense of wonder that he found in elucidating the nature of the universe and the regularity of its laws, but the metaphor carried the unintended implication that (if regular winding and occasional repairs are disregarded) the clock does not need the subsequent intervention of the clockmaker for each tick.

Deism did not survive. Ian Barbour explained why:

> *The waning of Deism can be attributed primarily to its own inherent weaknesses. The Cosmic Designer, who started the world-machine and left it to run on its own, seemed impersonal and remote – not a God who*

cares for individuals and is actively related to man,
or a Being to whom prayer would be appropriate. It is
not surprising that such a do-nothing God, irrelevant
to daily life, became a hypothesis for the origin of the
world or a verbal formula which before long could be
dispensed with completely.[9]

Thomas Huxley coined the word "agnostic" in 1869 at a party held to mark the formation of the short-lived Metaphysical Society, allegedly taking it from Paul's mention of the altar to "the Unknown God" in Acts 17:23.[10] Uniquely of the four belief paradigms, the name for this was created by its advocate. Huxley quickly lost control of the term. There is a story that Benjamin Jowett, the Master of Balliol, replied to an undergraduate who proclaimed himself an agnostic, "Young man, in this university we speak Latin not Greek, so when speaking of yourself in that way, use the word ignoramus." It was quickly recognized that agnosticism could be a veneer: "In nine cases out of ten Agnosticism is but old atheism 'writ large.'"[11]

If Deism is now rather a period piece, it has to some extent been superseded by its apparent antithesis, first in the form of creationism, and more recently in the form of so-called intelligent design. Creationism, in its most extreme form, denies much of the scientific consensus about the processes of evolution in the origin and development of species. It is often associated with a belief that the universe is much younger than the generally accepted value in cosmology of 13.7 billion years or so. The intelligent design movement has complex origins. Politically it arose from the requirement in America to eliminate instruction about God from state education, and hence to abandon any insistence that creationism should be taught as an alternative model to evolution. Intellectually it arose from the writings of people such as Phillip Johnson, a law professor at the University of California at Berkeley who sought to argue that scientists, with an astonishing degree of apparent collusion, were pursuing a materialist (= atheistic) agenda.

Intelligent design identifies phenomena in biology whose evolutionary origin demands further explanation, and claims that such phenomena provide evidence for "Intelligent Design". To avoid mixing education and religion, in the USA its advocates do not identify the designer as God, but this is the implication. Some writers in the ID movement assert that the complexity of the biological world could not have arisen without some independent steer from the intelligent designer.[12] I do not know of any colleagues at my own university who find such arguments either convincing or useful. Even for remarkable organs such as eyes there is a growing amount of evidence that evolutionary development may occur through different pathways, a phenomenon known as convergence (see Chapter 16 by Simon Conway Morris).

The idea of sporadic intervention by God is as unsatisfactory theologically as it is scientifically. Suppose the set of all observed phenomena is drawn as a circle in a diagram. Now imagine a boundary separating those phenomena which we understand at some level from those which we do not understand. If we ascribe those which we understand to science and those which we do not understand to God (or at least to an intelligent designer), then as science progresses, more and more can be explained by science, leaving less and less to God. This may be why some people assert the demise of faith in the face of the inexorable advance of science. But such a picture is wrong in almost every respect. First of all, the size of the circle is growing rapidly, maybe growing faster than the area of the territory containing what we understand. Indeed, to say that we understand something is an imprecise statement; the best that we can usually do is to understand an observation to a given level of explanation. But both of these objections are trivial compared with the fundamental mistake of ascribing phenomena either to science or to God, as though these were alternatives. As the inscription over the entrance to the Cavendish Laboratory says, in our scientific studies we are discovering how God makes the world work.

A Jewish colleague recently told me how much he had enjoyed reading Francis Collins' book *The Language of God*.[13] Collins is head of the Human Genome Project in the US. He is a believer, and writes with considerable authority about the composition and function of genes. My colleague commented that he detected the greatest sense of worship in the book when Collins was writing about science that is now very well understood, and he contrasted this with those who claim to feel most secure in their faith when they find topics in science that have not yet been elucidated. As Charles Coulson, the founding Professor of Theoretical Chemistry at Oxford wrote: "When we come to the scientifically unknown, our correct policy is not to rejoice because we have found God; it is to become better scientists."[14]

The God who reveals himself

For me the only tenable position is theism. God's activity in creation and his activity in history are of a single piece. While there are successive stages in the narrative in Genesis, there is no satisfactory point which would function as a divide between creation and subsequent history. On the contrary, the opening chapter of Genesis seems to be put there to say, in effect, that the God whom you are going to read about in the following pages and whom you may know through your community and through your own experience, is exactly and precisely the one who is responsible for the whole physical existence of the universe and your place in it. The inscription over the entrance to the Cavendish Laboratory says that scientists are finding out how he does it. This is why the believer can enjoy complete integrity between worship in church and research in the laboratory.

The pleasure that comes from learning about what someone has created can be a stepping stone to deeper knowledge through more direct communication. Joseph Addison was born on 1 May 1672, in Wiltshire. He studied at The Queen's College in Oxford. His Latin verses gained him admission to Magdalen College as a demy, a term for a scholar which arose from the fact that their food allowance was half that of a fellow. He was elected a Fellow of the College in 1698, whereupon his food allowance presumably doubled. Having written several works of poetry and prose, he turned to essay-writing for the *Tatler*. In 1711 he published the first issue of the *Spectator*. He died of asthma, complicated by dropsy, in Warwickshire in 1719. Addison's famous "Ode" to the glory of God (after Psalm 19:1–6) first appeared in *The Spectator*, no. 465, 1712. It was set to music by Benjamin Britten in his *Noye's Fludde*:

> *The spacious firmament on high,*
> *With all the blue ethereal sky,*
> *And spangled heav'ns, a shining frame,*
> *Their great original proclaim:*
> *Th' unwearied Sun, from day to day,*
> *Does his Creator's power display,*
> *And publishes to every land*
> *The work of an Almighty Hand.*
>
> *Soon as the evening shades prevail,*
> *The Moon takes up the wondrous tale,*
> *And nightly to the list'ning Earth*
> *Repeats the story of her birth:*
> *Whilst all the stars that round her burn,*
> *And all the planets, in their turn,*
> *Confirm the tidings as they roll,*
> *And spread the truth from pole to pole.*

What though, in solemn silence, all
Move round the dark terrestrial ball?
What though nor real voice nor sound
Amid their radiant orbs be found?
In Reason's ear they all rejoice,
And utter forth a glorious voice,
For ever singing, as they shine,
"The Hand that made us is Divine."

Although Earth's rotations take place in silence, this does not mean that God does not speak. The observations of astronomy can indeed prompt human reason to an awareness of God, which can then come into sharp focus in the Word of God. My Grandfather, George Wallace Briggs (1875–1959), a Canon of Worcester Cathedral, expressed it in a hymn which can be sung to the tune of Beethoven's "Ode to Joy":

God has spoken by His prophets,
Spoken His unchanging Word,
Each from age to age proclaiming
God, the one, the righteous Lord.
Mid the world's despair and turmoil,
One firm anchor holding fast;
God is King, His throne eternal,
God the first, and God the last.

God has spoken by Christ Jesus,
Christ, the everlasting Son,
Brightness of the Father's glory,
With the Father ever one;
Spoken by the Word incarnate,
God of God, ere time began,
Light of light, to earth descending,
Man, revealing God to man.

> *God yet speaks by His own Spirit*
> *Speaking to the hearts of men,*
> *In the age-long Word expounding*
> *God's own message, now as then;*
> *Through the rise and fall of nations*
> *One sure faith yet standing fast,*
> *God is King, His Word unchanging,*
> *God the first, and God the last.*

The fusion of the world of information and the physical world should not come as a surprise to the Christian believer. It was foreseen in the Old Testament, where the Word of God often has the property of being effective in the world. In the opening chapter of his Gospel, John describes how the Word became physical. The term $\Lambda o\gamma o\varsigma$ (*Logos* or Word) conveys a *double entendre*, no doubt intended. In Greek thought it was the rational principle of the universe of Stoic and Platonic philosophy. In Jewish thought it could describe God's revelation in which his thought was communicated through his speech. John takes both of these meanings and explicitly identifies them with God himself, and then states that in Jesus the $\Lambda o\gamma o\varsigma$ was physically embodied. The early Christians were quick to see the implication of this for every aspect of their lives. What is probably one of their earliest hymns bases the attitude which they should have to each other on what they find in Jesus:

> *He was in the form of God; yet he laid no claim*
> *to equality with God, but made himself nothing,*
> *assuming the form of a slave. Bearing the human*
> *likeness, sharing the human lot, he humbled himself,*
> *and was obedient, even to the point of death, death on*
> *a cross!*
>
> **(Philippians 2:6–8)**[15]

The resurrection is the best-documented miracle of the Christian faith, but the incarnation is no less significant. "The central miracle asserted by Christians is the Incarnation. They say that God became Man. Every other miracle prepares for this, or exhibits this, or results from this."[16] We have yet to see what the eventual impact of quantum information will be. The significance of the Word becoming flesh is already well established.

Notes

1. Berry, R. J. (2008), *Science & Christian Belief*, 20: 147–61

2. *Proceedings of the London Mathematical Society*, series 2, 42: 230–65, 1937.

3. *Proceedings of the Royal Society of London*, A, 400: 97–117, 1985.

4. *Physics Letters*, A, 217: 188–93, 1996.

5. *Physics Review Letters*, 77: 793–97, 1996.

6. *Physical Review Letters*, 82: 944–47, 1999.

7. *Journal of Physics – Condensed Matter*, 18: S867–83, 2006.

8. *Science & Christian Belief*, 16: 101–22, 2004.

9. Barbour, Ian (1966), *Issues in Science and Religion*, SCM.

10. Hutton, R. H., owner of the *Spectator*, in a letter dated 13 March 1881.

11. *Saturday Review*, 819 (2), 26 June 1880.

12. For example, Michael Behe (1996), *Darwin's Black Box*, Free Press.

13. See Chapter 7.

14. Coulson, Charles (1953), *Christianity in an Age of Science*, Oxford University Press, p. 16.

15. *Revised English Bible*.

16. Lewis, C. S. (1947), *Miracles*, Geoffrey Bles, p. 131.

Chapter 4

From Spock to the Supernatural

Chris Done is a Professor of Astrophysics at Durham University, researching black holes. After a first degree at St Andrews, she did a PhD at Cambridge and then worked for NASA. She leads Alpha courses at her local church, and appeared in the BBC *Songs of Praise* episode marking the International Year of Astronomy.

Science really caught a hold of my imagination as a child. My Dad was a TV repair man when I was growing up, and there was often a TV with its back off on the kitchen table with glowing valves inside. But it was space in particular that fascinated me. I grew up in the late sixties and early seventies, so I saw some of the later Apollo moon landings, but it was *Star Trek* that made the bigger impact. This science-fiction journey across space and time with a crew who got excitement and adventure every week just seemed incredibly exotic to a girl from a fairly ordinary family from a fairly ordinary small town. And the member of the crew I most wanted to be like was Spock, the half-human, half-Vulcan science officer. Generally it was Spock who understood stuff (apart from emotion, of course) and Spock who could think his way through to a solution. My mind was made up; I wanted to be a scientist like Spock! And since I thought that scientists had to be atheists, I was going to be an atheist too.

Giving up faith was no real hardship as I didn't particularly have one – I got sent to Sunday school by my Mum, and had joined the choir in the local Anglican church because I liked singing. I didn't see any reason to change this – I still enjoyed singing, and if there was no God to offend, it didn't matter whether or not I was still in the choir. I wouldn't get confirmed as a teenager though, as there was no way I was going to say I believed when I didn't. Voicing this gave me some confidence, and I started saying at school that I didn't believe in God, and arguing with any of my friends who were brave enough to talk about their faith. In fact, by the time I got to seventeen, I was an evangelical atheist, quite convinced I was right.

At that time, a friend of mine became a Christian and with incredible bravery, she invited me to her baptism. And while I thought she was completely nuts, it was something important to her and I was pleased that she wanted me to be there. So I went, expecting dull and dreary hymns, for her to get sprinkled with some drops of water, and then for us all to get on with the day. What I got was quite shockingly different. I had never been to a church where people sang as if they actually meant the words, where they were clearly participating in an act of worship rather than standing there apparently embarrassed by the words they were mumbling. Even more disturbing was a sense that I can only describe as like the presence of God just behind my left shoulder, saying in an amused tone of voice, "So I don't exist, do I?" I remember thinking, "No, go away!!" and groaning inwardly at the logical contradiction of talking to a God I didn't believe in.

I could rationalize this, of course. Religion clearly has a powerful psychological hold on us, and I was still human despite my best efforts to be Spock. So this simply demonstrated that I was as psychologically susceptible to this stuff as the rest of the human race. But I decided to make myself feel better by arguing with the minister after the service. He let me explain to him (probably at length) why there was no God before he asked what I now recognize as the classic question: "Who do you say Jesus is, then?" I came back with the classic wrong answer of "A good teacher." By the time he'd explained to me why someone who went around saying he was God and accepting other people's worship could not possibly be a good teacher, my day was going seriously awry. Not only had I encountered (at the very least!) my own humanity, I now had encountered someone who could argue better than I could!

He lent me a couple of books about the evidence for Jesus being the Son of God – his life, death and his resurrection. I am a scientist and I am a sucker for evidence. Weighing evidence is what we do! And I was shocked to find that there was evidence! Evidence that Jesus lived, died, and worse from my point of view as an atheist, evidence that he was resurrected. Because of course, if the resurrection is true, literally true, then it validates everything Jesus says about himself in the Gospels. It means he was and is the Son of God, and if there is a Son, then there is also a God. Which would mean that I was wrong – a truly terrible thing for an arrogant seventeen year old to contemplate. But with a little new-found humility, I also found a little hope. Surely many prominent atheists had tackled these arguments before, and had thought of ways around them. So I made up my mind to go to the library and get out some good atheist books, and see how they addressed the evidence. This was in the days before the internet, and the only atheist I had heard of was Bertrand Russell (Richard Dawkins was not very famous at that time). Only as far as I could see, Russell's arguments were not at all on the specifics of Jesus and the resurrection, but seemed to go along the lines of "There isn't a God because there can't be a God because there isn't a God..." I did not find this convincing.

So, scarily, I found myself as an atheist in a position where I could see that there was enough evidence to support believing in Christianity in terms of a literally resurrected Jesus. I couldn't think of any other way to satisfactorily explain the behaviour of the disciples after the crucifixion. I could definitely imagine them running away, as the Gospel accounts say, and I could then imagine them some time later being racked with guilt, that they had abandoned their master and friend in his hour of greatest need. I could imagine them standing up publicly, and saying "This Jesus who you crucified… was a good teacher who showed us the way to God." But by their own admission (after all, it was they, not Jesus, who caused the Gospels and Acts to be written), they said something completely different. They said, "This Jesus who you crucified… has been raised to life by God." This was completely stupid, and they were going to die for it (most came to very sticky ends). People will die for all sorts of things, but generally not for something which they know is demonstrably false. The evidence was clear that they utterly believed that they had met with the risen Christ, not some nebulous mass hallucination, and their lives from this point on were completely transformed.

Evidence, of course, is not the same as proof, but very little in either life or science is built on formal (mathematically derived from axioms) proof. From what I could see, the evidence was enough to convince me that it was more likely than not that Christianity was true in terms of Jesus literally being raised from the dead. But I still didn't become a Christian, as I didn't want it to be true. I didn't want there to be a God, especially not the God of the Bible, who takes an interest in how we live our lives. I wanted to make my own decisions about how to live my life, to be free to choose what I wanted. But having been intellectually convinced, it was hard to live as though it didn't matter, so I eventually gave in. My prayer of repentance wasn't one I would have accepted if I were God. It was definitely more a grudging admission that I'd been wrong about him not existing, rather than thanks and praise for a Saviour!

If becoming a Christian was unexpected, so was what happened next. I was still thinking about faith as an intellectual position, a set of beliefs that we choose to adopt and choose to follow. But all the books I'd been reading about Christianity were stressing that it was much more about being friends with God than a set of rules. And I remember how the next day the world looked different – it was obviously the same, just my standard walk home from school – but the sky and trees looked different because now their beauty pointed to the God I was just getting to know. There was meaning behind them that spoke of love, not just the beauty of physics.

After the drama died down I got on with life – which to me meant astrophysics! But then I had some qualms. Now I was a Christian, surely I should do stuff that helped people, and astrophysics isn't exactly a socially relevant career. So I struggled with this for a while, but Jesus managed to convince me that he'd made me and knew me and in his opinion I'd make a rubbish doctor, but I might have the makings of a good astrophysicist. So I decided to give it a go! But then the next problem was I didn't think my Mum would be too keen on this, as it didn't lead directly to a good job. So I told her I was interested in studying engineering, which she was horrified by, as she thought that was all dirty overalls and big spanners and not for girls! After letting her struggle with this for a while, I said I'd changed my mind, that maybe engineering wasn't for me, and maybe I'd do... astrophysics instead! She was delighted, I got what I wanted, and everyone was happy!

It turned out that God was right (a nasty habit of his!), and I made a pretty good astrophysicist, so I went on to do a PhD at Cambridge on black holes. But somewhere in all of that I'd lost sight of Jesus and my faith became just a set of beliefs, without the relationship bit – both with Jesus and with other Christians – that makes it such fun. I'd never found a church at university – St Andrews is a very small town and there weren't a lot of churches to choose from and none of them at that time seemed like the church where I had become a Christian. I was a bit bemused at the start, and couldn't figure out why these churches were much less exciting than the one I'd been in at home. I'd never really encountered much teaching on the Holy Spirit and simply didn't know what was missing! But the outcome was that I got bored and drifted away from church. So going to Cambridge was a time for a new start and I decided I really was going to keep looking till I found an exciting church this time.

Cambridge being a bigger town, and me being a bit less clueless at twenty-two than at eighteen, meant that I did find one, one where Christianity was all about a dynamic relationship with God through the Holy Spirit, and life had a flavour of the excitement of Acts. While I don't pretend to understand the Trinity, my standard way to think about this is that the Holy Spirit is how Jesus is with us, and reveals God to us. But this also gets into the supernatural aspect of God – though for me this has never been that much of an issue. Even when I was an atheist I used to get cross at discussions in RE lessons at school on how all Jesus's miracles could be physically explained. To me, once you have believed in a God, a supernatural being, then it's obvious that supernatural stuff could happen, since any God who can make the physical universe and its laws can presumably suspend those laws in any time and way he chooses. So when I became a Christian, the idea of a God involved in the lives of his people in a direct way was not something I struggled with – apart from when his view differed from mine in terms of what I should do! One very early example of this was after a teenage row with my Mum about my new-found faith. I was praying about what to do to show her I was right (sadly, this was more important to me than repairing the relationship) – and felt God say, "Try doing the washing up." So I did the washing up and retired in a halo of sanctity, thinking, "Job done." But the next day I felt God say, "Do the washing up again"... and the next and the next. And funnily enough, the relationship got mended and I wasn't so concerned about whether or not she thought I was right. Anyone who does not think this is a miracle has not remembered being a teenager!

I have seen many similar miracles over the years – people being transformed by discovering the love of God in Jesus. I know someone with bipolar disorder. A year ago their new faith was all about them, and now they show care for others. I know someone who was suicidal after the death of her husband, who found new hope in being loved by God and new purpose in life by helping others. A God who changes us is truly miraculous. But when people talk of miracles they generally don't mean psychological, internal change – they mean physical healings or a change in the physical world. How do I view these as a physicist? The fact that we have physics shows only that God does not ordinarily choose to suspend the laws he made to hold the universe together, not that miracles cannot happen. This is not to say that all claims for miracles are genuine – people can react and overreact to emotion – but that there is the possibility. A friend of mine was in a very serious car accident, and had diffuse head injuries where anything and everything could be affected. She wasn't expected to live through the night and the doctors were saying that might well be for the best. Lots of people prayed, and she was home in a few months. It's not necessarily a miracle – bodies and brains are complicated things; maybe she was just lucky. But from a standpoint of faith, I'm glad everyone prayed! Jesus called his miracles "signs", and signs are only seen by people looking in the right direction. If you don't believe miracles can happen, there is always some way to explain them away – like me with my experience of the presence of God when I was an atheist, or by saying that bodies and brains are complicated things. But with faith that there is a God who hears and acts, then miracles can point to that God, and be a sign that he is near and is concerned with our lives.

I don't think my faith directly affects the way I do science, but certainly it has an indirect impact. It has an impact on my priorities in that it tells me that work is not the most important thing in life, much as I love what I do and love the opportunities I have had through it, such as when I continued my work on black holes as a postdoc at NASA, where an unexpected highlight was to be involved in an X-ray telescope which flew on the Space Shuttle, and to be part of the ground control room team! Another impact is that I try to have integrity in both the way I treat data and the way I treat my students and colleagues. There is nothing unusual in this; most of my colleagues do the same. And it certainly doesn't mean I have never published a paper which turns out with hindsight and new data to be wrong, nor does it mean I have never stuffed up human relationships. It only means that I try to work and live in the light of knowing a God who cares about truth and who cares about people. I did once try praying that God would show me how he'd made a particular piece of his universe that I was working on at the time. His response was along the lines of "What do you think I gave you a brain for? Work it out yourself!" – which didn't exactly help, but did make me smile. Obviously, God has no need for anyone to explain his universe – he knows exactly how it works. But I think he takes pleasure in us using the brains he gave us to explore his creation.

It was Galileo who said, "I do not feel obliged to believe that the same God who has endowed us with sense, reason and intellect has intended us to forget their use." I am sure that when I stand before God to give an account of my life, he will ask, "And what did you do with that brain I gave you?" And I am equally sure that he will not be impressed with an answer along the lines of "I thought all you cared about was faith, not intellect." The first commandment is to love the Lord your God with all your heart, soul, mind and strength. Soul – yes, faith is important, but so is our mind. So also is our heart – our emotions are not something to be feared like Spock, but are a part of what makes us human. And our bodies also – we can take joy in the physicality of life. Jesus said he came to give us life in all its fullness, so as Christians we are meant to be people who can demonstrate what it means to be fully human – not brains on sticks, nor emotions on legs, but heart, soul, mind and strength all used to the best of our ability is what glorifies the God who made us.

At several points I've talked about hearing the voice of God. For me this has never been an audible voice (the nice young men in their clean white coats don't need to come and take me away quite yet). What I mean by this is a part of my own thoughts that somehow doesn't sound like me – a voice in my own head whose sense and rightness is obvious, yet what it's saying is not something that was apparent to me immediately before. Again, this is not proof of the existence of God; you could say it's simply part of my thought processes. But I combine it with faith that God speaks to me, and it has transformed my life.

We all struggle sometimes with being accepted, and that includes me, even though I have a great family who love me and accept me. I am unusual and sometimes it shows. In a church context I can be very unexpected as a scientist and as a woman who does leadership; and in a work context I can be very unexpected as a Christian and as a woman in physics; and in social contexts I can be unexpectedly direct.

At one of these points when I was feeling that I was off the scale of other people's experience, this voice came and said, "Chris, do you understand gravity?"

"No," I replied in my head.

"If you thought about gravity every day for the rest of your life, would you understand it?"

I do think about gravity every day of my life as I work on black holes. "No," I replied.

"Would that change the fact that your feet stick to the floor?"

"No."

"Do you understand my love?"

"No." I'm not thick, so I could see where this was going, but still the voice continued:

"If you thought about my love every day for the rest of your life, would you understand it?"

"No."

"Would that change the fact that I love you?"

Somehow, in that moment I got a bit of a grip on what it means to be loved by God, that it is really not about what we do or don't do; we are simply loved, and he takes joy in me being who he made me to be.

Chapter 5

Can Science and Christianity Both Be True?

Professor Sir Colin J. Humphreys, CBE, FRS, FREng, Hon. DSc, FIMMM, FInstP, FCGI, FRMS. Educated at Luton Grammar School and Imperial College, London. Goldsmiths' Professor of Materials Science, University of Cambridge since 1992; previously Professor of Materials Engineering, Liverpool University, 1985–89. Director of Research, Department of Materials Science and Metallurgy, University of Cambridge since 2008. Director, Rolls-Royce University Technology Partnership in Advanced Materials since 1994. Director, Cambridge Centre for Gallium Nitride since 2000. Fellow, Selwyn College, Cambridge since 1990.

Dorothy Sayers is famous for her detective stories featuring Lord Peter Wimsey. She was also a Christian and in one of her books, *The Dogma is the Drama*, she records the following interview with a typical man in the street:

> *Question:* What is Christian faith?
>
> *Answer (by man in the street):* Resolutely shutting your eyes to scientific fact.

In a similar vein, Sir Richard Gregory, a former editor of *Nature*, wrote:

> *My grandfather preached the gospel of Christ*
> *My father preached the gospel of Socialism*
> *I preach the gospel of Science.*

These quotations illustrate the popular belief that science and Christianity cannot both be true. In my life the question, "Is Christianity true?" has cropped up in various ways and I will write about some of these in this chapter. It was as a science student at university that I first wrestled with this question. Problems I have faced since then have included whether the theory of evolution can be true. I will write briefly about these topics in this chapter, ending with a particular personal interest: the use of astronomy to establish the date of various biblical events.

Is Christianity true? A personal conclusion

I had come to London to study physics at Imperial College and my accommodation in the first year of my undergraduate life was like a scene from a play. I lived in a house in Chiswick. The landlady was French; she had lived in England for forty years, yet she only spoke six words of English. Her husband was Greek and he was a chef at a famous London club. Also in the house were two other students: Paul, a first-year pharmacist, and Michael, a medical student who had lived for several years in the house. Both the French landlady and her Greek husband were superb cooks, and we must have been the best-fed students in London. However, there was an unusual condition about living in the house – the landlady would only accept students who spoke French! I scraped by.

"By chance", Paul and Michael were both Christians. Paul had been brought up in a small denomination known as Strict Baptists. At university he rebelled somewhat against his strict upbringing, gave a mean imitation of Elvis Presley on the guitar, became highly extrovert and is the only person I have known literally to go out with a different girl every night of a particular week. Michael, on the other hand, was quiet and studious (and an Anglican). I had been brought up by Christian parents, went to church and Sunday school, and became a Christian at about age eleven. At school I believed that evolution was nonsense and gave my biology teacher a hard time! However, the year before I went to university I started having serious doubts about the existence of God and I rejected Christianity (without telling anybody).

I resolved to work the matter out in my first year at London. For me the key question was "Is Christianity true?" I decided to read through one Gospel, a little each night, and also one book about becoming a Christian. I started in a very sceptical frame of mind. I tried to imagine being there in first-century Palestine as Jesus spoke, and to think if the words made sense. I had never realized before how outrageous were many of the claims of Jesus. It seemed to me that there were only three possibilities: either Jesus was who he claimed to be, or he was mad, or it was all a cruel hoax. Similarly with the Resurrection: either it was true or else it was a cruel hoax. Which was correct?

I agonized over this for some weeks, and I did not find the answer obvious. I discussed the matter with no one. I felt it had to be between me and God, if there was a God. Finally I became convinced that Christianity was true, but – and this I found really surprising – I didn't want it. I rejected Christianity, knowing it to be true. I knew this was intellectually dishonest but I did not want to make the commitment. Having reached the stage of rejecting Christianity, I planned to stop going to church. However, Paul and Michael went, so I went along with them. In any case, there were some attractive girls at the church! I became a secret non-Christian.

After the Sunday night service the minister would have a group of us back to his house for coffee, biscuits and a chat. After leaving the minister's house on one particular night I found myself walking along the street with someone who worked locally whom I did not know at all well. As we were walking along the street he suddenly said he would like to be a

Christian and he asked me how. The others in the group were further up the road and well ahead of us. My brain raced as I considered the honest course of action. I was well able to tell him how to become a Christian, but would it be intellectually honest to tell him something I had chosen not to believe myself? On the other hand, I could tell him that I was not a believer, but would it be right for me to say something which might destroy his search for Christian belief? After a few moments of thought I said he should go and speak with the minister of the church. I then went back to my lodgings, knowing that I should no longer resist what I knew to be true, and that night I committed myself afresh to Christ. I was delighted that the other man did visit the minister and he too became a Christian.

A few months after my decision I started doubting again. Once more I went through the arguments whether or not Christianity was true, and again I decided it was. Doubts returned periodically, but slowly diminished. There were times when being a Christian was like walking on a tightrope. For me the key question each time was "Is it true?" I have not had these doubts for a number of years, but I have always had great sympathy for the disciple known as Doubting Thomas!

Scientific truth and Christian truth

So far I have been writing about the truth of Christianity. But how does this relate to scientific truth? There is a widespread belief that science and Christianity occupy different territories. Thus it is often held that science is concerned with the material world and Christianity with the spiritual world. A basic problem with any territorial model is that battles at the boundaries are probably inevitable. A famous general once said that one-country maps were useless because most battles were fought at the boundaries between two countries. I am unhappy with a territorial model for science because, although the limits of science can probably be defined today, they will have changed dramatically in 100 years' time. In principle I believe any topic should be open for scientific study. Similarly, I am unhappy with a territorial model for Christianity, since the God revealed to us in the Bible and through Christ is the God of all, both spiritual and material. Paul writes, "For in him [Christ] all things were created: things in heaven and on earth, visible and invisible… all things have been created through him and for him" (Colossians 1:16). Thus I believe that science and Christianity are concerned with the same territory: the universe and all that it contains – nothing is barred.

The building of truth

I have found it very helpful to think of truth in terms of a set of architect's drawings of a building. A complex building will have side views (elevations), views from the top (plans), and sections drawn at different levels. There will be common elements where two drawings meet. Each drawing (e.g. an elevation) is complete in itself. All drawings should fit together, although it is often very difficult for the untrained eye to see this.

The analogy with truth is obvious. Truth is a unity – there is one building of truth. However, more than one drawing is necessary for a full description. Each drawing is different because it is from a different viewpoint. Thus I believe that science and Christianity describe the same territory, the same building of truth, but from different viewpoints. The master architect has ensured that all the viewpoints fit together, but to the untrained eye that is often not easy to see.

It is dangerous to pursue analogies too far, but we can take the building-of-truth model a little further. We don't even have the individual drawings! It is as if each drawing is broken up into a jigsaw puzzle. Scientists are trying to reconstruct the jigsaw of scientific truth. We may feel that many of the pieces are now in position, but I suspect that we have only just started (the quantity of our scientific knowledge about the universe is much less that the quantity of our ignorance). Similarly with Christianity. Some pieces of the jigsaw are in the Old Testament, some key pieces were revealed to us by Jesus, further pieces were revealed to the New Testament writers, but still "we see through a glass darkly", as we try to reconstruct the Christian view of the universe, including mankind.

In attempting to understand an architect's drawing it is useful to focus on common boundaries – e.g., where a side elevation and an end elevation meet. Similarly in science and Christianity, common boundaries (of two incomplete jigsaws) are particularly important places through which the understanding of truth may be advanced, and a few more pieces put in the jigsaw. For example, was creation in six literal days? It is my belief that if the early chapters of Genesis are read without preconceptions (very difficult!), then it is not possible to be sure whether the author intended them to be literal or not. On the one hand, the creation account has a rather matter-of-fact style; but on the other hand, pictorial language is used. For example, the account describes "the tree of life", which few people take as a literal tree when it is later referred to in the last book of the Bible, the book of Revelation. However, science also reveals to us information about the creation of the world. Because the building of truth is a unity, the scientific viewpoint of creation can help to reconstruct the part of the Christian jigsaw of truth dealing with creation. We will return later to the creation/evolution issue. At this point let me emphasize a key general point: the God revealed to us through Jesus is the same God who is revealed to us through the scientific study of the universe he created. If conflicts arise, it is therefore because either our understanding of Christianity, or of science, or of both, is incorrect (i.e. we have misplaced some of the jigsaw pieces). I believe there can be no conflict if our understanding of science and Christianity are both correct.

What is distinctive about the scientific viewpoint of truth? The aim of science is to describe and understand the universe (including man) in terms of mechanisms, theories and laws. As a materials scientist I try to explain the macroscopic properties of materials (strength, electrical and thermal conductivity, etc.) in terms of the position and movement of atoms, ions and electrons. Scientists also use their understanding of mechanisms, theories and laws to predict the future. Scientists essentially ask the question "How?" and try to answer this question in terms of mechanisms. Thus the jigsaw of the scientific viewpoint of truth is built up.

What is distinctive about the Christian viewpoint of truth? Whereas scientists mainly ask the question "How?", meaning "How did we get here?", Christians mainly ask the question "Why?", meaning "Why are we here?" However, Christians also sometimes ask the question "How?" and scientists also sometimes ask the question "Why?" – there are common boundaries on the building of truth. Scientific truth is mainly objective (e.g., the pen I am writing this with has a certain mass which can be measured and agreed upon by scientists throughout the world). Christian truth is both objective and subjective, and the subjective part is important. Many aspects of reality can be known only by personal involvement – for example, the love of one person for another. The Christian truth that God committed himself to us through Jesus can only be known if we commit ourselves to him. The building of truth is therefore complex and contains both objective and subjective truth.

There is another important way in which the building of truth is complex – it contains different floors and levels. We first learn science in a simplified way. For example, we are taught at school that Ohm's Law ($V = IR$) is a universal law. Whereas it is true that V = IR holds in the everyday world, for extremely thin wires Ohm's Law breaks down. However, we don't teach school pupils about this exception; if we attempted to teach school pupils all the complexities of science, they would never learn anything! We start with simple truths and work up to more complex truths. So it is with Christianity. Paul writes of feeding new Christians on milk, like babies, but also that we should progress to a diet of meatier truths. Some scientific truths are unchanged, however much we learn: for example, the value of the speed of light seems to be a constant truth. Similarly, some Christian truths are unchanged on whatever level of the building of truth we consider them: for example, I believe the Resurrection to be an event in history which is both a milk-truth and a meat-truth.

Miracles

Can a scientist believe in miracles such as the Resurrection? To understand miracles we must first understand "normal" events. For scientists, normal events are described by theories and laws. Laws are well established theories which have survived many tests. Laws therefore describe the past: they do not prescribe the future (i.e. predict what must happen in the future) but they do raise our expectations to a very high degree. For example, we would be astonished if a predicted solar eclipse did not occur.

What is the Christian view of normal events? A few years ago one of the Christmas cards I received had on the front a picture of a chef holding in his outstretched hands a giant spherical Christmas pudding. Underneath the sender had written his own caption, the first line of a famous American spiritual: "He holds the whole world in his hands". It was a brilliant analogy. The chef was outside of, and distinct from, his pudding, yet the creative genius of the chef was within each morsel. The chef was upholding the pudding. He could be said to have created the pudding in a few hours, yet the ingredients had taken much longer to develop.

The analogy, of course, is obvious. God is both the creator and the upholder of the universe. Paul writing to the Colossians says: "All things have been created through him [Christ] and for him. He is before all things, and in him all things hold together" (Colossians 1:16–17). When Paul spoke to a non-Christian audience in Athens he said: "He… gives to all people life and breath and all things… In him we live and move and exist" (Acts 17:25–28, NASB). The message is clear: Christ continually sustains and upholds the universe, including mankind.

Some years ago Jonathan Miller presented a television series called *The Body in Question*. In one programme the television cameras filmed statues of famous men and a fountain in the garden of a stately home, and Jonathan Miller asked the question, "What is the human body more like; is it like one of these statues or is it like the fountain?" The obvious answer was that our body is more like a statue, but the cameras zoomed in to show them crumbling away, whereas the fountain was being constantly renewed. Jonathan Miller said the human body was more like the fountain: our body cells, skin, nails, etc. are constantly being renewed (of course, the analogy cannot be extended to old age).

The biblical picture of God is not of a being who created the universe like a statue (with a clockwork mechanism) and then left it to decay, like an absentee landlord. Instead God is depicted as constantly upholding the universe, both externally like the chef holding up the pudding, and also acting within the very fabric of the universe. The analogy I like best of God's upholding is that of the singer and the song. The song depends totally on being uttered by the singer, moment by moment. So it is, I believe, with God and the universe, including mankind. We owe our moment-by-moment existence to the upholding of God.

The consistency of God

Ringing through the pages of the Bible is the message that God is consistent and not capricious. For example, "seedtime and harvest, summer and winter, will never cease" (Genesis 8:22), or "Jesus Christ, the same yesterday, today and forever" (Hebrews 13:8, NASB).

Scientists who are Christians believe that because God is consistent, therefore the universe is consistent, and hence it can be described by theories and laws. There are some eminent science historians who argue that the reason science flourished in Europe in the seventeenth century (and not previously in ancient China, Egypt, India, Babylon or Greece, brilliant observers that they were of natural phenomena) was because many of the early European scientists (Newton, Kepler, etc.) were Christians who believed in a consistent God and an orderly universe. Thus Newton realized that the force of gravity on earth that attracted the anecdotal apple to the ground was the same force of gravity that acted throughout the universe and was responsible for the planets moving around the sun. Kepler said, "scientists try to think God's thoughts after him", and he looked for elegant mathematical models of planetary motion. These early scientists were driven by the belief that God and his creation were consistent and not capricious.

However, this raises a major problem concerning miracles. If at least some miracles are real events, how can this be reconciled with not only our scientific belief in an orderly universe but also with our Christian belief in a God who is consistent and not capricious? It is helpful to consider some specific miracles to see how this problem can be resolved.

Crossing the Jordan

Joshua 3:15–16 records: "As soon as the priests reached the Jordan the water from upstream stopped flowing. It piled up in a heap a great distance away at a town called Adam, while the water flowing down to the Dead Sea was completely cut off." Joshua then records that about 40,000 Israelites crossed over.

The Bible consists of various types of writing: history, poetry, parables etc. When considering miracles we must seriously ask the question whether the author intended his account to be understood as history or not. This is not always easy to decide; however, it seems to me that the above description in Joshua is meant to be understood as an historical event.

As a Christian I believe that God is all-powerful and can do anything. However, I also believe that he will not do anything that is against his character. Since God is a consistent God, I believe it is right always to look for a consistent, not a capricious, explanation of miracles. I therefore believe that we should always look first for an understanding of miracles in terms of scientific mechanisms, although I realize that not all miracles can be explained in this way (see later), at least not with our current scientific understanding.

Returning to the "crossing the Jordan" miracle, in 1979 Amos Nur, a geophysicist at Stanford University, studied in detail historical earthquakes in the Jericho fault. He found that in 1927 there was an earthquake which caused mud slides along the river Jordan at a place called Damia, about 40km north of Jericho. These mud slides temporarily cut off the flow of the river Jordan. Nur then found that Damia used to be called Adam, the place described in the book of Joshua as being where the river Jordan was stopped, and he also found records of other occasions when an earthquake had caused mud slides that had stopped the river Jordan in this way. He states: "Adam is now Damia, the site of the 1927 mud slides which cut off the flow of the Jordan. Such cut offs, typically lasting one to two days, have also been recorded in 1906, 1834, 1546, 1534, 1267 and 1160." Nur adds that the description of the stoppage of the Jordan in Joshua 3:15–16 is so typical of earthquakes in this region that little doubt can be left of the reality of this event in Joshua's time.

God is all-powerful and therefore stopping the flow of the Jordan could have been a special supernatural intervention of God. However, the key question to ask is not "What could God do?" but "What did God do?" Was stopping the Jordan a special intervention of God or was it due to a natural mechanism? We have seen that there is clear historical evidence of the Jordan being stopped by earthquake-produced mud slides many times in the past at precisely the place, Adam, specified in the book of Joshua. There is strong evidence therefore that an earthquake was the natural mechanism which stopped the Jordan in the time of Joshua. Does this mechanistic explanation mean that the event was not a miracle? No: it was still a miracle, but a miracle of timing. At precisely the time when Joshua and 40,000 Israelites needed to cross the Jordan an earthquake occurred causing mud slides which blocked the river's flow. God upholds the universe with perfect timing. Many "miracles" happen today through natural mechanisms. For example, materials scientists provide artificial hips that enable the lame to walk, surgeons perform cataract operations that enable the blind to see. Just because we can understand scientifically these modern healing methods does not make them any less the hand of God.

The burning bush

"Moses saw that though the bush was on fire it did not burn up" (Exodus 3:2). At first sight this description seems very curious. However, there are bush species, for example, *Dictamnus albus*, the flowers of which emit a volatile gas which can catch fire spontaneously if certain conditions are met simultaneously: intense sunlight, high temperature, large bush, many flowers open, no wind and no flying insects to disperse the gas. If all the above conditions coincide, the gas around the bush has a sufficient concentration and a sufficient temperature that its flash-point is reached. The gas then catches fire spontaneously and burns, although the bush itself does not burn (somewhat similarly, gas burns above a gas ring without the ring itself burning). This effect can be produced in a greenhouse, but a bush catching fire spontaneously is very rare in nature (it has been reported in Central Europe, near Warsaw, in 1965). It is rare in nature because of all the conditions that must be satisfied simultaneously.

Was the bush that Moses saw newly created by God for the occasion, or was it an existing bush the flowers of which emitted a volatile gas? Again, the key question to ask is not "What could God do?" but "What did God do?", given that God is consistent and not capricious. To me the answer is clear. This was an existing normal bush. However, at this particular time when Moses passed by the conditions were right for spontaneous combustion: many flowers emitting a volatile gas were open, there was no wind nor flying insects, etc. But the biggest miracle of timing was that when this spontaneous burning occurred, Moses was there, God spoke to him, Moses responded, he led God's people out of Egypt, and this (in popular language) changed the course of history.

I became so fascinated by the miracles in the Exodus account that I wrote a book called *The Miracles of Exodus*.[1]

The Resurrection

Are all miracles "miracles of timing" explicable in terms of natural mechanisms? I believe that many are, but others – for example, the healing miracles performed by Jesus and his Resurrection – we cannot explain by natural mechanisms (at least not with our present scientific knowledge). In these cases God appears to be operating differently from usual, but can this be if God is consistent and not capricious?

Imagine standing behind a pianist as he plays the piano from memory. If his fingers normally land on the white keys, but every time he goes to play an F he plays the black F sharp instead, you can deduce the key signature (G major) of the composition. The key signature is at the start of the musical score and it is the rule given by the composer for playing his music. God, the Master Composer of the universe, has established its key signature. We do not have the score of the universe, but by careful observation scientists can establish the rules by which it operates: we call these rules the laws of nature (of course, we may be wrong about some of these).

A musical composer is not bound by his own rules. He is free to decide that at a particular place in the music he wants an additional sharp or flat; these local deviations from the key signature rules are called accidentals. With a great composer these accidentals are never capricious; they are always carefully placed and consistent with what the composer wants to achieve. They make sweeter music. (Try playing a Beethoven sonata as written and then without the accidentals.) Similarly, God is not bound by the rules he has established for the universe. He is free to uphold it moment by moment in any way he chooses. However, he is a consistent God, and therefore any "local accidental", any change in his method of upholding, must be consistent with what he wants to achieve. It cannot be capricious, it must make sweeter music, it must be consistent with the overall purpose of God.

Jesus, the Son of God, had perfect love. It made more sense, not less sense, for him to heal the sick. It was totally consistent with his character. In Peter's first sermon, at Pentecost, he states that God raised Jesus from the dead, "because it was impossible for death to keep its hold on him" (Acts 2:24). Peter saw the Resurrection as being inevitable, not incredible. If Jesus really was the Son of God, then death could not hold him. The Resurrection fully accords with God being consistent, not capricious, and was planned by God before the creation of the universe.

Many people think of miracles as interventions of God, and people often pray for God to intervene in the world. While this may be a convenient way to think from our point of view, the notion of God intervening is inconsistent with the biblical picture of God upholding the universe moment by moment. God is not a passive God who sometimes intervenes: God is always active. On rare occasions he chooses to act differently from usual. On less rare occasions events occur which to us seem to be astonishing coincidences of timing. Both these types of events we usually refer to as miracles. Both are equally the hand of God.

Creation and evolution

I was brought up to believe that animals and plants did not develop over millions of years by a process of evolution, but that each species was directly created by God. This belief is called creationism and it is shared by a great many people. When I went to university I started to question the beliefs I had held, and later I wrote a booklet on creation and evolution, aimed at secondary school pupils (the booklet has recently been translated into Chinese). The key question to be asked is, "Is evolution or creationism true?"

An enormous amount has been written about evolution. One of the critical questions is how old is life on earth? According to the theory of evolution it is many millions of years old, whereas many creationists believe life to have originated only about 6,000 years ago. This is clearly a question that science should be able to resolve.

It is well known that the ages of trees can be determined by counting the rings in the trunk. This method of dating is called dendrochronology. Some trees live for an astonishingly long time. The oldest known living object, plant or animal, in the world is a tree: living bristlecone pine trees exist which are 4,900 years old. A tree's rings can vary a great deal in colour and thickness from year to year, depending on the local climate. By counting tree-rings from both living and dead trees, and matching characteristic patterns in them, a continuous tree-ring dating sequence has been built up, extending back 8,200 years. The importance of this dating method is that it is accurate and absolute.

If it is assumed that the early chapters of Genesis are literally true, and that the genealogies given in the Bible have no missing generations, then it is possible to reconstruct the human family tree, with Adam and Eve at the top. Bishop Ussher was the first to calculate from the genealogies the date when Adam should have been created: 4004 BC. Therefore if the early chapters of Genesis are interpreted literally, the world was created in 4004 BC.

However, we know beyond reasonable doubt that the trees existed on the earth 8,200 years ago. Thus either early Genesis should not be interpreted literally or the genealogies are incomplete (i.e. should not be interpreted literally) or both. We can say with reasonable certainty from tree-ring dating that those creationists who believe the world was created in 4004 BC are wrong.

Other creationists believe that the earth's age is about 10,000 years, that the early chapters of Genesis are literally true, but that the genealogies were not intended to be a totally complete record. To investigate these claims a dating method is needed that goes further back in time than tree-ring dating. Various such methods exist: radiocarbon dating can be used to date animals and plants for the last 70,000 years. For older specimens, particularly rocks, radio-uranium and radio-potassium methods can be used. These methods indicate that the oldest rocks known on earth are about 3,900 million years old, and that the ages of meteorites found on earth are about 4,600 million years. The earliest evidence for life comes from traces of the outlines of colonies of bacteria in rocks about 3,000 million years old. Sea snail fossils have been found which are about 600 million years old, and the first whales appeared about 50 million years ago.

There is therefore strong evidence that the earth is very old, and that different types of animals emerged at intervals of many millions of years. However, as we have noted above, many creationists believe the earth is only 10,000 years old, or even less. How can they believe this in the face of the scientific evidence? First, some creationists claim that radioactive dating methods are unreliable. But even if radioactive dates are wrong by as much as 100 per cent, which is extremely unlikely, the earth is still many millions of years old. Second, many creationists believe in the theory of Apparent Age, which is a very clever theory, but which strikes at the heart of the belief that God reveals himself to us through his created universe.

The creationist theory of apparent age

In 1857 Philip Henry Gosse published a book entitled *Omphalos: An Attempt to Untie the Geological Knot*. *Omphalos* is the Greek word for "navel". The navel is of course what remains when the umbilical cord is cut from a new-born baby. Did Adam have a navel, even though he was not born? Of course he did, said Gosse. God created him the way he intended all human beings to be. (In a 1990 issue of *New Scientist* the cover depicted Adam with a navel, and this was questioned in subsequent correspondence!) In the same way, Gosse argued, the trees God created were fully grown trees with rings in them: thus, although the creation took place in 4004 BC, Gosse argued that if we try to date it scientifically, it appears older. Modern creationists have updated this idea, so that it is argued that God created rocks in 4004 BC having an apparent age of 3,000 million years if dated using scientific methods.

Logically it is impossible to tell the difference between: (i) a world which really is very old, and (ii) a world which is young but has been given a perfect appearance of age.

However, sheer common sense suggests that (i) must be preferred to (ii). Again, the key question is not "What could God do?", but "What did God do?" God does not deceive us by leaving old fossils lying about. The God who created all life is the same God as he who reveals his creation to us. This is central to my beliefs as a scientist and as a Christian. Since our study of the world shows clearly that it is very old and that life has emerged over millions of years, then this is the timescale over which God has created life on earth. It follows that the early chapters of Genesis should not be interpreted literally.

For most of the time the universe has existed there has been neither man nor woman. We occupy just a tiny speck of space-time on one out of millions of planets. This makes me feel very humble. On the other hand, it has taken an immense journey through time to produce us. God is the Master Mind who planned this great journey: that makes us something special. Life on earth appears to have developed by a process of evolution; it is the general way in which God chooses to work. It fills me with wonder that the whole of the universe and the whole of life were encapsulated in the very first concentration of matter and energy, rather like a great tree is encapsulated in a tiny seed.

The major way in which Christians and non-Christians differ in their view of the theory of evolution is that for many non-Christians "pure chance, absolutely free but blind, is at the very root of evolution... Neither the duty nor the destiny of man have been written down" (so said the distinguished biologist Jacques Monod). Christians cannot agree with this because they believe that life has a plan and a purpose. The topics of scientific chance and classical chaos are complex and outside the scope of this chapter. Although both may play key roles in evolution, I believe that God is in charge and that evolution is the way he chose to carry out his creation. If life emerged from a primeval soup, then God was the Master Chef.

Dating biblical events

Christianity is not some vague set of beliefs: it is based upon real historical events – for example, the Crucifixion – and if we can pinpoint in time these events, we strengthen the historical basis of the Christian faith. We may also understand certain events better if we know when they occurred, and hence can set them precisely in the social and political climate of the time.

Chronology is the backbone of history, and most history textbooks are written around a framework of the dates on which certain events occurred. On the other hand, dates are strangely absent from most commentaries on both the Old and New Testament books, even though the writers of the Bible were often keen to date events according to their own calendar systems, usually based upon the reigns of kings. For example, Isaiah had an important vision "In the year that king Uzziah died" (Isaiah 6:1); John the Baptist started his ministry "In the fifteenth year of the reign of Tiberius Caesar" (Luke 3:1). We need to know the corresponding dates in our BC/AD calendar as a starting point for dating events such as the Crucifixion.

One of my young daughters once had a book called *Great Men of History*, which devoted a few pages to each person selected (I hope some women were included also!). In the front of the book was a list of the people featured, with their dates of birth and of death. Definite dates were assigned to each person except one, Jesus Christ, against whom was typed "born 4 BC (?), died AD 30 (?)". This uncertainty must raise doubts in the minds of some people about whether Jesus really existed, and

I have made it a particular personal interest to use my very limited spare time to try to pin down more accurately the dates of some important biblical events.

Science, particularly astronomy, has a key role to play in this, since ancient writings, including the Bible, sometimes feature astronomical events (e.g. eclipses) occurring in a certain year of the reign of a particular king. If we can identify the astronomical event and calculate when it occurred, and if the text is reliable, then we can have certainty and precision in dating the reign of the king. I find this use of astronomy and history applied to dating biblical events complicated and fascinating. It is like unravelling a mystery in a detective story with very limited clues. I would love to do this full time!

My first foray into this arena was to attempt to date the Crucifixion, with the help of an astronomer colleague. The date we determined, 3 April AD 33, was not a new date, but we produced some new evidence. It is important to realize that Christians will not always agree about matters because the evidence is often incomplete, or because our understanding is incomplete. In the case of dating the Crucifixion there is not enough evidence to be 100 per cent certain, but I would claim there is enough to say that there is a very high probability (say 95 per cent) that the date of the Crucifixion was 3 April AD 33. The biblical evidence fits this date remarkably well.

I was amazed at the interest shown in our paper.[2] I stopped counting after 500 reprint requests and letters were received in the first few weeks after publication. News about this dating of the Crucifixion featured in national daily papers as far afield as the USA, Australia, Singapore and even mainland China. Although there is widespread apathy towards the events of Christianity, we should not forget the widespread latent interest.

I have also studied the date of the birth of Christ by identifying the Star of Bethlehem as a long-tailed comet which appeared in 5 BC. I published this work in both an astronomy journal and in a theological journal.[3] Again, these publications created widespread public interest.

My *Nature* paper on the date of the Crucifixion caused me to think more deeply about some apparent contradictions in the Gospels about events in the final week of Jesus, particularly whether the Last Supper was a Passover meal (as described in Matthew, Mark and Luke) or before the Passover meal (as described in John's Gospel). I thought about this problem for many years, before finally realizing that Matthew, Mark and Luke used a different calendar from John when they described whether the Last Supper was a Passover meal or not. I identified this different calendar and used astronomy to reconstruct both the official Jewish calendar in the first century AD and also this different calendar, which I believe was an earlier Jewish calendar. This is somewhat similar to the way that Catholics and Protestants calculate the date of Easter using the Gregorian calendar, while the Orthodox churches (Greek, Russian, etc.) still use the earlier Julian calendar to calculate the date of Easter (which is why they normally celebrate Easter on a different date from Catholics and Protestants). I wrote about this in another book, *The Mystery of the Last Supper: Reconstructing the Final Days of Jesus*.[4] This book created large media interest, with articles about it appearing in daily newspapers throughout the world. The book has been translated into Russian, German, Portuguese, Japanese and Greek with a special reprint edition for the South Asian market. A Passion Play has been written based on the new chronology of the last week of Jesus given in my book. So once again we see that despite the increasing apathy and hostility towards Christianity in recent years, there is also tremendous interest in science and faith issues around the world.

I have found, and continue to find, great intellectual satisfaction from both science and Christian belief. There is much we do not understand in both. There are many challenges.

For example, do recent ideas about chaos have any relevance to free will? Upon re-reading this chapter I find that I have mainly concentrated on insights we can gain for Christianity from our knowledge of science. What about the reverse? I think the most important thing Christianity has taught me as a mechanistic scientist is not to lose my sense of wonder. What a brilliant creative genius God is to produce the universe and life in all its complexity, diversity and beauty, from a single small beginning. To a Christian, the heavens declare the glory of God.

Notes

1. Published in 2003 by HarperCollins in the USA and by Continuum in the UK. It has been translated into various languages and is now published by HarperOne in the USA, and there is an audio edition by Audible.

2. *Nature*, 306: 743–46, 1983.

3. *Quarterly Journal of the Royal Astronomical Society*, 32: 389–408, 1991; *Tyndale Bulletin*, 43: 32–56, 1992.

4. Cambridge University Press, 2011.

Chapter 6

Reflections of a Christian Working in Science and Conservation

Simon Stuart is a conservation biologist with undergraduate and doctoral degrees at Cambridge and ornithological fieldwork experience in Tanzania and Cameroon. He has worked for the International Union for Conservation of Nature (IUCN) since 1985, serving as Chairman of the Species Survival Commission since 2008. His work focuses on measuring species extinction risks, with a particular emphasis in recent years on amphibian declines. His work has a global focus, and he also serves as an International Trustee of A Rocha – Christians in Conservation.

Prologue

One July morning in 2007 I was sitting on the veranda of my hotel room in the Philippines reflecting on the state of creation. It was a beautiful view over the Verde Island Passage, between the islands of Luzon and Mindoro, a stretch of water which (according to my good friend, the ichthyologist Kent Carpenter – and he should know) contains more species of fish per unit area than any comparable area in the world, including the so-called "mega-diverse" countries of Indonesia and Malaysia. It has been called "the centre of the centre of marine shore-fish biodiversity".[1] It is an incredible area. The sea is teeming with what seems like an endless diversity of fishes, corals and other forms of life. And unlike so many other places, this exceptional ecosystem still seems to be more or less intact.

I was in the Philippines to attend a workshop reviewing the status of every species of reef-building coral in the Indo-Pacific – over 90 per cent of the 845 species of reef-building corals in the world. Our findings were, to put it mildly, sobering. The leading world experts on corals went through each species, one by one, to assess its level of extinction risk.[2] We concluded that, of the species for which there was enough information to assess their status, nearly one third were at risk of extinction. Of even greater concern were the findings that (a) the driving force in the decline of coral species is coral bleaching caused by elevated ocean temperatures; and (b) before the massive bleaching episode of 1998, less than 2 per cent of the reef-building corals qualified as threatened with extinction.

In less than a decade, the number of globally threatened coral species has increased fifteen-fold, and the situation continues to deteriorate. If this was not enough, decreased ocean alkalinity caused by the rapid build-up of greenhouse gases in the atmosphere is reducing ocean carbonate ion concentrations and the ability of corals to build their skeletons.[3] This could have a devastating effect on reef ecosystems in the coming decades, and we hardly factored it into our species-by-species threat assessments. In short, the gloomy results of the workshop were probably over-optimistic.

As I sat pondering these disturbing trends, and feeling the sadness of the ongoing loss of beautiful ecosystems and species, I felt God say to me that I should write a lament on the status of his creation. This alarmed me. I had no idea how to write a lament. But the invitation to contribute to this book has given me the opportunity to be obedient to God's clear message. This chapter is not a lament, but I hope it may be a precursor for it.

A young naturalist

I cannot remember a time when I was not fascinated by animals. I now believe that this is how God made me. It is part of how I tick. I was extremely fortunate to grow up in Dorset with an abundance of wildlife around me. I developed a fascination for birds, and had a number of rare species on my doorstep – dartford warblers, nightjars and hobbies. From early on I was also very interested in reptiles and amphibians, and two species very rare in Britain – the sand lizard and the smooth snake – occurred close to my home. All sorts of weird and wonderful animals found their way into our house. My parents, apparently unfazed, did everything they could to foster my passion, and I was surrounded by a vast array of natural history books which I read avidly. Later on, my mother enjoyed recalling how I used to write lists of threatened species from when I was very small. When I was sorting through her papers after her death ten years ago, I found some of these early writings! As someone who went on to work for many years on the *IUCN Red List of Threatened Species*, I was struck by how little my interests have changed! Looking back on it, my career path seems to have been pretty inevitable.

My good fortune continued. At the age of thirteen I started at Canford School where an amazing biology teacher named Tim Hooker took me under his wing. He taught me an enormous number of things (in addition to the regular biology curriculum), including how to count birds, how to identify them by their songs, how to catch reptiles and amphibians, how to identify fungi and which ones were edible, and how to cook the last! It did not stop there. Tim organized a friend and I to spend part of a summer on the Shetland island of Foula, where we learned to ring seabirds. I remember climbing down into a foul-smelling cave, and passing young Shags out to the ringing team at the entrance to the cave. They would then return the ringed Shag for me to replace carefully on its nest before passing out the next one. I loved it. After this, Tim arranged for me to visit Tanzania, beginning a love affair with Africa. He was a friend of chimpanzee expert Jane Goodall who was working in the Gombe Stream National Park on the shores of Lake Tanganyika. She needed someone to help teach her young son. I don't think I was much good at that, but teaching only took a few hours a day. The rest of the time was mine to watch birds, look for chimpanzees, baboons, red colobus and other monkeys, and to swim in the lake and experience being nibbled by a huge diversity of cichlid fish.

So thanks to my parents and Tim Hooker, by the time I went to Cambridge University, I had an impressive knowledge of the natural world. Then two most important things happened. In my first year at Cambridge I met Ann, another biologist in my year, who, ten years later, became my wife. Second, I became a Christian (as did Ann a few months before me). It was not that I had been anti-Christian before. As a small boy, I had been in the choir at Wimborne Minster and also attended a very Victorian prep school that closed soon after I left. I was taught the Bible there by an octogenarian teacher by the name of Mr Swell. Most people hated his lessons, but I loved them and benefited a great deal from them. Later on at Canford, a number of overtly Christian teachers impressed me with their sincerity and care for their pupils. But despite my interest in all things Christian, none of it made particular sense until I arrived in Cambridge. I was most attracted by the authenticity in the relationships among the Christian undergraduates, something that seemed amazing to me, as hitherto I had lived in the insecure teenage world of seeking to perform and impress in order to gain acceptance and significance. It was the uncomplicated love that the Christians had for each other, and above all for Jesus, that won me over. I suppose that my conversion was thoroughly postmodern in that I met Jesus, and welcomed him into my life, before I came to understand the gospel in more conventional terms. But he welcomed me nonetheless, and life has never been the same. It is the most important decision that I ever took, and one that I have never regretted.

My interest in the natural world continued to develop during my time in Cambridge. Looking back, I do not think that my science and Christianity intersected much. I always had the feeling that a career in conservation biology was God's calling, but it was many years before I came to understand that science and conservation could actually be God's work and part of my worship of him. While at Cambridge, my interest in Africa grew. I came under the influence of two academics, Con Benson (who was Curator of Ornithology in the University Museum of Zoology) and Keith Eltringham (who studied large mammal ecology and wildlife management in East Africa). Con was an old man when I met him, but for the few years that I knew him I had the privilege to be taught by the most knowledgeable expert on the avifauna of Africa. While still an undergraduate, I led two university expeditions to study the rare, endemic birds of the Eastern Arc Mountain range of Tanzania. Through these experiences I learnt something about leadership and managing people – as well as developing an abiding interest in African birds. I then went on to do a PhD on the biogeography and conservation biology of the Eastern Arc avifauna. Keith became my supervisor (and an excellent one he was) and Con was a key scientific advisor (though, sadly, he died shortly before I finished). I spent three years in the field in Tanzania before returning to Cambridge to write up my thesis.

A scientist in conservation

After my doctorate (in fact before it was completed) in 1983, I was recruited by the International Council for Bird Preservation (ICBP – now BirdLife International) to work on the African

Bird Red Data Book. My boss was Nigel Collar, one of the great characters in conservation at both a personal and intellectual level. It took us about two years to complete the book,[4] and I think it is fair to say that it set a new standard in the documentation of threatened species. When we started we wondered if enough information could ever be found to say anything meaningful about most of the species, but through extensive networking with a large number of ornithologists we were swamped in data, much of it previously unpublished. I learnt something then that I've found to be true time and time again. When one asks how much is known about a particular species, the usual answer is "nothing". But as one digs deeper, one discovers much more information than most people expect. There is a wealth of information out there to support conservation and to guide decision-makers, but most of it is not in forms that can be readily accessed or used. Much of my subsequent career has been devoted to making information available in such a way that it can be used to advance conservation (in other words, making lists again!).

While I was at ICBP I organized and led an expedition to Cameroon to learn about the rare forest birds, amphibians and mammals in the mountains in the west of the country. From this, ICBP developed its conservation programme in Cameroon, which continues to this day. In late 1985 I was recruited by the International Union for Conservation of Nature and Natural Resources (IUCN) and moved to Switzerland, where Ann already had a job teaching biology in the International School at Geneva. We married the following year and started our life together exploring the beautiful scenery and natural history of the Alps and the Jura. It was a wonderful start to married life. My particular job involved working for the IUCN Species Survival Commission (SSC). I have been with them ever since, in various roles which have taken me into an ever broader array of activities. I worked with many outstanding people, too many to name here, though George Rabb, the visionary Chair of the SSC from 1989 to 1996, stands out as a true leader. I had to learn about all sorts of things, such as fundraising, project management, staff management, office politics and the like.

For much of the time I seemed to be drifting further and further away from science. I became heavily involved in the process to develop the new IUCN Red List Categories and Criteria. The *IUCN Red List of Threatened Species* is the world's official listing of globally threatened animals and plants, and was the brainchild of Sir Peter Scott, who chaired the SSC for many years, up until 1979. However, the Red List in the 1980s was, to say the least, a haphazard affair. There were no hard-and-fast criteria for deciding what was, and what was not, allowed on to the list, and politics and personalities played a big role in decisions. IUCN's scientific credibility and impartiality were seriously at risk. Previous attempts to rectify the situation had failed for various reasons.

The turning point came in 1989 when a young scientist at the Institute of Zoology in London, Georgina Mace, was asked to come up with a new proposal for deciding whether, and how much, a species was threatened. Her proposals, made jointly with Russell Lande, broke new ground and provided the first quantitative criteria for assessing extinction risk.[5] I was given the task of being Georgina's link in the IUCN Secretariat, with the job of facilitating the development of an agreed set of rules to govern the IUCN Red List. The rules had to be scientifically robust but also acceptable to an essentially conservative SSC. Georgina and I ran numerous consultations involving scientists covering a wide variety of skills and experience (botanists and zoologists, marine, terrestrial and freshwater scientists, etc.) before coming up with a finally agreed approach. We learnt workshop facilitation the hard way by being thrown in the deep end. But in 1994 the IUCN Red List and Categories and Criteria were adopted. We upset some people, especially in government departments dealing with fisheries when they found that cod and bluefin tuna were listed as threatened. This led to further workshops and consultations, resulting in the not hugely changed version that exists today.

Over the years I became more senior in the IUCN Secretariat, and spent a lot of time on management and running meetings. I even ended up as Acting Director General at one point. But I was becoming increasingly separated from real conservation issues. Then a new opportunity arose. In 2001 I was given the chance to set up a new Biodiversity Assessment Unit, based in Washington DC, as a shared initiative of IUCN and the United States-based charity Conservation International (CI). Russ Mittermeier and Gustavo Fonseca at CI, both leading figures in the SSC, encouraged me to make this move, and after prayer Ann and I felt that it was the right thing to do. So shortly before 9/11, we moved to Washington with our two daughters, Claire and Jyoti. This became another exciting place for us to explore natural history (the salamanders of eastern North America are special, as are the warblers on their annual migration northward each spring).

My first task in my new role was to run the Global Amphibian Assessment (GAA) – the first ever review of the conservation status of all the world's 6,000+ amphibian species. Having spent years working on how to determine whether or not a species is threatened, we now actually had to put our system into practice. This was a fantastic project to work on, and I had an excellent team who did most of the leg work. We ran 16 workshops, worked with 550 scientists, and the results were launched in 2004 to worldwide media attention. We found that one third of the world's amphibians were at risk of extinction, that the situation was rapidly deteriorating, and that as well as familiar threats like habitat loss, amphibian extinctions were taking place because of a "new" fungal disease, chytridiomycosis, the incidence of which appears to be linked to climate change.[6] The GAA is currently being updated, and we now have four other major ongoing assessment projects on mammals, reptiles, and on marine and freshwater species. It was because of our marine project (the Global Marine Species Assessment) that I found myself in the Philippines in July 2007.

Integrating science and Christian faith

As mentioned above, my professional and Christian lives did not much interact. For sure, I knew other Christians working in conservation. But I lacked an over-arching theology to give me a holistic view of the world I inhabited. Looking back on it, I don't understand how I tolerated such a compartmentalized life, but I suspect that I was not atypical. However in 1999, Ann and I met Peter and Miranda Harris, the founders of A Rocha – Christians in Conservation. A Rocha is a family of Christian conservation organizations operating now in eighteen countries on all continents, and finding exciting and innovative means to demonstrate God's love for all that he has made (see www.arocha. org). Ann and I became friends with Peter and Miranda, and I became an International Trustee of A Rocha. After we moved to Washington Ann became A Rocha USA's first Education Director. It was through Peter and Miranda that we learnt what now seems blindingly obvious – that the gospel is about more than personal salvation (though obviously it includes that). We saw that the doctrine of creation is not something buried away in the early chapters of Genesis, but actually permeates the entire Bible. Not only did God make everything, and made it very good, but creation was affected negatively by the fall (Genesis 3:17; Jeremiah 12:4), and is encompassed positively by God's plans for redemption (Romans 8:19–22; Colossians 1:19–20). We started to see that the ecological crisis has a spiritual root. But God has not given up on his creation – he owns it and sustains it (Psalm 24:1–2; Leviticus 25:23). Indeed, creation exists with the purpose of displaying God's glory – as it most surely does (Romans 1:18–20; Revelation 5:13). The doctrines of creation and salvation are complementary; there is a sense that salvation is in fact re-creation (2 Corinthians 5:17). Peter and Miranda taught us that our work in conservation is an integral part of our Christian calling, and part of our worship of the Creator God.

Gradually I started to see all my supposedly secular conservation work as part of my Christian walk. Although I would probably always have claimed this, it now started to make sense theologically. I could now see the Global Amphibian Assessment, for example, as God's work. It was something that he wanted me to undertake, and the results enabled us to understand what is happening in God's world more clearly. Moreover, as I felt the pain and sadness of the decline and disappearance of some remarkable species, I now understood that this was in fact God's pain arising from his own deep love and care for all that he has made.

Creation in jeopardy

My work on the assessment of the threatened species (what is now called "biodiversity assessment") has enabled me to gain a privileged overview of what is really going on in Creation today. When I started out in conservation, we operated under a very simple paradigm. Species were threatened by definable threats. All we had to do was to identify the threatened species, find out what threatened them, and then design conservation programmes to alleviate these threats. When we spoke of threats, we meant things like habitat loss, over-harvesting, pollution and invasive species – all readily identifiable, and in principle resolvable through tried and tested means, such as protected area establishment and management, sustainable development programmes (often designed to provide local human communities with alternative livelihoods to the over-use of species), control programmes for invasive species, environmental education projects, and conservation legislation. All these things remain important, of course, but they are no longer anything like sufficient to stem ongoing extinctions.

Our biodiversity assessment work has, especially over the last ten years, shown that species are increasingly impacted by pressures that have no immediate remedy. One of the first indications that we are on uncharted territory was increasingly severe and frequent coral bleaching due to the warming of the oceans. Even if the world had the political will to take truly radical measures to address climate change, it would take decades to stabilize carbon dioxide levels, and consequently ocean temperatures and acidity can be expected to rise for the foreseeable future. In short, we have no immediate remedy for coral bleaching. The consequences of the widespread loss and degradation of coral ecosystems will no doubt have huge impacts on other species, and we are only just starting to look at the implications for coral reef-dependent fishes. The impacts on the human communities that depend on fisheries in coral reefs could also be extremely severe and lead to the loss of livelihoods among the poorest of the poor.

Another early sign that something new and disturbing was happening to the world's species came from the amphibians. Two particular stories caught public attention. In Australia, the two species of Gastric-brooding Frog – the only frogs that incubated their young in their stomachs – died out suddenly, one in 1981, the other in 1985. The disappearance of the golden toad in Costa Rica in 1989 attracted even more publicity. However, the Global Amphibian Assessment showed that these were far from isolated instances. We documented over 120 species worldwide which had experienced unexplained, dramatic declines. Many species could no longer be found. The disappearances had one thing in common – the species vanished from places that seemed to be well protected. There were no obvious, identifiable threats. The old paradigm wasn't working. We now know that these amphibian extinctions are mostly caused by the fungal disease chytridiomycosis, interacting with climate change. There is no known remedy for this disease in the wild – another threat for which we do not have a solution.

Sometimes, even apparently identifiable pressures that ought to have a solution seem to defy our best attempts at conservation. Our Global Mammal Assessment has highlighted the disastrous state of large mammal populations in East and South East Asia. Hunting for meat and traditional Chinese medicine has severely reduced numbers in species that were abundant only a few decades ago. This has affected not only the species we expect to be threatened, such as tigers and rhinos, but also most Asian species of deer, cattle and monkeys – in fact anything bigger than a rabbit. Traditional means of protection – legislation, law enforcement, and education – simply are not working. All this holds a bitter memory for me personally. In the late 1980s and early 1990s I devoted a lot of time to developing a conservation programme for the Kouprey – a large species of wild ox from Cambodia, Vietnam and Laos. Our efforts were too little and too late. The Kouprey is now almost certainly extinct due to hunting.

I could go on, but the message is clear. If we look at the global picture from a detached, secular, scientific perspective, there are very few grounds for hope. All the trends are downwards, and we lack the means to reverse many of the threats, even if we had the political will. But as a Christian, I now see things differently. We live in a Creation that is cared for and owned by a Father God who has made a covenant with "all living creatures of every kind on the earth" (Genesis 9:8–17). He is the God to whom we can sing:

How many are your works, Lord!
In wisdom you made them all;
the earth is full of your creatures.

There is the sea, vast and spacious,
teeming with creatures beyond number –
living things both large and small.

There the ships go to and fro,
and Leviathan, which you formed to frolic there.
All creatures look to you
to give them their food at the proper time.

When you give it to them,
they gather it up;
when you open your hand,
they are satisfied with good things.

When you hide your face,
they are terrified;
when you take away their breath,
they die and return to the dust.

When you send your Spirit,
they are created,
and you renew the face of the ground.

(Psalm 104:24–30)

I believe that God laments over the sorry state to which we have brought his Creation through our own selfishness, self-indulgence, greed, neglect and ignorance. He also holds us accountable:

Because of this [i.e., the sin of the people] *the land*
dries up, and all who live in it waste away; the beasts

*of the field, the birds in the sky and the fish in the sea
are swept away.*

(Hosea 4:3)

*How long will the land lie parched and the grass in
every field be withered? Because those who live in it
are wicked, the animals and birds have perished.*

(Jeremiah 12:4)

*As for you, my flock, this is what the Sovereign Lord
says: I will judge between one sheep and another, and
between rams and goats. Is it not enough for you to feed
on the good pasture? Must you trample the rest of your
pasture with your feet? Is it not enough for you to drink
clear water? Must you also muddy the rest with your
feet? Must my flock feed on what you have trampled
and drink what you have muddied with your feet?*

(Ezekiel 34:17–19)

*The time has come for… destroying those who destroy
the earth.*

(Revelation 11:18)

Hope

Yet God does not leave us entirely with lament and judgment.
He is also the God of hope – indeed, without him there is no
hope for his creation. We learn this from passages such as
Romans 8:19–23 and Colossians 1:15–20, teaching us that *"the
creation itself will be liberated from its bondage to decay and
brought to the glorious freedom of the children of God"*, and that
"God was pleased to have all his fullness dwell in him [i.e., Jesus],
and through him to reconcile to himself all things, whether things

*on earth or things in heaven, by making peace through his blood,
shed on the cross."*

However, God also gives us hope in the present time, not
just in the future. In a paper on "Conservation theology for
conservation biologists", Stuart *et al.*[7] put it this way:

> *Perhaps of greatest importance [in terms of reasons
> for dialogue between evangelicals and secular
> conservationists] are the resources that authentically
> Christian theology can bring to an otherwise bleak
> environmental situation by establishing the grounds
> for hope. By this we mean something more than simply
> the belief that at the end of time God will restore his
> creation and that the loss of the dodo from Mauritius
> and the golden toad from the Monteverde Cloud Forest
> in Costa Rica is therefore not the end of the story.
> Of course this future hope is an important one, but
> when we say "grounds for hope," we are referring to
> our present situation as well. Evangelical Christians
> are committed by their biblical beliefs not only to the
> conviction that God himself cares for His universe in
> a daily and ongoing way but also that He helps and
> guides people in their conservation efforts. We are
> therefore not on our own against the relentless forces of
> unsustainable development and rapacious materialism.
> Every time we celebrate a conservation success story
> such as the recovery of the white rhinoceros in southern
> Africa, we are strengthened in this present hope
> that God is working with us to redeem his creation.
> Furthermore, these present successes are a very real
> foretaste of even greater things to come on that day
> when God will fully restore all that He has made."*

It is easy to recount a catalogue of conservation failures. Looking back over the conservation initiatives with which I have been involved, a few have been complete failures (as in the case of the Kouprey), many are still ongoing and cannot yet be called successes (but without them things would probably have been worse), but a few are certainly successes. One in particular comes to mind.

In 1984 I led an expedition to Mount Kilum in western Cameroon. What we found there was most disturbing. The area has a unique fauna and flora, quite different from those on the other mountains in the region, with a number of species being found nowhere else in the world. But deforestation was rampant, and no effective conservation measures were in place at all. We reported on the situation to BirdLife International. To their great credit, they started a major conservation initiative on Mount Kilum which continues to this day, working with the local human communities. The most recent data show that the forest extent on the mountain is actually increasing, an incredible success given the strongly negative trends elsewhere in this region. I had no further involvement with the project after writing the report of our expedition, although some members of our team returned to Cameroon to continue conservation work there.[8]

I believe the Lord is looking after his world. During our 1984 visit, I took one day off to climb a peak overlooking Lake Oku, a stunningly beautiful crater lake on Mount Kilum, to spend a day in solitude with God. And these are the words that came to me as I contemplated the ongoing destruction of this very special place:

> "For my thoughts are not your thoughts,
> neither are your ways my ways,"
> declares the Lord.

"As the heavens are higher than the earth,
so are my ways higher than your ways
and my thoughts than your thoughts.

As the rain and the snow
come down from heaven,
and do not return to it
without watering the earth
and making it bud and flourish,
so that it yields seed for the sower and bread for the eater,

so is my word that goes out from my mouth:
It will not return to me empty,
but will accomplish what I desire
and achieve the purpose for which I sent it.

You will go out in joy
and be led forth in peace;
the mountains and hills
will burst into song before you,
and all the trees of the field
will clap their hands.

Instead of the thorn-bush will grow the juniper,
and instead of briers the myrtle will grow.
This will be for the Lord's renown,
for an everlasting sign,
that will endure for ever."

(Isaiah 55:8–13)

I could almost feel the trees clapping their hands. But I had no idea back then that this was God's prophecy for Mount Kilum. To believe that the conservation situation on the mountain could be turned round would have seemed ridiculous – the pressures causing the destruction of the forest were so great. My faith was not strong enough to believe that anything could be done about it. But God had his own plans for this place that he made and loved. He is indeed a God of hope.

Acknowledgements

I thank Ann Stuart, Sam Berry and Peter Harris for their helpful comments on an earlier draft of this chapter.

Notes

1. Carpenter, K. E. & Springer, V. G., "The center of the center of marine shorefish biodiversity: the Philippine Islands", *Environmental Biology of Fishes*, 72: 467–80, 2005.

2. IUCN (2001), IUCN *Red List Categories and Criteria: Version 3.1*, IUCN Species Survival Commission: IUCN, Gland, Switzerland, and Cambridge, UK; Mace, G. M., Collar, N. J., Gaston, K. J., Hilton-Taylor, C., Akçakaya, H. R., Leader-Williams, N., Milner-Gulland, E. J. & Stuart, S. N., "Quantification of extinction risk", *Conservation Biology*, 22: 1424–42.

3. Cooper, T. F., De'ath, G., Fabricius, K. E. & Lough, J. M. (2007), "Declining coral calcification in massive Porites in two nearshore regions of the northern Great Barrier Reef", *Global Change Biology*, 14: 1–10.

4. Collar, N. J. & Stuart, S. N. (1985), *Threatened Birds of Africa and Related Islands: The ICBP/IUCN Red Data Book*, Series 3, volume 1, Cambridge: International Council for Bird Preservation and International Union for Conservation of Nature and Natural Resources.

5. Mace, G. M. & Lande, R. (1991), "Assessing extinction threats: toward a re-evaluation of IUCN threatened species categories", *Conservation Biology*, 5: 148–57.

6. Stuart, S. N., Chanson, J. S., Cox, N. A. & Young, B. E. (2004), "Status and trends of amphibian declines and extinctions worldwide", *Science*, 306:1783–86.

7. Stuart, S. N. *et al.* (2005), "Conservation theology for conservation biologists", *Conservation Biology*, 19:1689–92.

8. Stuart, S. N. (1986), *Conservation of Cameroon Montane Forests*, Cambridge: International Council for Bird Preservation.

Chapter 7

What Do *You* Believe, Doctor?

Francis Collins has a PhD in chemistry and is a qualified physician. Since 2009, he has been the Director of the National Institutes of Health at Bethesda, Maryland, after directing the Human Genome Research Institute there. Before taking up the latter post, he developed the technique for "positional cloning" of genes in DNA and led a research team at the University of Michigan which was responsible for identifying the genes causing cystic fibrosis, Huntington's Disease, neurofibromatosis, and other diseases. He has been a strong protagonist for the privacy of genetic information and prohibiting insurance discrimination on genetic grounds. He is a member of the National Academy of Sciences of the US and a recipient of the Presidential Medal of Freedom. This chapter is based on an interview with Denis Alexander, published in Third Way in June 2008; a fuller version is contained in Collins's book *The Language of God* (Free Press, 2006).

My early life was uncomplicated but unconventional. At the end of World War II, my parents did the "sixties thing" twenty years before it became fashionable: they bought a ninety-five-acre farm and set about trying to create a simple agricultural lifestyle without use of farm machinery. It was a dirt farm in the Shenandoah Valley with no running water and few other physical amenities. My early years were a happy brew of pastoral beauty, hard farm work, summer theatre, and music. I thrived in it and grew up with the general sense that you had to be responsible for your own behaviour and choices, as no one else was going to step in and take care of them for you.

My three brothers and I were home schooled by my mother. She had no organized class schedule or lesson plans, but was incredibly perceptive in identifying topics that would intrigue a young mind. Learning was never something you did because you had to, it was something you did because you loved it.

Religion was not an important part of my childhood. When I was five, my parents sent my next oldest brother and me to become members of the boys' choir at the local Episcopal church. They made it clear that it would be a great way to learn music, but that the theology should not be taken too seriously. I followed those instructions, learning the glories of harmony and counterpoint, but letting the theological teaching wash over me without leaving any discernible residue. My interactions with God were limited to occasional bouts of bargaining. At about the age of nine I remember making a contract with him that if he would prevent the rainout of a Saturday night outing that I was particularly excited about, then I would promise never to smoke cigarettes. Sure enough, the rains held off – and I never took up smoking.

At the age of ten, we moved in town to be with my ailing grandmother, and I entered the public [state] school system. At fourteen, a charismatic chemistry teacher opened my eyes to the wonderfully exciting and powerful methods of science. The fact that all matter was constructed of atoms and molecules that followed mathematical principles was an unexpected revelation, and the ability to use the tools of science to discover new things about nature struck me at once as something of which I wanted to be a part. With the enthusiasm of a new convert, I decided to become a chemist.

In contrast, biology left me cold. It seemed to have more to do with the rote learning of mindless facts than the elucidation of principles. The overwhelming complexity of life led me to conclude that biology was rather like existential philosophy; there was not nearly enough logic in it to be appealing.

I went on to the University of Virginia, determined to pursue a scientific career. Like most college freshmen, I found my new environment invigorating, with so many ideas bouncing off classroom walls in the day and dorm rooms at night. Some of these invariably turned to questions about the existence of God. In my early teens I had had occasional moments of longing for something outside myself, often associated with the beauty of nature or a particularly profound musical experience. Nevertheless, my sense of the spiritual was very skimpy and easily removed by fellow students who took great delight in destroying any remnants of superstition, which is what they considered faith to be. A few months into my college career, I became convinced that while many religious faiths had inspired interesting traditions of art and culture, they held no foundational truth.

Though I did not know the word at the time, I became an agnostic, a term coined by the nineteenth-century scientist T. H. Huxley to indicate someone who simply does not know whether or not God exists. Some arrive at agnosticism after intense analysis of the evidence, while many others simply find it to be a comfortable way of avoiding arguments they find discomforting on either side. I was definitely in the latter category. In fact, my assertion of "Don't know" was really more "I don't want to know." As a young man growing up in a world full of temptations, it was convenient to ignore the need to be answerable to any higher spiritual authority.

After graduation, I went on to a PhD programme in physical chemistry at Yale, pursuing the mathematical elegance that had first attracted me to this branch of science. My intellectual life was bounded by quantum mechanics and second-order differential equations, and my heroes were the giants of physics – Albert Einstein, Niels Bohr, Werner Heisenberg, and Paul Dirac. I did not doubt that everything in the universe could be explained on the basis of equations and physical principles. Discovering that Albert Einstein, despite his strong Zionist position, did not believe in Yahweh, the God of the Jewish people, only reinforced my conclusion that it would be intellectual suicide for any thinking scientist seriously to entertain the possibility of God. The result was that my agnosticism graduated to an obnoxious atheism; I became the sort of person you would not have enjoyed lunching with, because I felt it part of my mission in life to point out that all that really mattered in life could be discerned by science and that everything else was irrelevant. I felt quite comfortable challenging the spiritual beliefs of anyone who mentioned them in my presence and discounted all such perspectives as sentimentality and outmoded superstition.

Two years into my PhD, my carefully structured life plan started to crack. Despite the excitements of theoretical quantum mechanics, I began to doubt whether this would be a life-sustaining pathway for me. It seemed that most of the major advances in quantum theory were fifty years old and my career was likely to involve nothing much more than seeking simplifications and approximations to make elegant but unsolvable equations a tiny bit more tractable. In practice, it seemed that my path would lead inexorably to a life of delivering an interminable series of lectures on thermodynamics and statistical mechanics to class after class of undergraduates who were either bored or terrified by them.

In an effort to broaden my horizons, I enrolled in a course in biochemistry and was exposed to the life sciences that I had previously shunned. Its effect on me was mind-blowing. The structures of DNA, RNA, and protein were laid out in all their satisfying digital glory. The ability to apply rigorous intellectual standards to understanding biology – something I had assumed impossible – was bursting forth with the discovery of the genetic code. With new methods for splicing different DNA fragments together (recombinant DNA), there seemed real possibility for applying all of this knowledge for human benefit. Biology had mathematical elegance after all. Life made sense.

All this happened at a time of vague unrest. I was twenty-two, married, and with a young child. When I was younger, I used to prefer my own company, but now social interaction seemed rather important. I began to question whether I was really cut out to do science and carry out independent research. After much soul-searching, I applied for admission to medical school. I was the guy who had hated biology because you had to memorize things. Could any field of study require more memorization than medicine? But something was different now: this was about humanity, not crayfish; there were principles underlying the details; and all this might ultimately help real people.

I rapidly found medical school was the right place for me. I loved the intellectual stimulation, the ethical challenges, the human element, and the amazing complexity of the human body. Even better, I found out how to combine this new love of medicine with my old love of mathematics. An austere and somewhat unapproachable paediatrician, who taught a grand total of six hours of lectures on medical genetics, showed me my future. He brought to class patients with sickle cell anaemia, galactosemia (an often-fatal inability to tolerate milk products), and Down's syndrome, all caused by glitches in the genome, some as subtle as a single letter gone awry.

I was astounded by the multiple consequences of those rare careless moments of the DNA copying mechanism. I was immediately drawn to genetics. It was December 1973 and no shadow of possibility of anything as grand and consequential as the Human Genome Project had entered any human mind, but the path I fortuitously started then led directly into participation in one of the most historic undertakings of humankind.

My medical course naturally brought me into contact with patients. Doctors enter some of the most intimate relationships imaginable with individuals who had been complete strangers until they fell sick. Cultural taboos that normally prevent the exchange of intensely private information come tumbling down. I found relationships with sick and dying patients almost overwhelming, and I struggled to maintain the professional distance and lack of emotional involvement that many of my teachers advocated.

What struck me profoundly about my bedside conversations with these good North Carolina citizens was the spiritual aspect of what many of them were going through. There were a significant proportion whose faith provided them with a strong reassurance of ultimate peace, be it in this world or the next, despite terrible suffering that in most instances they had done nothing to bring on themselves. If faith was a psychological crutch, it must be a very powerful one; if it was nothing more than a veneer of cultural tradition, why were these people not shaking their fists at God and demanding that their friends and family stop all this talk about a loving and benevolent supernatural power?

A turning point for me came when an elderly woman, suffering from severe and untreatable angina, asked me, "What do you believe, Doctor?" It was a fair question; we had discussed many other important issues of life and death, and she had shared her own strong Christian beliefs with me. I felt my face flush as I stammered out the words, "I'm not really sure." Her obvious surprise brought into sharp relief a predicament which I had been running away from for nearly all my twenty-seven years: I had never really seriously considered the evidence for and against belief.

That exchange haunted me. Did I not consider myself a scientist? Does a scientist draw conclusions without considering the data? Could there be a more important question in all of human existence than "Is there a God?" And yet there I found myself, with a combination of wilful blindness and something that could only be properly described as arrogance, having avoided any serious consideration that God might be a real possibility. Suddenly all my arguments seemed very thin, and I had the sensation that the ice under my feet was cracking.

This realization was thoroughly alarming. After all, if I could no longer rely on the robustness of my atheism, would I have to take responsibility for actions that I would prefer to keep unscrutinized? Was I answerable to someone other than myself? The question was too pressing to avoid.

I suspected that a full investigation would buttress my atheism. But I determined to look at the facts. Thus began a quick and confusing survey through the major religions of the world. Much of what I found in the potted versions of different religions (I found reading the actual sacred texts much too difficult) left me thoroughly mystified. I doubted that there was any rational basis for spiritual belief undergirding any of these faiths. Then I went to visit a Methodist minister who lived down the street to ask him whether faith made any logical sense. He listened patiently to my confused (and probably blasphemous) ramblings, and then handed me a small book off his shelf.

The book was *Mere Christianity* by C. S. Lewis. As I struggled to absorb the breadth and depth of the intellectual arguments therein, I had to accept that all my own constructs against the plausibility of faith were horribly naïve. Lewis seemed to know all my objections, sometimes even before I had formulated them. He invariably addressed them within a page or two. When I learned subsequently that Lewis had himself been an atheist who had set out to disprove faith on the basis of logical argument, I recognized how he could be so insightful about my path. He had travelled the same way.

The argument that most rocked my ideas about science and spirit was spelt out in the heading of Book One: "Right and Wrong as a Clue to the Meaning of the Universe". While in many ways the "Moral Law" that Lewis described was a universal feature of human existence, in some ways it was as if I was recognizing it for the first time. Some disagreements are mundane, like a wife criticizing her husband for not speaking more kindly to a friend or a child complaining "It's not fair" when different amounts of ice cream are doled out at a birthday party. Other arguments take on larger significance. In international affairs, for instance, some argue that the United States has a moral obligation to spread democracy throughout the world, even if it requires military force, whereas others say that the unilateral use of military and economic force squanders moral authority. In medicine, furious debates currently surround the question of whether or not it is acceptable to carry out research on human embryonic stem cells. Some argue that such research violates the sanctity of human life; others that the potential to alleviate human suffering constitutes an ethical mandate to proceed.

In every case, each "side" appeals to an unstated standard, a Moral Law. The concept of right and wrong appears to be universal amongst all members of the human species and apparently applies peculiarly to human beings. Though other animals may at times appear to show glimmerings of such behaviours, they are certainly not widespread, and in many instances animal behaviours from other species seem to be in dramatic contrast to any sense of universal rightness. It is the awareness of right and wrong, along with the development of language, awareness of self, and the ability to imagine the future, to which scientists generally refer when trying to enumerate the special qualities of *Homo sapiens*.

Is this sense of right and wrong an intrinsic quality of being human, or just a consequence of cultural traditions? Some have argued that cultures have such widely differing norms for behaviour that any conclusion about a shared Moral Law is unfounded. But is that really true? Lewis, a student of many cultures, calls this

> *a lie, a good resounding lie. If a man will go into a library and spend a few days with the* Encyclopaedia of Religion and Ethics, *he will soon discover the massive unanimity of the practical reason in man. From the Babylonian Hymn to Samos, from the laws of Manu, the Book of the Dead, the Analects, the Stoics, the Platonists, from Australian aborigines and Redskins, he will collect the same triumphantly monotonous denunciations of oppression, murder, treachery and falsehood; the same injunctions of kindness to the aged, the young, and the weak, of almsgiving and impartiality and honesty.*[1]

In some unusual cultures the law takes on surprising trappings – consider witch burning in seventeenth-century America. Yet when surveyed closely, these apparent aberrations can be seen to arise from strongly held although misguided conclusions about who or what is good or evil. If you firmly believed that a witch was the personification of evil on earth, an apostle of the Devil himself, would it not then be justified to take such drastic action?

The conclusion about the existence of a Moral Law conflicts with contemporary postmodernism, which argues that there are no absolute rights or wrongs, that all ethical decisions are relative. This leads to a series of catch-22s. If there is no absolute truth, can postmodernism itself be true? Indeed, if there is no right or wrong, then there is no reason to argue for the discipline of ethics in the first place.

Another widespread assumption is that the Moral Law is simply the consequence of Darwinian selection and selection for altruism. By altruism I do not mean the "you scratch my back, I'll scratch yours" kind of behaviour that practises benevolence to others in direct expectation of reciprocal benefits. True altruism is more interesting: the selfless giving of oneself to others with absolutely no secondary motives. When we see that kind of love and generosity, we are overcome with awe and reverence. Oskar Schindler placed his life in great danger by sheltering more than 1,000 Jews from Nazi extermination during World War II, and ultimately died penniless – and we feel a great rush of admiration for his actions. Mother Theresa has consistently ranked as one of the most admired individuals of the current age, though her self-imposed poverty and selfless giving to the sick and dying of Calcutta is in drastic contrast to the materialistic lifestyle that dominates our current culture.

C. S. Lewis explores this kind of selfless love in his remarkable book *The Four Loves*, pointing out that "*agape* love" can be distinguished from the three other forms of love he identifies (affection, friendship, and romantic love) which all can be more easily understood in terms of reciprocal benefit, and which we can see in animals besides ourselves. Indeed, *agape* love or selfless altruism presents a major challenge for the evolutionist. It is quite frankly a scandal to reductionist reasoning. It cannot be accounted for by the drive of individual selfish genes to perpetuate themselves. Quite the contrary: it may entail sacrifices that lead to great personal suffering, injury, or death, without any evidence of benefit. And yet, if we carefully examine that inner voice we sometimes call conscience, the motivation to practise this kind of love exists within all of us, despite our efforts to ignore it.

If the law of human nature cannot be explained away as cultural artefact or evolutionary by-product, then how can we account for its presence? There is truly something out of the ordinary going on here. To quote Lewis:

> *If there was a controlling power outside the universe,*
> *it could not show itself to us as one of the facts inside*
> *the universe – no more than the architect of a house*
> *could actually be a wall or staircase or fireplace in that*
> *house. The only way in which we could expect it to*
> *show itself would be inside ourselves as an influence*
> *or a command trying to get us to behave in a certain*
> *way. And that is just what we do find inside ourselves.*
> *Surely this ought to arouse our suspicions?*[2]

I was stunned by the logic of this argument when I encountered it. Here, hiding in my own heart as familiar as anything in daily experience but now emerging for the first time at age twenty-seven as a clarifying principle, this Moral Law shone its bright white light into the recesses of my childish atheism, and demanded a serious consideration of its origin. Was this God looking back at me?

And if that were so, what kind of God was this? Would this be a God who started the universe in motion 14 billion years ago and then wandered off to deal with other more important matters? No, this God, if I was perceiving him at all, must be One who desires some kind of relationship with those special creatures called human beings, and has therefore instilled this special glimpse of himself into each one of us. This might be the God of Abraham, but it was certainly not the God of Einstein.

There was another consequence of this growing sense of God's nature, if in fact he was real. Judging by the incredibly high standards of the Moral Law, this was a God who was holy and righteous. There was no reason to suspect that this God would be kindly, indulgent, or forgiving. The gradual dawning of my realization of God's plausible existence brought conflicting feelings: comfort at the breadth and depth of the existence of such a Mind, and yet profound dismay at the realization of my own appalling imperfections when viewed in his light.

I had started this journey of intellectual exploration to confirm my atheism. That now lay in ruins as the argument from the Moral Law (plus other issues) forced me to admit the plausibility of the God hypothesis. Agnosticism, which had seemed like a safe second-place haven, now loomed like the great cop-out it often is. Faith in God now seemed more rational than disbelief. It also became clear that science, despite its unquestioned powers in unravelling the mysteries of the natural world, would get me no further in resolving the question of God. Still beset by uncertainties of what path I had started down, I had to admit that I had reached the threshold of accepting the possibility of a spiritual worldview, including the existence of God. It seemed impossible either to go forward or to turn back. Years later, I encountered a sonnet by Sheldon Vanauken that precisely described my dilemma. Its concluding lines are:

> *Between the probable and proved there yawns*
> *A gap. Afraid to jump, we stand absurd,*
> *Then see behind us sink the ground and, worse,*
> *Our very standpoint crumbling. Desperate dawns*
> *Our only hope: to leap into the Word*
> *That opens up the shuttered universe.*[3]

For a long time I stood trembling on the edge of this yawning gap. But then, at last, I leapt.

Humility

In 1989, I spent some months at a small mission hospital at Eku in the Niger delta. It was unlike anything I had known.

There were never enough beds, so patients often had to sleep on the floor. Their families often travelled with them and took on the responsibility of feeding them. Oftentimes patients only arrived at the hospital after many days of progressive illness. Overwhelmed by the enormity of these problems, exhausted by the constant stream of patients with illnesses I was poorly equipped to diagnose, frustrated by the lack of laboratory and X-ray support, I grew more and more discouraged, wondering why I had ever thought that this trip would be a good thing.

One afternoon in the clinic a young farmer with progressive weakness and massive swelling of his legs was brought in by his family. Taking his pulse, I was startled to find that it virtually disappeared every time he took a breath. Though I had never seen this classic physical sign (referred to as a "paradoxical pulse") so dramatically demonstrated, I was pretty sure it meant that this young farmer had accumulated a large amount of fluid in the pericardial sac around his heart. This fluid was threatening to choke off his circulation and take his life. The only chance to save him was to carry out a highly risky procedure of drawing off the pericardial fluid with a large-bore needle placed in his chest. In the developed world, such a procedure would only be done by a highly trained interventional cardiologist, guided by an ultrasound machine, in order to avoid lacerating the heart and causing immediate death.

No ultrasound was available. No other physician present in this small Nigerian hospital had ever undertaken this procedure. The choice was for me to attempt a highly risky and invasive needle aspiration, or watch the farmer die. I explained the situation to the young man, who was now fully aware of his own precarious state. He calmly urged me to proceed. With my heart in my mouth and a prayer on my lips, I inserted a large needle just under his sternum and aimed for his left shoulder, all the while fearing that I might have made the wrong diagnosis, in which case I was almost certainly going to kill him.

I didn't have to wait long. The rush of dark red fluid in my syringe initially made me panic that I might have entered the heart chamber, but it soon became apparent that this was not blood. It was a massive amount of bloody tuberculous effusion from the pericardial sac. The young man's response was dramatic. His paradoxical pulse disappeared almost at once, and within the next twenty-four hours the swelling of his legs rapidly improved.

For a few hours after this experience I felt a tremendous sense of relief, even elation, at what had happened. But by the next morning, the familiar gloom began to settle over me. After all, the circumstances that had led this young man to acquire tuberculosis were not going to change. Even if he survived the disease, some other preventable disorder, born of dirty water, inadequate nutrition, and a dangerous environment, probably lay not too far in his future. The chances for long life for a Nigerian farmer are poor.

With those discouraging thoughts in my head, I approached his bedside, to find him reading his Bible. He looked at me quizzically, and asked whether I had worked at the hospital for a long time. I admitted that I was new, feeling somewhat irritated and embarrassed that it had been so easy for him to figure that out. But then this young Nigerian farmer, just about as different from me in culture, experience, and ancestry as any two humans could be, spoke the words that will forever be emblazoned in my mind: "I get the sense you are wondering why you came here," he said. "I have an answer for you. You came here for one reason. You came here for me."

I was stunned. Stunned that he could see so clearly into my heart, but even more stunned at the words he was speaking. I had plunged a needle close to his heart; he had directly impaled mine. With a few simple words he had put my grandiose dreams of being the great white doctor, healing the African millions, to shame. He was right. We are each called to reach out to others.

On rare occasions that can happen on a grand scale. But most of the time it happens in simple acts of kindness of one person to another. Those are the events that really matter. The tears of relief that blurred my vision as I digested his words stemmed from indescribable reassurance – reassurance that there in that strange place for just that one moment, I was in harmony with God's will, bonded together with this young man in a most unlikely but marvellous way.

Nothing I had learned from science could explain that experience. Nothing about the evolutionary explanations for human behaviour could account for why it seemed so right for this privileged white man to be standing at the bedside of this young African farmer, each receiving something exceptional. This was what C. S. Lewis calls *agape* love. It is the love that seeks no recompense. It is an affront to materialism and naturalism. And it is the sweetest joy that one can experience.

Truth

Most of the world's great faiths share many truths. Probably they would not have survived had that not been so. Yet there are also important differences, and each person needs to seek out his own particular path to the truth. After recognizing the bankruptcy of atheism and agnosticism, I spent considerable time trying to discern God's characteristics. I concluded that he must be a God who cares about persons, or the argument about the Moral Law would not make much sense. So Deism wouldn't do for me. I also concluded that God must be holy and righteous, since the Moral Law calls me in that direction. But this still seemed awfully abstract. Just because God is good and loves his creatures does not, for instance, mean that we have the ability to communicate with him or to have some sort of relationship with him. I found an increasing sense of longing for that, however, and I began to realize that this is what prayer is all about. Prayer is not, as some seem to suggest, an opportunity to manipulate God into doing what you want him to. Prayer is instead our way of seeking fellowship with God, learning about him, and attempting to perceive his perspective on the many issues around us that cause us puzzlement, wonder, or distress.

Yet I found it difficult to build that bridge toward God. The more I learned about him, the more his purity and holiness seemed unapproachable, and the darker my own thoughts and actions seemed to be in that bright light. I began to be increasingly aware of my own inability to do the right thing, even for a day. I could generate lots of excuses, but when I was really honest with myself, pride, apathy, and anger were regularly winning my internal battles. I had never really thought of applying the word "sinner" to myself before, but now it was painfully obvious that this old-fashioned word, one from which I had previously recoiled because it seemed coarse and judgmental, fitted quite accurately.

Into this deepening gloom came the person of Jesus Christ. During my boyhood years sitting in the choir loft, I really had no clear idea who Christ was. I thought of him as a fairy tale, a superhero in a "just so" bedtime story. But as I read the actual account of his life for the first time in the four gospels, the enormity of Christ's claims and their consequences gradually began to sink in. Here was a man who not only claimed to *know* God, he claimed to *be* God. No other figure in any other faith made such an outrageous claim. He also claimed to be able to forgive sins, which seemed both exciting and utterly shocking. He was humble and loving, he spoke remarkable words of wisdom, and yet he was put to death on the cross by those who feared him. He was a man, so he knew the human condition that I was finding so burdensome, and yet he promised to relieve that burden: "Come unto me all ye that labour and are heavy laden, and I will give you rest" (Matthew 11:28, KJV).

The other scandalous thing that the New Testament eyewitnesses said about him and that Christians seemed to take as a central tenet of their faith, was that this good man rose from the dead. For a scientific mind, this was difficult stuff. But, on the other hand, if Christ really was the Son of God, as he explicitly claimed, then surely of all those who had ever walked the earth, he could violate the laws of nature if he needed to do so to achieve a more important purpose. But his resurrection had to be more than a demonstration of magical powers. What was the real point of it? After much searching, I could find no single answer – instead, there were several interlocking answers, all pointing to the idea of a bridge between our sinful selves and a holy God. Some commentators focus on the idea of substitution – Christ dying in the place of all of us who deserve God's judgment for our wrongdoings. Others concentrate on redemption – Christ paid the ultimate price to free us from the bondage of sin, so that we could find God and rest in the confidence that he no longer judges us by our actions, but sees us as having been washed clean. Christians call this salvation by grace. But for me, the crucifixion and resurrection also provided something else. My desire to draw close to God was blocked by my own pride and sinfulness, which in turn was an inevitable consequence of my own selfish desire to be in control. Faithfulness to God required a kind of death of self-will, in order to be reborn as a new creation.

How could I achieve such a thing? As had happened so many times previously, the words of C. S. Lewis captured the answer precisely:

> *But supposing God became a man – suppose*
> *our human nature which can suffer and die was*
> *amalgamated with God's nature in one person – then*
> *that person could help us. He could surrender His will,*

and suffer and die, because He was man; and He could
do it perfectly because He was God. You and I can go
through this process only if God does it in us; but God
can do it only if He becomes man. Our attempts at this
dying will succeed only if we men share in God's dying,
just as our thinking can succeed only because it is a
drop out of the ocean of His intelligence: but we cannot
share God's dying unless God dies; and He cannot die
except by being a man. That is the sense in which He
pays our debt, and suffers for us what He Himself need
not suffer at all.[4]

Before I became a believer in God, this kind of logic seemed like
utter nonsense. Now the crucifixion and resurrection emerged
as the compelling solution to the gap that yawned between God
and myself, a gap that could now be bridged by the person of
Jesus Christ.

And Lewis had yet another word for me:

A man who was merely a man and said the sort of
things Jesus said would not be a great moral teacher.
He would either be a lunatic – on a level with a man
who says He is a poached egg – or else He would be the
devil of hell. You must make your choice. Either this
man was, and is, the Son of God: or else a madman
or something worse. You can shut Him up for a fool,
you can spit at Him and kill Him as a demon; or you
can fall at His feet and call Him Lord and God. But let
us not come with any patronizing nonsense about His
being a great human teacher. He has not left that open
to us. He did not intend to.[5]

Lewis was right. I had to make a choice. A full year had passed since I decided to believe in some sort of God, and now I was being called to account. On a beautiful fall day, hiking in the Cascade Mountains during my first trip west of the Mississippi, the majesty and beauty of God's creation overwhelmed my resistance. As I rounded a corner and saw a beautiful and unexpected frozen waterfall, hundreds of feet high, I knew the search was over. The next morning, I knelt in the dewy grass as the sun rose, and surrendered to Jesus Christ.

I do not mean by telling this story to evangelize or proselytize. Each person must carry out his or her own search for spiritual truth. Christians all too often come across as arrogant, judgmental and self-righteous. Christ never did. But the overarching principle of love and acceptance appears throughout Christ's teachings in the New Testament. It is the most important guide of how we are to treat others. In Matthew 22:35 Christ is asked about which is the greatest of God's commandments. He answers simply, "Love the Lord your God with all your heart and with all your soul and with all your mind. This is the first and greatest commandment. And the second is like it: Love your neighbour as yourself."

Deciphering God's instruction book

I often wonder if I would have decided to pursue genetics if I had been a committed Christian when I made the decision. My first published paper on human genetics was when I was a research fellow in genetics at Yale in the early 1980s. It was based on DNA sequencing, which was a very laborious undertaking at that time. We knew relatively little then about what the genome might contain. No one had actually seen the chemical bases of an individual human gene under the microscope. Only a few hundred genes had been characterized, and estimates of how many genes the genome might contain varied wildly. Even the definition of a gene was in disarray – simple definitions that a gene constitutes a stretch of DNA that codes for a particular protein had been shaken by the discovery that the protein-coding regions of genes are interrupted by intervening DNA segments called introns. Depending on how the coding regions are subsequently spliced together in the RNA copy, one gene could sometimes code for several different (albeit related) proteins. Furthermore, there were long stretches of DNA in between genes that didn't seem to be doing very much; some even referred to these as "junk DNA", though a certain amount of hubris was required for anyone to call any part of the genome "junk", given our level of ignorance.

Despite these uncertainties, I decided to pursue the genetic basis of certain diseases that had so far resisted all attempts at discovery. Foremost among these was cystic fibrosis (CF), the most common potentially fatal genetic disorder of north Europeans. We knew that CF patients had thick, sticky secretions in their lungs and pancreas – but we had no real clue as to the likely function of the gene that must have gone awry. All we knew was that somewhere in the 3 billion letters of the DNA code, at least one letter had gone wrong in a vulnerable location. We couldn't read all 3 billion pairs of letters, but we could randomly shine a flashlight on a few million here, a few million there, and look for any correlation with the disease. We had to do this hundreds and hundreds of times, but the genome is a bounded set of information – if we kept at it, we were confident of locating the right neighbourhood. And then in 1985, to the astonishment and delight of scientists and families alike, we accomplished it – demonstrating that the CF gene must reside somewhere within a 2 million base-pair segment of DNA on chromosome 7.

But 2 million base pairs is a lot of genetic information. How could we find the CF gene itself? My team and I invented a method called "chromosome jumping", which allowed us to move across our 2 million base-pair target in pogo-stick leaps, rather than crawling along in the traditional way. The search was like a detective story – we knew the mystery would eventually be solved on the last page, but we didn't know how long it would take to get there. There were clues and blind alleys aplenty. After getting excited for the third or fourth time about a possible answer, only to have it collapse the next day because of new data, we stopped allowing ourselves to be very optimistic about anything. We found it hard to keep explaining to colleagues why we hadn't found the gene yet, or alternatively why we hadn't just given up. At one point, seeking another metaphor to explain the difficulty of the problem, I even went to a local farm to have my picture taken holding a sewing needle while sitting atop a large haystack. It was four laborious years before we found the answer. The cause of cystic fibrosis in the majority of patients was a deletion of just three letters of the DNA code in the protein-coding part of a previously unknown gene. Soon after, we and others were able to show that this mutation and other less common misspellings in this same gene, account for virtually all cases of the disease.

Sorting out cystic fibrosis was supposed to be one of the easier genetic tasks – it was a relatively common disease and one which followed Mendel's rules of inheritance precisely. How could we ever imagine extending this work to the hundreds of rarer genetic diseases that urgently needed unravelling? Even more challenging, how could we penetrate diseases like diabetes, schizophrenia, heart disease, or the common cancers, where we know hereditary factors are critically important but where many different genes are involved. If there was to be any hope of succeeding in these more difficult circumstances, we simply had to have detailed and accurate information about every nook and cranny in the human genome.

Clearly a complete genome sequence would be enormously valuable. Hiding in the vast instruction book would be the parts list for human biology, as well as clues to a long list of diseases which we understand poorly and treat ineffectively. For me as a physician, the possibility of laying open the pages of this most powerful textbook of medicine was extremely compelling. Arguments about the wisdom of a Human Genome Project raged furiously during the late 1980s (Cook-Deegan, 1994). While most scientists had to agree that the information would eventually be useful, the sheer magnitude and cost of the project made it seem almost unattainable. It was Jim Watson, Director of the Project, the co-discoverer of the DNA Double Helix and at that time the unrivalled "rock star" of biology, who convinced Congress to take a risk on this new endeavour.

Then two years later, I succeeded Watson as Director. Being quite happy at the time at the University of Michigan and having no ambition to be a federal employee, I initially declined interest in the post. But it haunted me. There was only one Human Genome Project. This was only going to be done once in human history. If it succeeded, the consequences for medicine would be unprecedented. As a believer in God, was this one of those moments where I was somehow being called to take on a larger role? Here was a chance to read the language of God, to determine the intimate details of how humans had come to be. Could I walk away? I have always been suspicious of those who claim to perceive God's will in moments such as this, but the awesome significance of this adventure, and the potential consequences for humankind's relationship with the Creator, could hardly be ignored.

Visiting my daughter in North Carolina in November 1992, I spent a long afternoon praying in a little chapel, seeking guidance about this decision. I did not "hear" God speak – in fact, I have never had that experience. But during those hours, ending in an evensong service that I had not expected, a peace settled over me. A few days later, I accepted the job.

This is not the place to describe the next ten years. They were a wild roller-coaster of experiences. The original goals of the Human Genome Project were incredibly ambitious, but we set aggressive milestones and held ourselves accountable for achieving them. There were moments of great frustration. There were tensions when Craig Venter, the leader of the company soon to be named Celera, announced that he would carry out large-scale sequencing on the human genome, but would file patents on many of the genes and keep the data in a database that would require significant payment for access. The idea that the human genome sequence might become private property was deeply distressing. Even more of concern, questions began to be raised in the Congress about whether it made sense to continue to spend taxpayers' money on a project that might better be carried out in the private sector – though the data from the Celera team was not readily available, and the scientific strategy that Venter aimed to pursue was almost certain to fail if a truly finished and highly accurate sequence was ultimately desired. A constant stream of claims of higher efficiency poured out of the well-oiled Celera public relations machine, which also sought to label the public project as slow and bureaucratic. Given that the work of the Human Genome Project was being done in some of the world's finest universities by some of the most creative and dedicated scientists on the planet, that was hard to take. Yet the press loved the controversy. What most observers seemed to miss was that this was not, at its core, a debate about who would do the work faster or cheaper (both Celera and the public project were now well situated to deliver on this). It was instead a battle of ideals – would the human genome sequence, our shared inheritance, become a commercial commodity or a universal public good?

Interest in "the race" became increasingly unseemly and threatened to diminish the importance of the goal. It was resolved in a private meeting over beer and pizza. Dr Venter and I worked out a plan for a simultaneous announcement. The result was that on 26 June 2000, I found myself standing next to the President of the United States in the East Room of the White House announcing that a first draft of the human instruction book had been determined. Three years later, in the month that marked the fiftieth anniversary of Watson and Crick's publication on the Double Helix, we announced the completion of all of the goals of the Human Genome Project. As the project manager of the enterprise, I was intensely proud of the more than 2,000 scientists who had accomplished this remarkable feat, one that I believe will be seen a thousand years from now as one of the most major achievements of humankind.

For me as a believer, the uncovering of the human genome sequence held additional significance. This book was written in the DNA language by which God spoke life into being. I felt an overwhelming sense of awe in surveying this most significant of all biological texts. Yes, it is written in a language we understand very poorly, and it will take decades, if not centuries, to understand its instructions, but we had crossed a one-way bridge into profoundly new territory.

Human evolution?

We now have data from the study of multiple genomes. An important consequence of this has been the ability to compare our own DNA sequence with that of other organisms. If one picks the coding region of a human gene (i.e. the part that contains the instructions for a protein), there will nearly always be a highly significant match to the genomes of other mammals. Many genes will also show discernible although less perfect matches to fish. Some will even find matches to the genomes of organisms such as fruit flies and roundworms. In some particularly striking examples, the similarity extends all the way down to genes in yeast and even to bacteria.

What does this mean? At two different levels, it provides powerful support for Darwin's theory of evolution, i.e. descent from a common ancestor with natural selection operating on randomly occurring variations. At the level of the genome as a whole, a computer can construct a tree of life based solely upon the similarities of the DNA sequences of multiple organisms. Bear in mind that this analysis does not utilize any information from the fossil record, or from anatomical observations of current life forms. Yet its similarity to conclusions drawn from studies of comparative anatomy, both of living organisms and of fossilized remains, is striking. Second, Darwin's theory predicts that mutations within the genome that do not affect function (i.e. those located in "junk DNA") will accumulate steadily over time. Mutations in the coding region of genes, however, are expected to be observed less frequently, since most of these will be deleterious and only a rare event will provide a selective advantage for retention during the evolutionary process. That is exactly what is observed. This latter phenomenon even applies to the fine details of the coding regions of genes, exactly what Darwin's theory would predict. If, as a creationist might argue, these genomes were created by individual acts of special creation, why would this particular feature appear?

In the mid nineteenth century, Darwin had no way of knowing what the mechanism of evolution by natural selection might be. We can now see that the variation he postulated is supported by naturally occurring mutations in DNA. These are estimated to occur at a rate of about one error every 100 million base pairs per generation. (That means, by the way, that since we all have two genomes of 3 billion base pairs each, one from our mother and one from our father, we all have roughly 60 new mutations that were not present in either of our parents.) We now have the tools to track these events.

Some critics of Darwinism insist that there is no evidence for "macroevolution" (major change in species) in the fossil record, only of "microevolution" (i.e. incremental change within a species). They argue that although we have seen (for example) finch beaks change shape over time as food sources changed, we haven't seen new species arise. This distinction is increasingly seen to be artificial. For example, a group at Stanford University is engaged in an intense effort to understand the wide diversity of body armour in stickleback fish. Sticklebacks that live in salt water typically have a continuous row of three dozen armour plates extending from head to tail, but freshwater populations from multiple different parts of the world, where predators are fewer, have lost most of these plates.

The freshwater sticklebacks apparently arrived in their current locations 10,000 to 20,000 years ago after widespread melting of glaciers at the end of the last Ice Age. A careful comparison of the genomes of the freshwater fish has identified a gene, EDA, whose variants have repeatedly and independently appeared in freshwater situations, resulting in loss of the plates. Interestingly, humans also have an EDA gene, and spontaneous mutations in that gene result in defects in hair, teeth, sweat glands and bone. It is not hard to see how the difference between freshwater and saltwater sticklebacks could be extended, to generate all kinds of fish. The distinction between macroevolution and microevolution is arbitrary; larger changes that result in new species are a result of a succession of smaller incremental steps.

Applying evolutionary science to sticklebacks may be one thing, but what about ourselves? The study of genomes leads inexorably to the conclusion that we humans share a common ancestor with other living things. This evidence alone does not, of course, *prove* a common ancestor; from a creationist perspective, such similarities could simply indicate that God used the same design principles over and over again. Notwithstanding, the detailed study of genomes has rendered that interpretation virtually untenable. Take the human and mouse genomes, both of which have been determined in detail: the overall size of the two genomes is roughly the same and the inventory of protein-coding genes is remarkably similar. But other indications of a common ancestor appear when one looks hard. For instance, the order of genes along the human and the mouse chromosomes is generally maintained over substantial stretches of DNA. In some instances, this correlation extends over substantial distances; virtually all of the genes on human chromosome 17, for instance, are found on mouse chromosome 11. While one might argue that the order of genes is critical in order for their function to occur properly, and therefore a designer might have maintained that order in multiple acts of special creation, there is no reason from current understanding of molecular biology that this restriction should apply over substantial chromosomal distances.

Even more compelling evidence for a common ancestor comes from the study of what are known as ancient repetitive elements (AREs). These arise from "jumping genes", which are capable of copying and inserting themselves in various other locations in the genome, usually without any functional consequences. Mammalian genomes are littered with such AREs, with roughly 45 per cent of the human genome made up of such genetic flotsam and jetsam. When one aligns sections of the human and mouse genomes, one can often identify AREs in approximately the same location in the two genomes. Some of these will have been lost in one species or the other, but many of them remain in a position that is most consistent with their having arrived in the genome of a common mammalian ancestor. Of course, creationists might argue that these are actually functional elements placed there by the Creator for a good reason and our discounting of them as "junk DNA" merely betrays our current level of ignorance. And indeed, some may play important regulatory roles. But others severely strain the credulity of that explanation. The process of transposition often damages the jumping gene. There are AREs throughout the human and mouse genomes that were truncated when they landed, removing any possibility of their functioning. The point to note is that one can very frequently identify a decapitated ARE in parallel positions in the human and the mouse genome. Unless one is willing to take the position that God has placed these decapitated AREs in these precise positions to confuse and mislead us, the conclusion of a common ancestor for humans and mice is virtually inescapable. This kind of recent genome data thus presents an overwhelming challenge to those who hold to the idea that all species were created *ex nihilo*.

At this point, godless materialists might be cheering. If humans evolved strictly by mutation and natural selection, who needs God to explain us? To this, I reply simply: I do. The comparison of chimp and human sequences, interesting as it is, does not tell us what it means to be human. I do not believe that DNA sequence alone, even if accompanied by a vast trove of data on biological function, will ever explain certain special human attributes, such as the knowledge of the Moral Law and the universal search for God. Freeing God from the burden of special acts of creation does not remove him as the source of the things that make humanity special, and of the universe itself. It merely shows us something of how he operates. In fact, for those like myself working in genetics, it is almost impossible to imagine correlating the vast amounts of data coming forth from genome studies without the foundations of Darwin's theory. As Theodosius Dobzhansky, a leading biologist of the twentieth century (and a devout Eastern Orthodox Christian) has said, "Nothing in biology makes sense except in the light of evolution."[6]

If evolution is true, is there any place left for God? Arthur Peacocke, a distinguished British molecular biologist who subsequently became an Anglican priest and has written extensively about the interface between biology and faith, in his book *Evolution: The Disguised Friend of Faith?*[7] recalls the statement of a Victorian theologian, that "Darwinism appeared [at a time when science seemed to be pushing God further and further away] and, under the disguise of a foe did the work of a friend."[8] Now that we have laid out the arguments for the plausibility of God on the one hand, and the scientific data about the origins of the universe and life on our planet on the other, can we find a happy and harmonious synthesis? My answer is in the infinite God, who created the universe and established natural laws to govern it, including the marvellous mechanism of evolution to populate it with living creatures. Most remarkable of all, God used the same mechanism to give rise to us – special creatures with intelligence, a knowledge of right and wrong, free will, and a desire and ability to have fellowship with Him.

Conclusion

If you have made it this far with me, I hope you will agree that both the scientific and spiritual worldviews have much to offer. Both provide differing but complementary ways of answering the greatest of the world's questions, and both can co-exist happily within the mind of an intellectually inquisitive person living in the twenty-first century. Nevertheless, science alone is not enough to answer all the important questions. Even Albert Einstein saw the poverty of a purely naturalistic worldview. Choosing his words carefully, he wrote, "Science without religion is lame, religion without science is blind." Faith is not the opposite of reason; faith rests squarely on reason, but with the added component of revelation. The meaning of human existence, the reality of God, the possibility of an afterlife, and many other spiritual questions lie outside of the reach of the scientific method. While an atheist may claim that those questions are therefore unanswerable and irrelevant, that does not resonate with most individuals' experience. John Polkinghorne uses music to make this point:

> *The poverty of an objectivistic [or reductionist]*
> *account is made only too clear when we consider the*
> *mystery of music. From a scientific point of view, it*
> *is nothing but vibrations in the air, impinging on the*
> *eardrums and stimulating neural currents in the brain.*
> *How does it come about that this banal sequence of*
> *temporal activity has the power to speak to our hearts*
> *of an eternal beauty? The whole range of subjective*
> *experience, from perceiving a patch of pink, to being*
> *enthralled by a performance of the Mass in B Minor,*
> *and on to the mystic's encounter with the ineffable*
> *reality of the One, all these truly human experiences*
> *are at the centre of our encounter with reality, and they*
> *are not to be dismissed as epiphenomenal froth on the*
> *surface of a universe whose true nature is impersonal*
> *and lifeless.*[9]

Science is not the only way of knowing. The astronomer, Arthur Eddington, used to tell of a man who set out to study deep-sea life using a net that had a mesh size of three inches. After describing many wild and wonderful creatures from the depths, he concluded that there are no deep-sea fish smaller than three inches in length. If we are using the scientific net to catch our particular version of truth, we should not be surprised that it does not catch the evidence of spirit.

Nearly five centuries ago, Copernicus argued:

> *To know the mighty works of God, to comprehend*
> *His wisdom and majesty and power, to appreciate*
> *in degree the wonderful working of His laws, surely*
> *all this must be a pleasing and acceptable mode of*
> *worship to the Most High, to whom ignorance cannot*
> *be more grateful than knowledge.*

It is time to call a truce in the war between science and spirit. The war was never really necessary. It has been initiated and encouraged by extremists on both sides, sounding alarms that predict imminent ruin unless the other side is vanquished. Science is not threatened by God; it is enhanced. God is most certainly not threatened by science; he made it all possible. So let us together seek to reclaim the solid ground of an intellectually and spiritually satisfying synthesis of *all* great truths. That ancient motherland of reason and worship beckons all sincere seekers of truth to come and take up residence there. Answer that call. Abandon the battlements. Our hopes, joys, and the future of our world depend on it.

Notes

1. Lewis, C. S. (1967), *Christian Reflections*. Hooper, W. (ed.), Eerdmans.
2. Lewis, C. S. (1977), *Mere Christianity*, Fount (originally published by Geoffrey Bless, 1942), p. 21.
3. *A Severe Mercy*, Harper & Row.
4. Lewis, C. S. (1977), *op. cit.* p. 50.
5. Lewis, C. S. (1977), *op. cit.* p. 45.
6. Dobzhansky's expression could be regarded as disagreeably arrogant. It should be read in its context, which was an article commenting on a request from the Grand Mufti of Saudi Arabia to his ruler, King Faisal, to suppress evolution because it was a spreading heresy.
7. Peacocke, A. R. (2004), *Evolution: the Disguised Friend of Faith?*, Templeton Foundation Press.

8. Moore, A. (1889), "The Christian doctrine of God", *Lux Mundi*, 57–109, Gore, C. (ed.), London: John Murray, p. 99.

9. Polkinghorne, J. (1988), *Belief in God in an Age of Science*, Yale University Press, p. 18.

Chapter 8

A Talent for Science

Professor Sir Ghillean T. Prance, MA, DPhil, Fil Dr, VMH, FRS. Educated at Malvern College and Keble College, Oxford. New York Botanical Garden (1963–88), becoming Senior Vice-President for Science and Director of the Institute of Economic Botany. Director, Royal Botanic Gardens, Kew, 1988–99. Visiting Professor, Reading University; Visiting Professor, Yale University, 1983–88. Scientific Director, Eden Project. Foreign Member of the Academies of Science of Brazil, Denmark and Sweden. President, Association of Tropical Biology, 1979–80, American Association of Plant Taxonomists, 1984–85, Systematics Association, 1989–91, Linnean Society, 1997–2000, Institute of Biology, 2000–2002, Christians in Science, 2002–2008. Distinguished Service Award, New York Botanical Garden, 1986. Diploma Honra ao Merito, Instituto Nacional de Pasquisas, da Amaazonia, 1978. Linnean Medal, 1990. Order of the Rising Sun, Japan, 2012. Author of *Earth Under Threat* (Wild Goose, 2004), *Go to the Ant* (Wild Goose, 2013). Biography by Clive Langmead, *A Passion for Plants* (Kew Publishing, 1995).

The problems of my interest in both botany and the Christian faith began at an early stage – I was six years old and we were living in the Isle of Skye. One Sunday morning as I was walking to church with my parents I spotted a roadside flower that interested me and picked it. It was a harebell or bluebell of Scotland (*Campanula rotundifolia*). I was then in trouble for disgracing the family in public by doing such a thing on the Sabbath. After church I was sent to my room without lunch. My annoyance was not so much that I was punished, but that my parents were being unfair, since they did not really adhere to the strict local customs; their justification was that the opinion of the neighbours and of our hostess, cousin Margaret, was what mattered. I am glad to say that in the long run that misadventure did not deter my interest either in botany or the church.

I was brought up in a nominally Christian environment where church was an important part of family life, and many of our activities revolved around the parish life of a small Cotswold village church. However, it was not until my first term at Oxford University that I made a firm commitment to the Christian faith and the teaching of the Bible. This was through the ministry of the Oxford University Christian Union (OICCU). After hearing the gospel preached on my first two Sundays at Oxford, I accepted Christ on the third, and I soon became an active member of OICCU and served on their executive committee as prayer secretary.

The good teaching received there and from Saint Ebb's Church in Oxford gave me firm grounding for the future. After leaving Oxford I spent twenty-five years in the USA and Brazil, during which time I was a member of the First Baptist Church, White Plains, New York. In Brazil, in the course of my botanical fieldwork, I had the opportunity to travel widely on the mission field and to support the activity of local churches, especially the First Baptist Church of Manaus. As tropical deforestation has accelerated I have become progressively more active in ecological issues, and as a consequence also in creation theology and the Christian basis for environmental protection.

The first problem that I faced on my conversion was which path my future should take. I was naturally anxious to serve my newly found Lord to the best of my ability, and soon after my conversion I began to consider whether I was being called to a full-time ministry. In fact, I went as far as a Church of England selection committee where I was accepted as a candidate for ordination.

It was the wisdom and counsel of my future father-in-law, himself an Anglican clergyman, that was most helpful at this stage in my career. He pointed out the talents I had in botany and that from as early as I could remember I had collected plants. At school I had few botany lessons because my biology master said that I already knew more than I was likely to learn in his classes! Actually, I learned a great deal on field trips with him all over the British Isles, and this gave me the strong botanical grounding that has helped me throughout the rest of my career. My father-in-law explained that this knowledge of botany was a talent given from God and that I should use it to the glory of the Lord. He expounded to me in a helpful way Romans 12:4–7, about the use of spiritual gifts, and it was perhaps at that time that I began to recognize my botanical background as a God-given gift. The result was that I made a positive decision to serve God through a career in botany and to seek to do it well as part of my Christian testimony.

I have never regretted that decision; it has been confirmed in the many ways in which I have had opportunities to serve the Lord during the course of my work as an Amazonian explorer botanist. There is no doubt that I have been a better, more dedicated, and successful botanist as a result of my Christian faith; my faith and desire to serve the Lord through the quality of my work has helped me to work harder and more conscientiously. An attitude that has always troubled me is that of Christians who are too busy with church activities and other Christian pursuits to perform their jobs satisfactorily. That cannot be a good testimony to a living faith in Jesus Christ, yet it is a frequent occurrence. I was strongly advised by my father-in-law to strive for excellence in my studies and my career; I have always been extremely grateful for his wise, yet at the time difficult, advice to follow.

Perhaps the reconciliation between faith and science is easier for a biologist than for those in other areas of science, for biologists have the opportunity to study the working of creation. The question that is always asked of a biologist with a Christian faith is, "How do you reconcile your belief in God with the theory of evolution?" For me, that has never been a real difficulty.

I was brought up in evolutionary thought from an early age and before I was fifteen years old had studied in the field the camouflage of moths on tree bark, the pollination of bird's foot trefoil, and many other examples of evolution. I first read Darwin's *Origin of Species* just after going to Malvern College as a thirteen-year-old. The wonders of creation are just as great whether God created in a single step or used the gradual mechanism of evolution. My subsequent research on intricately co-evolved relationships between plants and animals of the Amazon rainforest has confirmed rather than reduced my awe at the greatness of creation. The *Epiphyllum* cactus flower which I studied has a tubular flower which is eight inches long, with nectar at the base of the tube. Its hawkmoth pollinator has a tongue eight inches in length with which it can reach the nectar at the bottom of the tubular flower, providing a perfect match between the morphology of the plant and the insect because they have co-evolved together. To me this is both a fine example of co-evolution and of the perfection of God's creation. God saw that it was good!

The scientist Christian can get into some amusing and difficult situations. During my travels around Amazonian Brazil I have always looked for local churches and sought to link up with them and encourage their work in any way possible. However, there is not always a clear understanding that a scientist can also be a Christian. Any foreigner entering a local church in a small town in Amazonia is automatically assumed to be a missionary. On my first Sunday in the First Baptist Church of Manaus, Brazil, I was asked by a deacon for biographical details in order to be welcomed during the service by the pastor. I explained to my questioner that I was a botanist from the New York Botanical Garden working with the local research institute and that I was also a Christian layman. After writing extensive notes he asked, "What mission did you say you were from?" Again, I thought that I explained my situation well, and he left with his notes. I was asked by the pastor to stand and was introduced to the congregation as Dr Prance from the "New York Botanical Missionary Society"! It is sad that even in a large city church a foreign Christian is automatically associated with full-time mission work. Where are all the Christian laymen? Do they go on holiday from church when they travel as tourists or on business to Manaus or other tropical cities? I have been blessed so often on my travels through attending worship in a foreign city where I did not understand a word of the language. The unity in Christ is the same.

I once spent a few weeks in the northern frontier town of Boa Vista (the capital of Roraima State in Brazil). I attended the local Baptist church which had a wonderful pastor who befriended me. On my last Sunday there, he asked me to preach at the evening service, and I gladly accepted. He stood up in the pulpit and introduced me with the usual nice words, and then informed his congregation that here was the proof that man was not descended from monkeys. A biologist scientist was about to preach. As I got up to follow this introduction I was thinking of 1 Corinthians 8:13: "Therefore, if food is a cause of my brother's falling, I will never eat meat, lest I cause my brother to fall." I was careful to affirm that church where I could, and to preach the gospel faithfully without touching on any controversial subject that might have caused my brothers in the church to stumble, and as a result there was considerable response to my preaching.

Perhaps one of the most difficult classes I have ever taught was in response to the request of a pastor of a fast-growing, theologically conservative church in Manaus. It had reached the stage in its development where, for the first time, teenage members were entering university. The pastor expressed his concern to me and to a Brazilian scientist member of the church (Warwick Kerr, a well-known geneticist) that many of the young church members dropped out of church when they went to university because of the conflict between their conservative theology and the evolutionary and atheist beliefs of their university teachers. We were asked by this wise pastor to teach a Sunday school course on creation and evolution, amid considerable criticism from his church members. In the course we looked at both the scientific details and the biblical teachings on creation: it helped this group of young people to use their intellectual abilities for matters of faith and prepared them for the university scene. Here we were helping to harmonize science and Christian faith for a group of people who had come from the opposite end of the spectrum to me, through a strong faith in the Creator rather than an extensive knowledge and interest in his creation. Our experiment worked because when I return to that church today, I always meet some of that class who have survived their launch into the world without becoming part of it. At times it was not easy for us to take barbed words from some of the church deacons, but we helped to produce a new generation of thinking Christians in that church, and they continue the work with today's youth.

Conservation and stewardship

I first went to the Amazon region in 1963 to study plants and to collect material for basic taxonomic work. During the first ten years of my exploration in Amazonia I was privileged to travel widely and had a wonderful opportunity to carry out research in the region, with little concern for environmental issues. It was a time of learning about the plants and the animals with which they interact. The more I understood complicated pollination mechanisms by bats, beetles, birds and butterflies, and the ways in which plants defend themselves against the hoards of leaf-eating predators, the more I marvelled at creation. By 1973, however, the situation in Amazonia had changed drastically and large-scale development, accompanied by massive destruction of the forest, had begun. For example, the TransAmazon Highway and its colonization plan was inaugurated in 1970 by President Medici of Brazil. While teaching an ecology field class at Altamira, on the TransAmazon Highway, with environmental ecologist Robert Goodland, I began to realize how serious the issue of deforestation of tropical rainforest had become. We could see that much of the devastation was in vain, for projects that were unsustainable were being undertaken. For instance, unproductive land was being used as cattle pasture, but could support less than one cow per hectare over the eight-year lifetime of the field before it had to be abandoned altogether. Cattle farming was being sustained by a completely false economy of tax incentives and land speculation.

This first-hand experience of the futility of much of the deforestation led me gradually to change the emphasis of my research interests to a much more applied approach. I worked far more on economic botany and became concerned about some of the environmental problems related to the use of tropical rainforest. This involved both the search for new plants of possible economic use and the study of the ecology and land use systems of the Amazon Indians. I am sure that I was able to make this change in direction more easily because of my Christian faith and the consequent concern for justice and peace.

However, it was my faith that was strengthened from this experience because finally my botany and my faith came together; the dichotomy between work as a scientist and my church life had ended. The two began to strengthen and to complement each other in a new way rather than being separate compartments of my life. The biblical command of Genesis 2:15 to till and to keep (literally, to serve and preserve) the land began to take on a new meaning for me. I could add my own list of the wonders of creation to those of the psalmist who wrote Psalm 104, that wonderful hymn of creation.

As my interest in Christian ecology has grown under the guidance of the Holy Spirit, so has my sadness that the church has been slow to respond to this issue – the care of God's creation. The much-quoted John 3:16 tells us that "God so loved the cosmos that he gave his only begotten Son". Colossians 1:15 reaffirms that the redeeming work of Christ was for more than the benefit of man, the one creature made in his image. Verse 17 (NASB) says, "He is before all things, and in Him all things hold together", and verses 19–20 say, "For it was the Father's good pleasure for all the fullness to dwell in Him, and through Him to reconcile all things to Himself, having made peace through the blood of His cross; through Him, I say, whether things on earth or things in heaven." Those of us who are reconciled to God in Christ are also reconciled to his creation, and the only chance of survival for that creation is if those who are reconciled defend the creation. Today, many people look to New Age beliefs on which to base their environmental action. It is particularly important for those who know and worship the Creator rather than creation to be at the forefront of environmental protection.

Perhaps one of the common temptations for an environmentally concerned ethnobotanist, who has spent considerable time living among indigenous people, is to embrace the animist beliefs which often make them strong protectors of the environment. This is where the New Age movement would have us go.

On my first expedition to the tropical rainforest I had an experience which I have never forgotten. After a long flight in a small plane to the remotest part of Suriname – two days by dugout canoe and two days on foot – we finally reached the base camp of the botanical expedition that I was to join for the next three months. After only a few minutes of exploration around the camp, I was excited to discover a flowering tree of the genus *Licania* on which I had worked for my doctoral thesis at Oxford. I asked the expedition leader, whom I had met for the first time thirty minutes previously, to arrange for the collection of herbarium specimens of the tree. He asked Frederick, our Suriname cook, to cut down the tree so that I could collect the samples. Our leader was quite annoyed when Frederick refused to fell the tree and an argument ensued. Frederick reluctantly agreed to fell the tree, but only after half an hour so that he would first have time to appease his deity, the "bushy mama". Later, after a time of ritual and prayer, Frederick cut the tree while chanting a song to the bushy mama blaming the white man for this unnecessary destruction. The tree fell and I excitedly gathered my collections from the flowering branches that were now on the ground. This incident is certainly the reason that I have preferred using tree climbers rather than the axe on my own expeditions. However, it is one of the many ways in which I have encountered nature protection in the religious beliefs of the rainforest dwellers. The forest is often under the care of much better protectors with the indigenous peoples than with the Western missionaries who replace their culture.

I have not fallen for the temptation of following the animist beliefs of the Indians because of the personal experience of my faith in Christ and the working of the Holy Spirit. My experience of such beliefs has led me to search the Scriptures more ardently for the many ways in which they teach a rich creation theology and thereby provide a firm basis for understanding the need to protect rather than destroy the earth. It has also led me to become involved in "missionary earthkeeping" – using every opportunity to encourage missionaries to accept the Bible's teaching on caring for creation. It is vital that when the church sends out missionaries to remote areas, they are well versed in Christian ecology based on the principles of stewardship that are so explicit in the Scriptures. This is not only relevant to Christian work in the rainforest, but is also essential nearer to home.

However, when I attend one of the meetings of Christian ecologists (such as A Rocha or Christian Ecology Link), the common lament of the participants is that they are lone voices as defenders of creation in their home churches. This has certainly been my own experience, although it is encouraging for me to receive an increasing number of invitations from churches to speak on ecological issues and more recently to have a pastor in my local church who is steeped in creation theology. As I have become more involved in environmental issues, I have not just attempted to introduce more green issues into the churches, but rather, my research interests have been stimulated by my faith. The two aspects that have been most helpful are the study of creation and the Creator, and the biblical basis for justice and equity. It is no longer enough for me merely to classify and describe the plant species of the Amazon forest; I must also use my research data to address issues of deforestation, pollution, starvation, climate change and other problems that surround us today. I am a much more concerned person because my faith helps to remove more selfish motives.

Christians can make a difference. In 2006 I took part in a conference in Manaus, Brazil organized and sponsored by the head of the Orthodox Church, His All Holiness Patriarch Bartholomew. It brought together about fifty each of theologians from various denominations, scientists, journalists, and local and national politicians. The considerable media attention the conference received led to the banning of cutting down more rainforest to plant soybeans. This was an activity organized by Christians that resulted in a major environment improvement.

I began this chapter with a childhood episode that might have caused me to be against a strict observance of the Sabbath.

However, the God-given principle of rest on the seventh day is part of a biblical ecology (Exodus 23:10–11; Leviticus 25:1–13); it has also been one of the greatest strengths to my career. Since accepting Christ at Oxford, I have always used Sunday as a day of rest and worship, and have never done any work on Sunday unless on an expedition where the programme must continue regardless of the day of the week. I am where I am today because I am a workaholic who has always worked long hard hours. But this has never extended to Sunday; the Creator knew what he was doing when he rested on the seventh day.

As I have studied indigenous agricultural systems, I have come increasingly to appreciate the need for land as well as humans to rest, and the wisdom of the biblical principle of fallow. It is significant that the principle of fallow in Exodus 23:10–11 is also "that the poor of your people may eat; and what they leave the wild beasts may eat" (rsv). This is another example of the richness of biblical ecology that we need to appreciate in the church today as we face the green movement and New Age beliefs. A scientist is often under great pressure to work solidly seven days a week. Enthusiasm for a research project can easily lead one into a seven-day week. The fact that this has never been a possibility in my mind has been a great strength to me and has helped both my work and my faith.

In March 1990, the Brazilian Minister for the Environment echoed the word of Lynn White, in his 1967 paper that blamed Christianity for the current ecological crisis.[1] The Minister said, "Christianity is at the root of the destruction of nature and the rainforest. Once you invent a god separate from nature, nature does not matter any more. It's something to use as you please. The Hindus, the Buddhists, saw nature as perfect and tried to harmonize with it." The challenge for the future is to set this record straight and to show that those who know the Creator through a relationship with his Son, Jesus Christ, also become the stewards of the creation with which we have been entrusted.

This makes the work of the Christian ecologist all the more important and challenging for the future.

Notes

1. White, L. (1967), "The historical basis of our ecologic crisis", *Science*, 155: 1203–07.

Chapter 9

Man – Dust with a Destiny

Dr Montagu G. Barker, MB, ChB, FRCPEd, FRCPsych, DPM. Educated at Hutchesons' School, Glasgow, and St Andrew's University. Consultant Psychiatrist in Bristol and Clinical Lecturer, Department of Mental Health, University of Bristol, 1968–1992; subsequently Emeritus Consultant, United Bristol Health Trust. Also Visiting Professor, Union Biblical Seminary, Pune, India from 1989. Author of *Psychology, Religion and Mental Health* (Rutherford Press, 2000).[1]

Scientism

My early training in the 1960s was marked by the recent discovery and development of the new tranquillizers and antidepressants which, added to electroconvulsive therapy, benefited – and continue to benefit – patients with severe mental illness, however misused such treatments may sometimes be. There seemed to be a new breakthrough in "scientific psychiatry" which could reduce all psychic suffering to genetic predisposition and abnormal brain physiology, for there was now a physical treatment which could "cure". Some of the most vigorous exponents of this approach wrote highly popular texts, such as Dr William Sargant's *Battle for the Mind*. In his book, Dr Sargant equated brain and mind, and all mental (including religious) experiences were reduced to physiological reactions. His physiology and psychology were severely criticized and rejected by many scientists, but his general equation of mental and spiritual experiences remained unassailed by the same scientific world.

My own training was in a school of psychiatry which professed rigorous exploration of all aspects of a patient's physical, mental and social development before assessment and treatment. But I was intrigued to discover that although careful histories were demanded on upbringing, sexual development, relationships and employment, the patient's goals in life and religious beliefs (or lack of them) rarely merited a mention; the failure of a doctor to elicit such information was never criticized. Even less attention was paid to the significance of such belief or lack of it in terms of how persons conducted their lives, unless the presenting symptoms and distress were expressed in specifically religious terminology.

As a trainee psychiatrist I became aware that most of my senior colleagues would seek only the clinical symptoms of their patients and ignore attitudes and value systems, viewing these as entirely personal matters not to be explored by the psychiatrist. A few would take a direct and usually hostile approach, tending automatically to blame strongly held religious views as being as least partly causal of a patient's illness. My interest in these matters provoked an invitation to review the subject of "Religion and Psychiatry" at the weekly postgraduate meeting. By the mid-sixties, there had been only one major paper on the subject of religion and psychiatric illness in the fifty-year history of the leading British psychiatric journal; and that paper seemed to have been included only because it was a special guest lecture traditionally published in the journal each year. My own thesis was that a truly scientific approach within psychiatry could occur only where the patient's beliefs and goals, religious or otherwise, were explored along with the whole life situation. Everyone lives in accordance with some belief, whether expressed in religious terms or not, and to neglect the significance of this within a patient's life reduces that person in some way and makes him or her less than human.

Thirty years on, the materialist and determinist bias to the understanding of psychiatric illness still has its followers. In an academic meeting exploring various approaches to understanding and treating depressed patients, a leading academic psychiatrist recently declared that he preferred to see patients as "biological organisms predisposed by their genetic inheritance and subjected to certain life events". The organic factors and the events affecting a patient's life were looked upon as legitimate subjects for study, but the person's own beliefs and the framework within which he understood and ordered life and events were looked upon as irrelevant.

It is an attitude dissected by Richard Holloway, the former Bishop of Edinburgh, when he wrote:

> *This is my dilemma... I am dust and ashes, frail and wayward, a set of predetermined behavioural responses, programmed by my genetic inheritance and by social context, riddled with fears, beset with needs whose origins I do not understand and whose satisfaction I cannot achieve, quintessence of dust, and unto dust I shall return. Who can expect much of that?*

But he went on to say:

> *There is something else in me; there is an awareness that, truly, I am not what I am; and what I am and what I am not is what I truly am. Dust I may be, but troubled dust, dust that dreams, dust that has strange premonitions of transfiguration, of a glory in store, a destiny prepared, an inheritance that one day will be my own.*

Relativism

These words reflect a change of emphasis that has taken place in the psychiatric profession. A new generation of psychiatrists, nurtured in the swinging sixties and influenced by a growing interest in "consciousness", "awareness" and "spiritual" values, began to search for "personal growth, character transformation, psychological rebirth and even mystical experience". Physical methods of treating psychiatric illness and even the diagnostic categories of traditional psychiatry were severely criticized. By the 1970s there was a burgeoning of "talking treatments", more technically known as psychotherapies and counselling programmes. Where Bishop Holloway had sought to direct his hearers to that longing for God the Creator innate in the hearts of all men, the new therapists offered fuller understanding and "self-actualization" through an ever-increasing number of psychotherapy programmes. One American writer spoke of the seventies as the "me decade" because of the preoccupation with "my needs" and "let's talk about me" approaches.

All this undoubtedly indicated a deep spiritual hunger. It was illustrated by one of my colleagues who described his own pilgrimage from "rational humanism" to "devotional humanism", by which he meant a discovery of a need for meditation and personal values based upon what now would be called "green issues". Words such as "fulfilment", "wholeness" and "integration", often described in almost spiritual terms, began to appear in psychiatric texts, although any attempt to see these as deriving from a religious or theistic context was met with a sharp rebuttal.

This development, coupled with pluralism with its many philosophical positions and religious beliefs, has led to psychiatrists becoming increasingly aware that they can no longer ignore the belief structures and the value systems of their patients. Their attitude became that either these are cultural variants and "true" and valid for the individuals concerned but requiring no response from scientific psychiatry, or, as one leading psychiatrist expressed in a paper to the Royal Society of Health, "There is a significant element in life and health to do with meaning, which is concerned with the direction of one's life... the psychiatrist should allow the patient to develop and express his own spiritual values..." He went on to suggest that one of the functions of the psychiatrist may be "helping the patient to find his god".[2]

The fact that antidepressants and other psychotropic medication have been so successful in treating the more severe psychiatric disorders has led to increasing attention being directed to lesser disorders. An example of this is the anxiety and depression which often occur in family relationships. In the 1950s, marital problems and their associated distress would have been dismissed by many psychiatrists as inappropriate referrals to a psychiatric clinic. By the 1970s, marital problems and marital therapy merited a whole section in a postgraduate text on *Recent Advances in Psychiatry*, where it was argued that it was "better to encourage the breakup of a relationship which was unfulfilling for one or other party where there was the possibility of forming a more fulfilling relationship subsequently".[3] This was in spite of the fact that the author acknowledged that there were no scientific or follow-up studies available to support his suggestion and that second marriages have a higher rate of breakdown than first ones. At the time, it was received wisdom that children would be happier to be removed from a situation where their parents were constantly bickering or in conflict. My own reflection was that children more often wished their parents to remain together, and, if forced to make such a choice, were influenced more by where security seemed to lie; where their teddy bear was tended to be more influential than which parent to select. This was quite apart from the observation that every broken relationship makes it more difficult to believe in the permanence of any subsequent relationship. It was the pioneering and persistent work of a practising Christian, Dr Jack Dominian, who patiently conducted studies in his Family Research Unit in London, which confirmed the high degree of mental and physical illness arising out of divorce and family breakup, quite apart from the enormous cost to the nation economically.

These issues have rightly gained the attention of the press and have resulted in much closer scrutiny of the assumption that *desires* are the same as *rights*, and one's own fulfilment is good. A *Times* leader (21 May 1990) commented:

> *The 1960s consensus that quick and easy divorce was in the best interests of all parties is increasingly open to doubt. Experts now say that we have underestimated the damage done to children by divorce. Moreover a surprising number of people who get divorced then regret it. The problem seems to be that once an unhappy couple approach a lawyer they are driven to divorce as inexorably as the military mobilisations in the summer of 1914 led to war.*

It has to be said that many psychiatrists and social scientists were not far behind the alleged activity of the lawyers in the pressure put upon individuals, even within a so-called therapeutic situation. Even if there was no attempt to impose values and beliefs upon patients or to bring emotional pressure to bear upon individuals in a time of great vulnerability, I often felt that there was less than honest dealing with such individuals when the specialists too readily accepted the value system of the patient under treatment.

The psalmist in Psalm 8:4 asked the question "What is man?", and the writer of Ecclesiastes debated with himself regarding the meaning of life. The lusty Roman poet Ovid, with no background of Jewish thought or contact, nevertheless echoed the words of St Paul in Romans 7 when he said, "I see the better things and I agree with them, but I follow the worse." Such questions are asked as often today as in former days; one leading psychiatrist identifies this as "man is still searching for a map of man". His own solution was that provided by traditional psychoanalysis. In this century the emergence of biological and behavioural sciences has produced several "maps of man", from psychoanalysis to behaviour modification, in an attempt to understand man and thereby to heal or resolve his tensions. One researcher on human sexuality summed up his conclusions after decades of study and research in the following words:

> *Paradoxically further study of the continually*
> *increasing volume of publications has led to less*
> *firm opinions than before. Increasing awareness*
> *of the complexities of the subject brings with it the*
> *realisation that on many issues it would be wise to*
> *suspend judgment pending further research. Indeed*
> *one conclusion that can be expressed without fear of*
> *contradiction is that much more needs to be learnt*
> *about human sexuality even before quite elementary*
> *questions can be answered with any degree of*
> *confidence.*[4]

Experience suggests that further research could make him even less sure.

One of the prerequisites of the "ideal psychiatrist" is "the ability to be detached at times from any value judgment", able to be "accepting and totally free of prejudice (an ability only found in those who genuinely possess very well defined values and have a personality that is mature)."[5] It is an error to believe that only those without well-defined, and hopefully thought-out values are tolerant and accepting. On the contrary, the absence of such values and beliefs may be dangerous.

Dualism

Harry Williams, writing of his experience as a psychiatric patient, stated:

> *A psychiatrist should be chosen because he is a skilled psychiatrist and not because he is a good Catholic or reads the Bible every morning. I have a lasting suspicion of people who are known as a* Christian *dentist or a* Christian *doctor or a* Christian *psychiatrist or a* Christian *chiropodist. Invariably it means that they are bad at their craft. God is honoured by a dentist being a good dentist, not by his singing hymns.*[6]

He rightly points to the fear of psychiatrists in the minds of many Christians who protect themselves and their beliefs by insisting on a "Christian psychiatrist". I agree entirely with this and strongly believe that the prerequisite of a good psychiatrist is that he should be someone respected as a person of ability, integrity and of good standing among his colleagues, including non-psychiatrists. I do not believe that it necessarily helps for the worldview of the patient to be understood by the psychiatrist; what is important is the open acknowledgment and discussion of where worldviews differ and an acceptance by both psychiatrist and patient as to the limits upon such issues. Openness and honesty is often all that is necessary in order to establish a good therapeutic relationship between doctor and patient, even when worldviews and value systems are disparate.

However, the philosophical and antireligious bias of Freud, especially as portrayed by some of his followers, has led to the public perception of psychiatrists as generally being anti-God and hostile to Christian belief, even though Freud's views have not been a dominant influence upon the practice of psychiatry in this country. Few psychiatrists in Britain hold the rigid philosophical and reductionist views of men like Maudsley, Freud and Sargant, and they would be unhappy to stray far from such a position in their practice. This has had a generally beneficial result in ensuring a pragmatic approach to the severer forms of psychiatric illness, ensuring treatment with proven and scientifically assessed methods of treatment.

The same has not been so true when psychiatrists have dealt with patients with lesser forms of psychiatric disorder, with some of the results mentioned previously. This has led to a fear of the practice of psychiatry in many Christian medical students and young doctors; although they are attracted to dealing with patients on a broader basis than purely the physical, they are unhappy with the reputed hostility of psychiatrists to religious faith. They are often confirmed in this view by senior doctors, not least those known for a Christian commitment but sceptical about the value of psychiatry, largely out of deficiencies in their own training. Such individuals often profess to be fearful for the continued spiritual wellbeing of any Christian who should enter into the practice of such a subject. I personally am grateful to the canny Scots physician who quietly encouraged me in my medical student days, on the ground that "There is a need for Christians to practise psychiatry and demonstrate that it is possible to be truly scientific in one's thinking and at the same time committed to Christ."

A small pamphlet which I wrote, called *Starting Psychiatry*, was published to help Christian medical students embarking on their psychiatric studies and experiencing difficulties with the special problems posed by the nature of the suffering of these patients and special language and approaches of psychiatry.[7] It is a booklet which remained in print for several years and has, I hope, contributed something to the changed attitudes which have resulted in many more Christian doctors being prepared to pursue a career in psychiatry.

In it I focused upon the need for Christian and non-Christian alike to examine their attitudes, lest they be guilty of smuggling their own special prejudices and preconceptions into their practice of medicine. Such self-examination is not easy, as it means calling into question one's own beliefs, standards and objectives in life when faced with patients, and colleagues who would hold very different views on life and may have quite deliberately and specifically rejected a Christian standpoint.

Unfortunately, there is still a strongly held view among both Christians and non-Christians that mental illness is something to be ashamed of, and that it is self-induced. The approach to the mentally ill adopted by such individuals is to search for some approach, often a panacea, along the lines that if only one's diet, exercise, lifestyle or some procedure is rigorously held to, then all mental disorder will disappear. In some Christian circles, conversion, or special healing procedures, or exorcism would be spiritual counterparts. These, of course, are no different from the "nothing but" approaches so frequently encountered in the philosophical framework of the materialist and atheist, and are equally reductionist. The temptation to resort to quick solutions is always present. Anything which appears to offer *solutions* and *cure* is always more seductive and attractive than the preparedness to accept that in human behaviour and illness, *resolution* and *relief* is more usual. Inexperience and lack of familiarity with patients often leads the medical student and young psychiatrist to become impatient with a person who "won't be cured", and to take a punitive approach to them. Among Christians there is the often-expressed belief that "if only" a patient would become a Christian then all difficulties would disappear. In fact, quite the reverse may occur. Becoming a Christian may produce extra conflict in a person who finds himself at greater variance with his family and with colleagues as he faces challenges to an established lifestyle.

Often there is a dualism in Christian thinking which reduces everything in life to either the organic or the spiritual, and refuses to look at research which demonstrates that our experiences and mental processes are a complex interaction of the effects of our genetic background, family and upbringing, life events, and goals in life. Some Christians are reluctant to look at the very human issues behind their illness and instead demand "spiritual remedies" from the Christian psychiatrist, having already exhausted their normal spiritual mentors. The plethora of "how to overcome..." books in secular bookshops have their parallel in Christian books supporting a thriving Christian alternative medicine, avidly backed by those keen to have a personalized medicine but not prepared to subject the claims of such "Christian therapies" to proper evaluation.[8]

Conclusion

Psychiatrists are faced with many who lived their life in such a way that pain, grief and depression have been the almost inevitable fruit of their conduct, and others who have had unfulfilled goals and objectives in their work and relationships. The psychiatrist has to explore the roots of his patient's behaviour, help him retrace his steps and find a new purpose for going forward in life. Whatever happens, no psychiatrist should force his own belief or faith upon a patient. Such an act would be a fundamental transgression of the professional nature of the doctor/patient relationship which can never be an equal relationship, and even less so where the patient's judgment may be impaired and vulnerability increased by psychiatric illness. Sadly, many Christians have felt that their problems have been blamed entirely upon their Christian viewpoint, but it also has to be said that many Christian patients have refused to examine how little thought-through and reality-based their own faith has been. As a result, they have criticized unjustly their psychiatrist, be he non-Christian or Christian, for seeking to explore discrepancies in their own belief and behaviour.

Perhaps the reason why the medical profession has a significantly higher incidence of alcohol abuse and suicide than many professions derives from the fact that such issues are seldom raised in the training of medical students or postgraduates. Trying to deal with patients who have presented with deliberate self-harm, diseases incurred by abuse, in addition to those who have suffered from the malevolence of fate or even members of their own family, brings distress and even despair which cannot always be assuaged by more research, more precise definitions or increased devotion to one's work.

The theologian, J. I. Packer, has said:

> *Man is a biologically developed, language-using, tool-making, social, economic, political animal with a complicated physiology and even more complicated psychology... and that is to say nothing about the historical and philosophical contributions to our understanding of man.*

That does not mean that we ought to interpret biblical language as equivalent to any behavioural jargon in vogue; this would reduce ultimate truth to dependence on a limited culture-dependent understanding of man. It does not mean that we should read Freudian concepts into biblical terminology, equating the ego with the soul and the superego with conscience. It does not mean that we should use biblical terminology and words as though Scripture had to include some allusion to every possible discovery of man, or that the Bible is a mini-treatise in psychology or behavioural sciences. It does mean that we have to use the insights of all that science and research have made available in the realm of human experience and conflict, while remaining sceptical as to these being the last word.

As a psychiatrist I have to deal with the lives of men and women in illness, conflict and tension. But I myself need to be wrestling at the same time with the biblical revelation regarding the human condition and man's ultimate need. The first illumines the second, but the second gives the context within which the first is to be understood and explored. Here is the framework within which I approach my patients and assess the current practice of psychiatry, aware that there is no easy synthesis but an ongoing fight against a blinkered scientism on the one hand and an easy believism on the other. Even "good doctors" can slip into either error.

At the end of the day, the psychiatrist who is a Christian knows the limitations of his work. He knows that new discoveries will be made about God's creation and about human behaviour. But he also believes that something new happened when God the Creator of all came to live among men in the Person of Jesus, that he died on a cross for us and rose again from the dead to bring new life to all who put their trust in him. This is at the heart of my life.

As a psychiatrist, I am tempted to agree with the writer of Ecclesiastes who said that there was nothing new on the face of the earth. Finding a meaning in life and a god who suits undoubtedly helps people, but it is possible to miss or refuse to meet the only God who is the basis of all life. I cannot give a meaning for life to be dispensed like pills and therapy; I can receive the confessions of wrongs and listen to the outpourings of guilt so that people feel better, but only Jesus Christ can forgive and remove guilt. As a psychiatrist I can encourage, challenge and direct people to act differently, but only the

Spirit of God ultimately gives people new power to act as God wills; I can explore possibilities and ways of living a better and different life, but Jesus Christ is the only Person who has said, "I *am* the way and the truth and the life. No one comes to the Father except through me" (John 14:6). These are strong words which draw their credibility from the life, teaching, death and resurrection of Jesus Christ, and it is to him that I seek to witness as a Christian.

Notes

1. Barker, M. G. (2000), *Psychology, Religion and Mental Health*, Rutherford Press. Bristol Templeton Lectures (1995).

2. Sims, Andrew (1988), "The Psychiatrist as a Priest", *Perspectives in Public Health*, 108:160–163.

3. Crown, Sidney (1971), *Recent Advances in Psychiatry*, Duckworth, p. 201.

4. West, D. J. (1977), *Homosexuality Re-examined*, Duckworth, p. 316.

5. Jaspers, K. (1963), *General Psychopathology*, Manchester University Press, pp. 808–09.

6. Williams, H. (1982), *Someday I'll Find You*, Mitchell Beazley, p. 167.

7. Barker, M. G. (1971), *Starting Psychiatry*, CMF.

8. I have explored these issues further in chapters in Malcolm Jeeves (ed.) (1984), *Behavioural Sciences: A Christian Perspective*, IVP, pp. 230–45; and Nigel Cameron and Sinclair Ferguson (eds.) (1986), *Pulpit and People*, Rutherford House, pp. 89–102.

Chapter 10

From Nanotechnology to Macro-Organizations: Engineering Atoms and More

John Wood is currently Secretary-General of the Association of Commonwealth Universities and has honorary chairs at Imperial College and University College, London in materials and nanotechnology respectively. Among his academic positions he was Head of Department of Materials and Dean of Engineering at Nottingham University, and then Principal of the Faculty of Engineering at Imperial College. For a time he was Chief Executive of a UK Research Council and has chaired a number of boards advising the UK Government and latterly the European Commission on the future of research with a special emphasis on research infrastructures and massive data sets. On behalf of the European Commission he co-chairs the Global Research Data Alliance and is spokesperson for the Commission on Science 2.0.

If the English are a nation of shopkeepers then my family is indisputably English. My parents accepted this role and assumed I would do the same. Trade and materialism made the world go round and those who did not hold this view were considered scroungers. Conversation at home was never about religion, science was never mentioned and there was no time for academics (heads in the sky). This was the world I knew as a small boy; my parents' friends shared it and, apart from a boy next door who told me he wanted to be a missionary since he had read a Jungle Doctor book, I assumed this was what the world was like.

I was born shortly after the end of the Second World War into an utterly conventional home. I was rather backward at reading at my first school (Kidlington Primary, near Oxford); my only saving grace was that I appeared to be good at "sums". Then, when I was nine, my father was doing well and we moved to what is still the family home looking onto the back of Blenheim Palace.

As an only child and living in the countryside north of Oxford, I became quite a loner. I often spent whole days wandering around the local woods or burying myself in books at home. One of the authors that I loved was Anthony Buckeridge who wrote the "Jennings and Darbyshire" books about two boys at a boarding prep school. With no thought about what it really meant, I badgered my parents to let me go to boarding school. To my amazement, one day while visiting my grandparents who lived in Broadstairs on the south-east tip of England, I was taken to St Lawrence College, a boarding school at Ramsgate, which in those days was a five-hour drive from my home in rural Oxfordshire, and given a test to take in the headmaster's study. Why St Lawrence? It turned out that my grandparents' next-door neighbour taught the piano at the prep school and clearly believed it to be suitable for me. It was. Unknown to either myself, or I suspect my parents, St Lawrence was a school with a firm Christian ethos. Even today the prep school (where I started) states that it has a "well-established aim: to offer a supportive, caring environment, based on traditional Christian values, where children are given every opportunity to fulfil their potential."

I did not know this when I arrived and was rather surprised at the number of boys whose parents were missionaries or clergymen. I felt out of place. This came to a head my first Sunday. After chapel we had to read and learn a few verses from the Bible. Guess what? Wood J.V. (87) did not have a Bible! The number 87 was my school number and as a prime number, always shouts out at me when I see it anywhere as "my number"; it remains almost my identity. Swiftly a very old, ink-blotched Authorized Version of the Bible was found and the appropriate page found for me. With this inauspicious start I began my spiritual journey. School life involved Bible study in the dormitory, morning and evening prayers, chapel on Sunday. I did not question any of it.

Nor were Christianity and religion the only things I was ignorant of when I arrived. Other boys in my class had been at the school for at least two years before I arrived and had studied Latin and French – which I hadn't. In a rather weird way, my spiritual journey became linked to a particular Latin verb. Each Saturday morning we practised the hymns for the following day. Our head of music was also head of classics. As he walked into the school hall he would click his fingers and we would all start chanting "*cognosco, cognoscere, cognovi, cognitum,*" followed by five possible English equivalents, one of which was "I understand." By the time we had finished chanting, he had arrived at the piano and we plunged into the first hymn.

One evening in my second term, some of the masters showed us a film of a summer camp on the North Norfolk Coast at a place called West Runton. My imagination was captured by the thought of living under canvas, playing outdoor games, and the general knock-about atmosphere, coupled with the boyish enthusiasm of the teachers. I wanted to sign up immediately but persuading my parents was not easy. It was apparent to me and I guess to them, that I was now immersed in a totally different culture to the one at home. However, they relented and off I went.

I now encountered hearty Christianity with a vengeance! Stuffing straw into a cotton sack to make a mattress which quickly became a haven for earwigs, battling with keeping water out of the tent when it poured, all contributed to an atmosphere in which the Christian message was clearly explained. At the time I thought I had given my life to Christ as a result, but in retrospect I think that first camp was really when I started to turn. I took my Scripture Union Bible notes home, but the rhythm of home life soon took over. I felt guilty. The same happened the next year and by my third visit, when I was thirteen, I thought that I would never make it as a Christian. However, there were other plans.

There was a young enthusiastic Oxford graduate at the camp who suggested I read a small booklet. It told the life of John Newton, the ex-slave trader who came to know Christ in a spectacular way. Here was a man who did not fit in and called himself "the old blasphemer". Since I felt I did not fit in, the story immediately spoke to me, or rather I should say, God spoke to me. To many John Newton is known as the writer of such hymns as "Amazing Grace", "How sweet the name", and "Glorious things of thee are spoken", which are still sung with gusto around the world. He is probably much better known nowadays, not least through the film *Amazing Grace* which starred Albert Finney.[1]

Formal science at my prep school was almost non-existent. My only memory, perish the thought, was chasing some liquid mercury around on my desk as we tried to make a thermometer. One redeeming activity was the so-called "science club". Each term a metal coffin would arrive called the "Esso science kit". It had one simple experiment to be done each week. I have a vivid memory of one experiment which required a tiny bottle of dilute sulphuric acid to be taken out of a sealed canister. The tension in the room could be felt as this highly dangerous substance emerged from its container. I have completely forgotten what the point of the experiment was but it instilled in me a sense of wonder and surprise. Probably more influential, at that time, was an article in a magazine I read showing how small an atom was. I kept returning to that article and dreaming about atoms. That love has stayed with me ever since. When I became Dean of Engineering at Nottingham University many years later, I was challenged by other heads of departments (who had elected me) that I was not a true engineer. In a flash of inspiration (or so I thought at the time) I declared that as a materials scientist I was an "atomic engineer" building engineering structures starting with atoms.

I subsequently moved up the road to the senior school where I was fortunate to be in a house run by a strong Christian teacher called Donald Drew. He was a disciplinarian but a very positive leader who encouraged us all to think through everything we did in life, including our faith. In house rugby matches he would encourage us from the touch-line with exhortations such as "Smite the Amalekites, lads!" Years later the writer Os Guinness dedicated a book entitled *Fit Bodies, Fit Minds – Why evangelicals don't think and what to do about it*[2] to Donald Drew, "who first taught me to think and to think Christianly." I can vouch for that; he gave me a wonderful legacy.

There was no doubt the school focused on training us to be good Christian citizens who should have a mission in life. Sunday by Sunday, old boys who were missionaries would come and tell us about the great need to evangelize the world.

While the academic side of life was encouraged, it was not put on a pedestal and I sort of meandered into focusing on science, thinking that I could still enjoy music, history and English as a scientist, although I probably would not be able to enjoy or understand science if I majored on arts subjects. By this stage I had disappointed my parents by telling them that I did not wish to take over the family firm. However, I confess I did not put much effort into my academic studies and concentrated rather on music and theology. Around the age of sixteen I came across *Honest to God* by Bishop John Robinson. At the time this book was causing huge eruptions in church circles, yet for me it was as if a veil had been lifted from my eyes. I had started to react badly to the sanitized Christianity of school and the

Christian Union. Glib stock book answers did not satisfy me. I started reading around the authors Robinson quoted and eventually came to Dietrich Bonhoeffer's *Letters and Papers from Prison* (subsequently I read his *The Cost of Discipleship*). It became the book that has been most influential in my life. Here was a man talking about real Christianity at the coal-face, someone who eventually gave his life for it. In the most recent edition the opening sentence comes like a bombshell: "Cheap Grace is the mortal enemy of the church. Our struggle today is for costly grace." I realized that much of what I had absorbed of Christianity was cheap grace, words and doctrine that could be rattled off without thinking, a clean and honest lifestyle, a faith with no depth.

As far as further education was concerned, I really did not know what to do. I loved physical and inorganic chemistry but hated organic. Organic chemistry seemed to consist of memorizing reactions rather than understanding them. I could see no point in that, whereas for physical and inorganic chemistry, I could see the rationale of understanding what could happen, starting from basic atomic structure. I knew I could never survive chemistry at university because I would not be able to avoid organic. I decided to go on a week's placement at the research laboratories of the International Nickel Company – the nearest thing I could find to my chemistry interests. That week was an eye-opener for me. Looking down a transmission electron microscope for the first time showed that metallurgy was the way for me.

At about the same time, my housemaster, sensing my lack of direction, sent me to an Industrial Psychologist who, after a series of tests, said straight out, "You should do metallurgy at Cambridge!" Unfortunately I had done virtually no work for my exams, so Cambridge was out. During my work experience Sheffield University had been recommended, and amazingly I scraped in. In a sense this choice was confirmed for me since the motto of Sheffield University is *Rerum Cognoscere Causas* ("To understand or search behind the causes or reasons for things"). Thank goodness I had the meaning of *cognoscere* drummed into me at school! There was one problem. My father refused to apply for a grant so I could go. In the end I was offered scholarships by industry. I took one with what became British Steel Corporation, Special Steels division.

Having just scraped in, I now discovered my true love, physical metallurgy (involving microscopy and atoms) and thermodynamics. At the same time I was railing against the established church which seemed to me to be not engaged in the real issues of society. I had never seen such poverty as I found in parts of Sheffield. This was in the late 1960s at the height of student unrest in the UK and I took my full part in it, demonstrating against the war in Vietnam, seeking social justice for the poor, and so on. All this meant that I struggled to reconcile my love for my subject (which could seem an indulgence) with what I thought was my Christian duty to change the world. It all came to a head in my final year. Should I give up science and go into some type of Christian ministry? One afternoon I walked for several hours around some of the slum housing in Sheffield and eventually got back to my room, where I went down on my knees and told God, "I give up."

While it can be explained in many ways, I believe I heard God say, "At last. Now use the talents you have been given." This may sound melodramatic but for me it was very real; my ministry was to be in the science I loved. I went for broke; I felt I needed to test my vocation further. I applied to Cambridge to do a PhD. Having only just got into university, I came out with the top degree and medal for my final year. In many ways, something that took place straight after was even more affirming. I had an invitation from Donald Drew who had left school teaching and was now at a place called L'Abri in Switzerland assisting Francis Schaeffer, the Christian philosopher. I camped down there on the floor next to an ex-heroin addict and went to lectures where I heard Schaeffer announce that we could ask any questions of God, since he is big enough to take them, although the answer he gives may be unexpected. Here at last was an intellectual base to all the tensions I had. I went to Cambridge with a renewed vision. I immediately plunged myself into a mission church on the edge of town where students did not go. Social housing, broken families, problems with the law were the norm there. Yet the church had become fully involved with the issues and I was soon swept up with putting my faith into action. Oh, and yes, my doctorate was on transmission electron microscopy and trying to fool atoms to be in places that thermodynamically they did not want to be. I subsequently called myself an "atomic anarchist".

After a couple of fellowships and promises of more, I wanted to stand independently and took a lectureship at the relatively new Open University to start a research base in materials science. The contrast with Cambridge could not have been greater. My driving force was to give others who had not had the chances I had had, an opportunity to become excited about the world around them. Also, I wanted to be my own boss and show I could start something from scratch. One thing about the OU was that all conventions were challenged. Was what was in the textbooks really true? Several times we found that ideas had just been assumed to be correct, and rather like the trivial answers I had been given at school to my faith questions, they did not stand up if one tested their validity. Yes, we needed to fully understand the causes of things if students at home were to have a chance.

During my time at the OU two significant things occurred. The first was that I took a short sabbatical at Kyoto University in Japan. My wife and I had decided to use the time there to decide our future mission together. The result was the setting up of the "Stables Christian Centre", a charity based at our home in rural

Bedfordshire which ministers to the socially disadvantaged and has been in existence for thirty years as I write. The second was that I traded in my future study leave of one day a week to be a consultant to industry. I had been given the first Grunfeld Medal awarded by the Institute of Materials for a young person. The company that had endowed the medal invited me to work with them. I had several other consultancies with industry and I found the mixture of academic and industrial research balanced well. It is fair to say that the industrial research really broadened my mind and influenced much of my future research work. Most of my research was focused on "non-equilibrium processing of materials" for a wide range of potential uses, including medical applications.

I learnt other things too – such as knowing what makes the board of a company tick (treating them as people, not just as objects to get money from); and understanding that a good idea is just the start, and the real question is, "Is there a business here for us?" The other side of the coin is to make sure the company understands the needs of students and research assistants by involving them fully in the total project and not treating them as a side issue. I used to say to fellow academics who were going to visit a company, "Find out their share price and profits-to-earnings ratio and try to discover the personal interest of the managing director. Start with where they are at." I also find this the right approach to discussing my faith with others. Too often we start with ourselves.

Subsequently someone suggested I apply to be professor and head of department of material science at Nottingham University. I arrived for the interview to find that I was to have dinner with the four other candidates, one of whom had been my tutor when I was an undergraduate, and another had been a visiting professor in our group when I was a postgraduate. Amazingly, I was offered the job. I believe I was the youngest endowed professor of materials in the country at the time;

I was certainly the second youngest in the department. The department had not performed well and had been about to close. The vice-chancellor told me I had five years to see what I could do and have fun. I negotiated my one day a week in industry as part of the deal. Re-energizing a demoralized department was not easy. I had to lead from the front on three main issues: focus the strength of the teaching by collaboration with other departments; increase research expectations by undertaking more adventurous research; and deal with some critical personnel problems. The last point was the most difficult for me personally, but removing two of the academics had a dramatic effect on others. One member of staff suddenly sprang to life after years of inactivity. The funds started to come in from several sources to support research. I saw it as my job to cultivate new areas by collaborations both with other members in the department and by encouraging outside links. I brought in a friend from industry to look critically at what our strengths were. This was a revelation and in some ways hard to take. Links started with not only the other science and engineering departments but with the medical school, archaeology, and food science. Although I had my own large research group, I felt it my duty as head of department to support all members of staff in achieving their potential. I have ever been mindful of Jesus' teaching on the use of talents, making the most of our gifts. Indeed, I see this is one of the biggest sins of our churches – that members are not encouraged in this way.

Soon after I arrived at Nottingham a visitor sporting rough chin stubble came to my office. He introduced himself as a professor of materials from the University of Cluj-Napoca in Romania. He was amazed that I knew the city. I had camped there as a student in 1972 on my way to Armenia through the south of the then Soviet Union. This chance encounter started a long collaboration in helping turn round the teaching and research in materials in that university. It enabled several young staff, who are now the leaders in both the university and the city, to come and work with me. As a result the city made me an honorary citizen and the university gave me an honorary doctorate. I retain a great love for that country, which has had to endure so much. Even as I write, I am actively involved with a young Christian Romanian scientist about how his faith can relate to his Orthodox background.

In 1994 the British government published a critical white paper called *Realising Our Potential*. This revamped the research councils into what is more or less their current structure and created an Office of Science and Technology, part of whose mission was to undertake "foresight" exercises. These were based on a technique used in Japan using the Delphi forecasting methodology. A similar method was adopted in the UK and one panel focused on materials. Although I was included in the survey, I became very critical of the methodology on the grounds that it led to a lowest common denominator approach rather than encouraging risk taking. I was somewhat taken aback to be asked to take over as chair and to lead the second report by the OST. This was baptism by fire, combining great fun with great responsibility. The advice of my panel could change the course of public investment in research. I had to learn how the civil service and ministries worked, deal with industrial lobby groups and irate academics, cope with science counsellors in foreign embassies, and on top of all that, motivate the panel. We produced the first report on the potential impact of nanotechnology on the UK economy, created a schools' pack on future materials (led by Colin Humphreys – see Chapter 5) and persuaded a number of industrial sectors to undertake their own assessment of their future. One of the ministers I had to deal with was Alan Johnson (subsequently Home Secretary), who asked me to give a view to trade union leaders in the sector on the future of the UK's metals industry. I told them the truth – that there was no future in the UK for high-volume low-cost metal production – and encouraged them to look to new high-added-value products. I faced a barrage of criticism. Two days later British Steel announced the closure of a major steel plant!

As a result of this experience I found I was now bored with the everyday life of an academic. Nonetheless, I was amazed to be appointed as head of the Council for the Central Laboratory of the Research Councils (CCLRC), one of the eight research councils at that time. With 1,800 staff and two main sites in the UK and no idea how large-scale international science was done, this was baptism by fire yet again. The decision had been taken to house the UK's new synchrotron at the Rutherford-Appleton Laboratory in Oxfordshire rather than with the existing synchrotron based in Daresbury near Manchester. Immediately I was in the firing line with an existing vote of no confidence in the management by the unions and intense pressure from politicians. What to do as a Christian? I have two simple principles: first, treat people as God sees them and, secondly, tell the truth. I went to see all involved and also published the external report on the state of morale in the organization that had been suppressed by the previous management. This was one of the times as chief executive where I felt my faith was under attack. In the main I was dealing with passionate scientists both in the organization and in universities who were often much brighter than I was but did not see the big picture. The most challenging aspect of the job was in future science policy for the UK and internationally. I firmly believe that God wanted me in the job, but how to express my faith in this arena without appearing crass?

There were three things that helped and one that did not. Starting with the negative: I was looked upon with deep suspicion by leaders in the church I attended, who thought I was questioning the basis of Christianity in the way I asked fundamental questions about the world around us, both physically and socially. Students and parents at our home church had a desperate need for help on the relationship between science at school and their own personal faith, and would come to me for advice, yet it was with utmost difficulty that I was able to put on the excellent course "Test of Faith" produced by Ruth Bancewicz from the Faraday Institute at Cambridge. I found this isolation was common among several other Christian scientists I knew. Some of us formed a mutual mentoring group which was a great source of encouragement and strength.

Through this group I got to know David Ford (Professor of Divinity at Cambridge) and asked him for advice on what might loosely be called "Christian proclamation in the public square". I was given this advice from the Nicene Creed: "I believe in one holy, catholic and apostolic church".

- *One:* not like Elijah, thinking I am the only one, but God has others for me to be one with.

- *Holy:* set aside by God for this purpose, chosen.

- *Catholic:* able to be part of the universal church.

- *Apostolic:* commanded to pass on the good news from one generation to another.

- *Church:* Christ centred, or as Schaeffer constantly said, "the cross plus nothing".[3]

The third plank was attending a Trinity Forum event on "Inspiring Leadership" about the role of personal character and integrity for positions of leadership.

Subsequently I have taken on many international roles, ranging from chairing the European Strategy Forum for Research Infrastructures, producing the first roadmap for large-scale research, to chairing the European Research Area Board setting the research vision for the next twenty years. These and other roles have led me to re-examine the faith-based vision of the early pioneers of the European Union, especially with respect to research and our current attitude today. To my amazement, there has been a tremendous openness to discussing the role of faith and values among many influential people in Europe and beyond, including Commissioners, Members of Parliament, heads of universities and directors of large corporations.

My love of atoms and energetics has led me in strange and unexpected paths. I am reminded of the number of times throughout the Bible where God asks, "What do you see?" It is then that God reveals his purposes. We live among a people who Jesus says (quoting Isaiah), "will be ever hearing but never understanding, will be ever seeing but not perceiving."

For myself, I have been helped in my personal understanding by many books, especially Dietrich Bonhoeffer's two books and David Ford on the Creed mentioned earlier, together with accounts of those who have sought hard to follow the way God has for them, such as John Newton and the Clapham Sect members who wrestled with the 'Establishment' in the 19th century.[4] I am grateful the verb "*cognosco*" was drummed into me in my early school life.

Notes

1. See Aitken, Jonathan (2007), *John Newton – From Disgrace to Amazing Grace*, Continuum.

2. Hodder & Stoughton, 1995.

3. Ford, David (2007), *Christian Wisdom: Desiring God and Learning in Love*, Cambridge University Press.

4. Tomkins, Stephen (2010), *The Clapham Sect*, Lion.

Chapter 11

Surprise and the Value of Life

Andy Gosler is University Research Lecturer in Ornithology and Conservation at Oxford University where he holds a joint position between the Edward Grey Institute of Field Ornithology and the Institute of Human Sciences. Fellow in Human Sciences at Mansfield College, Oxford. Chair of the Institute of Human Sciences, Oxford University, 2008–2011. Educated at Aberystwyth, Reading and Oxford Universities. Co-Convenor of OxPeace – the Oxford University Network for Peace Studies. Editor of Ibis (British Ornithologists' Union), 1998–2006. Tucker Medal of British Trust for Ornithology, 1999. Union Medal of British Ornithologists' Union, 2012. Originator and Director of EWA, the Ethno-ornithology World Archive. Fellow of the Linnean Society of London. Fellow of the International Ornithologists' Union.

I doubt that there can be any surprise greater or more personally significant than that of the non-believer who finds faith in middle age. But when that dawning comes from within a lifetime's study of (indeed passion for) evolution, others might share in that surprise. The issue of surprise is a major theme that I shall return to, but I should give some outline of my history, as much for me as for you, to try to understand how I came to faith. In retrospect, I see that my personal search for truth through science has also been a search for personal truth, to find myself, so that ultimately science and faith have become intimately interwoven.

Home life

Some of my earliest recollections are of sitting on our kitchen table drawing horses: horse after horse, in walk, trot, canter and gallop and from every angle my young mind and hand could manage. I must have been about four, and I had discovered amongst my father's books a slim volume entitled *How to Draw Horses*; I was captivated. I was captivated by the elegant lines, the agility and the movement I found in the simple sketches within that book; but there was more, because the book also had some simple anatomical drawings showing how the final form depended on the underlying skeleton and muscles. I was fascinated by the anatomy and by the transformation of skeletal articulation through the astonishing complexity of musculature into the beauty of the whole animal that had so captured my attention. *How to Draw Horses* was one in a series of *How to Draw...* books from which my father had several titles including hands, ships, children, planes, trees and portraits, but none so touched me as did *Horses*. I think it is from that spark that my interest in biology, and more specifically in the relationship between biological form and function, began. It probably also explains why, thirty-five years later, I learned to ride, but that is another story.

Horses were not all that fascinated me at the age of four. I remember giving my poor mother a hard time with a stream of rather metaphysical questions. As I recall, these did not centre so much around the obvious "Where did I come from?" as around the idea of eternity. I think I had been asking about stars and the answer had involved space and that it went on for ever without end. Having learned to count, I was also aware that numbers must go on forever, as should time (or so we thought then). It may be because these things all demanded my attention at such a young age that they have been at the centre of my personal search throughout my life. Whatever the answers turned out to be, they would have to satisfy an interest in anatomy and eternity.[1]

Looking back, with regard to religion I see my childhood to have been a confusion of issues, a fact which undoubtedly reflected my parents' own positions. I came from a Liberal Jewish family in West London, for whom Jewish identity had validity and value independently of any understanding (profound or otherwise) of God. That identity was about whom we were and where were our roots, an issue that might have had particular significance for Jews living in the long shadow of the Holocaust (my own grandfather had lost a sister in Bergen-Belsen just a month before the end of the war). I rarely spoke to my mother about God, but I believe she felt his presence strongly in her life. My father's Judaism is more social and cultural; he has for many years considered himself an atheist, partly because of what he perceived as bigotry and hypocrisy within religion, two things about which he warned us children (I am the second of three sons). Despite all the inconsistencies that I might have experienced through all this in my childhood, I now regard the open-mindedness that I inherited from my parents, which has now allowed me to find faith, as one of the greatest tributes to them. My brothers and I were nurtured in a free-thinking, loving atmosphere for which I shall always be grateful.

To be raised simultaneously both within a faith (for example, we attended Sunday school where we learned about Jewish history, the festivals, and to read Hebrew) and also in a generally secular household, was confusing enough, but from the age of five, morning prayers at school included the Lord's Prayer, and while we were not allowed to go carol-singing with our school-friends, we did have a Christmas tree, and received Christmas cards and presents, because my parents didn't want us to feel left out. And so I learned about Jesus at school, but was told at home that Jews considered him to be a prophet. It would be many years before I would think about this independently for myself. My early attempts to reconcile all this, especially in the light of my rapidly growing interest in evolution, dinosaurs and then birds, were too confused to be of value to me and so, after Bar' Mitzvah, it was probably inevitable that I would lapse into a slightly restless agnosticism (actually apathy would be a better description). From then until my awakening of faith in the late 1990s, I was simply uninterested in religious matters; indeed I would have regarded it as too strong a *commitment* to have labelled myself an atheist!

Birds

An interest in dinosaurs, which developed from my close attention to a colouring book on the subject bought during an early visit to the Natural History Museum at South Kensington, gave way at the age of ten to the interest in birds that has sustained me ever since. Birds, bird-watching and ornithology ruled my teens. I think my parents were quite concerned because it wasn't obvious to them (or to me, for that matter) how one might make a living from birds: the opportunities then were far scarcer than they are now. At that time, living in Ealing, the routes and timetables of the London buses and Underground dictated my travels. Favourite haunts included Richmond Park, where I saw many birds that were uncommon nearer home, including my first woodpeckers, owls, kingfisher, warblers, flycatchers, redstart and unexpected waterfowl including, on one occasion, a red-throated diver. At Osterley Park I saw my first tree sparrows and bramblings, and at Perivale Wood (owned by the Selborne Society) I helped with a Common Bird Census and was invited to join the Management Committee as a Junior Representative. Through the Selborne Society I also learned about the Revd Gilbert White and his *Natural History of Selborne* and by implication that a passion for natural history, albeit pre-Darwin, could be compatible with a devotion to God.

I must admit that at that time my interest in birds was so exclusive that I didn't much notice other forms of life. I learned to identify all the common trees, shrubs and more significant herbs, but this was more because they were essential components of habitat, or provided food, for birds, than because they interested me for their own sake. Likewise for invertebrates: if they weren't bird food, they didn't exist to me. Despite this, perhaps extreme, focus on birds, although I enjoyed seeing new species, adding them to my life-list was never a goal. I was a frequent visitor to the Bird Gallery of the Natural History Museum, where I learned a great deal about form and function, evolution, ecology and systematics – that is, not just how to distinguish one species from another. In addition to a delight in evolution that developed from my museum visits, my feeling that this place, with its shrine-like monuments to Darwin, Huxley and Owen, was itself a cathedral to natural history developed in me a sense of relationship between biology and spirituality. But it was not a sense that this science, which revealed so much about the history of life, had replaced God. Rather, it was that God was more powerfully present, more real, *here* than anywhere I had known. I think this sense is also captured by the final paragraph of Darwin's *Origin of Species*,[2] and perhaps this reveals something of his own spirituality.[3] As I have probably indicated, the inspiration that I felt from evolution presented no great threat to any position of faith that I had; indeed quite the reverse. I had, for example, been taught (consistently on this point) at school, home and in synagogue, that the Genesis text was not to be taken literally: its meaning and value lay in the relationships between God, humanity and the natural order that it revealed through allegory. It therefore came as a shock in later life to discover, probably from reading Richard Dawkins' *The Blind Watchmaker*, that some people regarded Genesis as historical fact.[4]

Value and values – intrinsic and contingent

There was another side to my avian obsession, which was significant in my personal development. I came to regard birds – each species – as precious, uniquely evolved, irreplaceable and therefore of inestimable value, a view which has been the ground for my personal conservation ethic ever since. Furthermore, I felt that if the value of each species arises through its being a unique evolutionary "event" (as indeed is each individual life), then that value is independent of my valuing of it as a human observer – that is, its value is intrinsic, and not contingent. It followed that extinction was the greatest loss imaginable, and the fact that we humans were the cause of most, if not all, extinctions in recorded history, meant that there must be something seriously wrong with my own species. I came at this time to regard humans (as I still do) as the most destructive force on the planet; and the fact that most people I met, including friends and family, seemed oblivious of the damage we were causing, and seemed to regard extinctions as nothing more than an occupational but inevitable hazard of human progress, made me deeply sceptical of any progressive modernist narrative, and seemed to reinforce my view that humanity was irredeemable. It also seemed clear that religion, with its apparent anthropocentricity, was simply part of the problem: it could have nothing to offer for the solution.

It was through reading Environmental Biology at Aberystwyth University that I began to see the world beyond birds, even though while there I did train and qualify as a bird ringer (a "bander", in US terminology). Studying ecology, I began to see a unity in nature that my avicentric perception had hidden from me and, more significantly, that all organisms exist in relationship to every other – be they mates, prey, predators, parasites, or indeed habitats. With the wider perspective of ecology, I began to appreciate that while *I* might perceive birds as distinct entities of seemingly greater value than anything else (including humans), that perception could not reflect reality. There was no rational ground for believing that birds had any greater value than any other organism. In other words, I realized that my view of the natural world was unsustainable and it gradually changed, but it was replaced not by an atheistic nihilism, but by a perception of the grandeur and value of *all* life.

In the process of asking whether birds have any greater value than any other organisms, the question inevitably arises as to whether they have any less, and in particular where human beings fit in. Although humans routinely assume that they have greater value than any other animal, isn't that anthropocentrism precisely *the* problem? The question then arises of whether life itself has any value. As an undergraduate, I read Richard Dawkins' *The Selfish Gene*,[5] which argued that nothing had any absolute value from an evolutionary point of view: either value was anthropogenic or anthropocentric, in which case a life's value could only ever be what humans ascribed to it; or contingent upon some ecological role (for example, pandas might value bamboo). Whilst I might accept this as an intellectual exercise (even though it contradicted my own relating of value to evolutionary uniqueness), I was deeply troubled by it at a practical level, because my personal experience suggested that most humans *didn't* value nature. If we couldn't argue for nature conservation from the ethical standpoint of its intrinsic value, this left only utilitarian arguments. It was already clear to me that utilitarian arguments for conservation, by themselves, were inadequate because they implied that if no human use were found for a particular species its extinction could be considered no loss. Of course, we now see that extinctions do not happen like this, via the filter of human scrutiny, since in the biological holocaust of anthropogenic deforestation, pollution and climate change that is now underway most losses will in fact be of species that won't even have been described when they are snuffed out of existence.

So *The Selfish Gene* troubled me, not because it robbed me of God, but because it robbed life itself of any value: Dawkins argues that the origin of genes preceded life, in the sense that life arose only as a means to perpetuate genes – lifeless, unthinking, uncaring chemistry. Furthermore, he suggests that a sign of maturity is being able to recognize one's anthropocentric valuing of life for the "mistake" that it really is. But hang on – life *is* wonderful *and* amazing, and perhaps even good! It depends heavily on co-operation at higher levels of organization than that of the gene[6] – a fact which is all the more wonderful if it truly arose in the manner that Dawkins describes, and life exists in all its glorious fullness (love, joy, pain, suffering, warts and all) only at the level of the whole organism, the individual, and not at that of the gene (chemistry). Moulded by selection through the lives and deaths of organisms, the *value* of a gene lies in its contribution to, or potential for, life. Dawkins' attempt to reverse the natural view that *life* gives *genes* value is an aspect of *The Selfish Gene* that I could never accept.[7] Indeed, I could not help feeling that any biologist who argues that life has no value has lost the plot. But how does one reconcile these issues? Dawkins' view was that if the facts trouble your worldview, that's unfortunate, but your worldview was wrong. This is a plausible intellectual standpoint, but it ignores the possibility that *the facts* considered by Dawkins were not, in fact, the whole truth.[8]

Oxford and atheism

After taking a Master's degree in plant taxonomy at Reading University, I came to Oxford to work as a field assistant in the Edward Grey Institute of Field Ornithology (EGI). Shortly afterwards, I was awarded a studentship, and so had fees to work for my doctorate in ornithology; at last I was making a living from birds. I was surprised at Oxford to find that most people, even in the EGI, were not as passionate about birds as I was, and the issue of the *value* of life soon emerged for me as a material one. It did so because bird welfare seemed to be a more significant issue for me than for some of the zoologists around me. Whether or not my perception was correct, it seemed that they had accepted the *Selfish Gene* view of life so thoroughly that they had extrapolated it to their working relationships with animals.

Because of my bird-ringing qualification, I soon found myself with sole responsibility within the department for training students in ringing techniques. This enabled me to instil in them from the outset that the welfare of a wild bird in their hands was a matter of significant responsibility (a bird is more than just a data point on a graph). The coming of the Animals (Scientific Procedures) Act in 1986 raised ethical issues much more sharply than before for everyone engaged in animal-related work, including ecological studies. Despite its shortcomings, it is largely thanks to this that it is no longer possible to pay mere lip-service to ethical issues in animal research, and my appointment in the 1990s to the Ethical Review Committee of the Zoology Department brought the issue of value strongly into focus.

Through the 1980s and 1990s I became increasingly dissatisfied with the arguments for atheism that I found promoted gratuitously in my biology reading. Hitherto I had been content to ignore God, but I was now being forced to think about the issue. For example, having read a surprisingly strong scientific argument *for* the existence of God in Peter Medawar's *The Limits of Science*,[9] the best argument for demolition that he could muster in the next chapter was that it "defied common sense"! I had long held the view, based on my rudimentary understanding of quantum mechanics, that for a scientist "common sense" was the last refuge of the desperate. Furthermore, in the opening to *The Problems of Evolution*,[10] Mark Ridley had pointed out that the very notion that species were not immutable (i.e. that they evolved), itself, defied common sense. So common sense gets us nowhere. Indeed, since my view that life has value was part of *my* common sense, it must at least be as valid a position as Medawar's, even if it proved not to be scientifically sustainable. I began to realize that the conclusion that God did not exist did not come inexorably from any real science, but from the systematic annihilation of straw men – from simplistic literal readings of Genesis, "common sense", and an absolute confidence in the "meaning" of the *Selfish Gene* model, which itself might be wrong – as argued by philosophers[11] and increasingly by biologists.[12]

In other words, whilst I had (I thought) been content not to consider God in my life in any way, shape or form, through reading standard biology texts I was being made to consider the evidence for atheism, and frankly I wasn't impressed. The thought dawned then that if the best arguments for atheism were so weak, it must follow that God really might exist, and that this must be the most important thing that anyone could ever know. Browsing in a second-hand bookshop in Oxford one day, I came across a book entitled *Believing in God* by a Dominican priest, Gareth Moore.[13] I was delighted by its sanity, and its humility, and it fascinated me. I started to read books at the interface between science, philosophy and faith.[14] A new perception opened – a very light in my darkness.[15]

Theology, biological conservation and information

Through the 1990s I also immersed myself increasingly in the scientific literature associated with biological conservation, and here crystallized, at last, the ethical paradox to which I had become sensitized. In addition to the (to me unsatisfying) utilitarian arguments for conservation (along the lines that somewhere in the rainforest may exist a cure for cancer), I read time and again the explicit statement that a valid ground for conservation was that life had "*intrinsic value*" – that is, value by virtue simply of its existence and independent of any human (or other organic) valuer.[16] The authors never elaborated on this, perhaps because they were aware of the metaphysical nature of this claim (and its biblical roots). However, it often became clear elsewhere that they personally (or culturally) subscribed to a *Selfish Gene* worldview – that life could have no value beyond the relative and contingent value that humans placed on it. It was as if the authors didn't believe their own statement intellectually but nevertheless felt it so strongly to be their personal motivation as conservationists (as did I) that they should sneak it in under the reader's radar and hope nobody questioned it too deeply. So forcibly has the inconsistency struck me that I have made a point of asking colleagues whether they believe that life has "intrinsic value". Invariably (so far) they answer yes, but when questioned further as to where this value originates, I simply get blank expressions and shrugs. This is important. Because of it, I have witnessed the distressing spectacle in a seminar of a committed and dedicated (judged by his own work) conservationist arguing himself out of his own sense of commitment because he suddenly recognized the contradiction in his own philosophy. Thankfully, this was not a permanent injury, but the point is highlighted: we have to explore the notion of intrinsic value.

I must make clear here that my coming to faith in Christ did not rest on a single issue such as the value of life. It was a holistic redefining of perspectives that came together through every aspect of my life: relationships with people and animals, science, teaching, art, music, philosophy, bird-watching, horse-riding, everything, and the common denominator was love: the light in the darkness of blind indifference. Indeed, the views presented here on intrinsic value developed after my acceptance of Christ (I was baptized in 2000), and I regard them as some of the fruits of my new life in Him.[17] I shall argue that intrinsic value is real, and that it is reflected in the information content of existence. Important in developing this view has been the recognition of an association between value and rarity (think of antiques) or irreplaceability, and the fact that ecologists often measure bio-diversity using a statistic derived from Information Theory.[18]

Materialists argue that nothing exists but matter and energy. Yet clearly there is another, essential, phenomenon: information. What *is* information, and where in the matter–energy realm does it exist? Even for the materialist to argue that only matter and energy really exist, information is necessary, a fact which causes the statement itself to implode.[19] We tend to think of information essentially as a mathematical concept, but it is more than this. For example, we accept that DNA "carries" information, yet it cannot be observed directly (it must be interpreted). There is therefore a sense in which information seems to be transcendent, independent of the matter and energy with which it is associated. Yet even more than this: it is intimately involved with dynamic process as well as material existence. It can be said that everything that exists, in both the energy–material and mental realms, is inseparably associated with, or exists simultaneously as, information.

Information is of course associated with the concept of a "signal", which is distinct from "noise". For this insight we owe a great debt to Claude Shannon, a mathematician and engineer working for the Bell Telephone Laboratories in the 1940s. Shannon recognized that information (the signal) is the antithesis of entropy (noise), and that entropy declines as information increases. Hence we can argue that since, within this universe, everything that exists, either realized or potential, is a manifestation of information, we might regard information as the signal of existence, as opposed to the noise of chaos: information is the very light in the darkness – *Dominus illuminatio mea*.

The mathematical formulation of information, which measures the quantity of information in a signal, and from which ecologists derive their diversity index, was also developed by Shannon, and is known as the Information Statistic. This statistic is based on the quantity p, which represents the probability of an event. Shannon described this quantity as its "surprise" because rare, or less probable, events are more surprising.[20] As Shannon's statistic is regarded as the essential mathematical definition of information, the concept of surprise is seen to be inherent to our understanding of information itself.

So information is intimately bound up with the rare event, the improbable. Now, considering a (broadly evolutionary) biological series such as bacterium, fish, frog, mouse, chimpanzee, human, suggests that what essentially has been going on through organic evolution has been an increase in surprisingness, in information, as well as (as it happens) an increase in the relative ability to apprehend information itself (i.e. cognitive ability). It may be that the order of this series also matches your instinctive order of valuing these organisms (unless you are an ornithologist), and I suggest that this might reflect an innate ability to recognize information content, which tends to lead us to value the rare, the improbable, the surprising.

It is clear, however, that we do not value things only because they are rare; our sense of value involves a further component. Further insight here might be found from the analogy with antiques, suggested earlier, for which provenance is also important. As my anthropologist friend John Paull pointed out, a chipboard desk is still a chipboard desk irrespective of how old or rare it is, but if it had been James Cook's chipboard desk (John is Australian), we might view it differently. Provenance then is an important component of the information associated with an item contributing to its rarity, and our appreciation of value. In the special case of life too, I suggest we must consider provenance.

Wonder and surprise

The point is that existence, all that exists, exists *as* information. This means that it appears to us, within this universe, to be improbable, and therefore surprising. Since we equate value with rarity, and improbability (surprise and information content) is simply the rarity of an event, in equating information with value we recognize an important congruence, which most of us might accept (indeed, we might even argue from common sense in this regard):

- existence is more surprising (in the sense that it has more value) than non-existence;

- life is more surprising (has more value) than non-life;

- complex life is more surprising (has more value) than simple life;

- conscious life is more surprising (has more value) than non-conscious life;

- self-aware life is more surprising (has more value) than non-aware life; and,

- perhaps most surprising, then, is life that contemplates its very existence.

We must be very clear what we mean here by "intrinsic value", because our very existence is endangered by hubris if we misunderstand it. We know that the Earth's biosphere can function (indeed it did so for millions of years) without humans, but it cannot function at all without microbes. Thus in terms of value to the planet's ecological functioning, microbes are demonstrably more valuable than humans. However, this is not *intrinsic* value, it is value for a specific purpose (Gaia),[21] it is *contingent* value. But this demonstrates forcibly that *we* should not value organisms differently by virtue of differences in their intrinsic value: all have their utilitarian value to the functioning of the whole. The significance for conservationists of defining intrinsic value lies in terms of recognizing a value that exists metaphysically and independent of our being.

In recognizing the need for a metaphysical perspective in defining intrinsic value, I was struck by the fact that John's Gospel tells us that in the beginning was the Word – that is, before all things, was the signal: information; nothing was ever made except by the Word. Furthermore, as my relationship with God has developed, I have also come to associate him with surprise. This became clear to me not only from the many references to surprise found in texts of Christian testimony (e.g. C. S. Lewis – *Surprised by Joy*;[22] Gerard Hughes – *God of Surprises*;[23] Colin Russell – *Surprised by Science*;[24] and Tom Wright – *Surprised by Hope*[25]) but also from the numerous wonderful "coincidences" that have attended my own coming to faith. William Temple wrote: "When I pray, coincidences happen, and when I don't, they don't." Non-believers may say that coincidence is just that – it is noise and carries no information, and thus has no value: it is certainly not evidence of God's immanence. But I had forty-two years in which to assess the "background rate" of coincidence in my life, and the last fourteen years stand out for me: the coincidences *have* had value for me, and by implication they carried information, they were not noise. I will give a brief taste.

In 1999 my wife and I had to put our books into temporary storage. In packing them I found myself holding a Bible. Partly because I had never made much sense of the Old Testament, and partly because the atheist writers had made me curious about Christianity, I started to read the Gospels. What I found was a Jesus who sounded like my father: hot on the issues of religious bigotry and hypocrisy, and not at all what I'd been led by the atheists to expect. That Christmas Eve I attended midnight service at our parish church (Holy Trinity, Headington Quarry), supported by my wife Caroline for whom (unlike me) this was not alien territory. Caroline had come from an Anglican family, but had lost her faith years earlier, and indeed I should like to dedicate this testimony to her for so wonderfully supporting my own faith while still lacking belief in God herself.

The preacher at that service was Tom Honey (now a Canon at Exeter Cathedral), whom I already knew as a birdwatcher and who had been at the same school as me in Ealing (where he had known my older brother). His sermon was precisely what I needed at that time. I started going regularly to the church and, having decided to accept baptism in the autumn, worried about how to tell my parents. A friend wisely counselled me to write and tell them, giving them the reasons for my decision as best I could – and to invite them to the baptism service. I was baptized by the Bishop of Oxford. My parents accepted my invitation and were delighted by their warm welcome in our church. They were even more delighted by the Bishop's very sympathetic sermon on the relationship between Christianity and Judaism. And when my mother and I asked the Bishop if he had been aware of my background and he replied that he had not, he too was moved to learn of the surprise value to us of his address.

God, creation and improbability

The argument I have presented suggests that exploring the nature of information more fully may provide deeper insights into the true nature of reality. Information exists most powerfully in the mental realm; it is surely the very stuff of consciousness and of relationship, whether mathematical, ecological or personal. If all "things" (material and spiritual) exist as information, while some also exist, or are "realized", as matter–energy, then might we consider the soul as the information "image" of the living being, including the consciousness of that being as well as the information associated with physical form, function and process? If this is in any sense correct, perhaps we might gain yet further insight into what is meant by being created in the "image" of God.

Space does not permit me to elaborate on the value of the support that I have received for my Christian journey from friends, family and indeed colleagues (though they are probably unaware of this), but the value I have come to see in humans through these relationships, gives me hope that our species might be redeemable after all. I have come to recognize that while humans are indeed the most destructive species on the planet, this is because of the broken relationship with God described allegorically in Genesis, which results in the perception of *Homo sapiens* as the centre of all things. The irony of this is palpable since, for example, an evolutionary argument for atheism is that religion is irrational precisely because of its anthropocentricity.

But it is this broken relationship, this falling out of love, that has resulted in the distorted judgments that result from utilitarian ethics, and the inability to recognize the value, indeed sanctity, of life. The crucifixion gives the lie to the notion that God delights in the suffering of creation;[26] the resurrection shows the potential value of surprise. The present environmental crisis is ultimately a consequence of human greed, of selfishness, of the poverty and criminality that arise from these, and of ignorance. Consequently, and contrary to the assumptions of my youth, I have found that Christ's teachings have much to offer us by way of salvation from this crisis.

Two final points. First, while the very fact of existence appears surprising to us as we contemplate it from within a universe where the occurrence of events is contingent on probability, it seems unlikely that this should be so for God; if he created the universe, it cannot surprise him that it exists.

While this says nothing about the nature of God's interaction with the extant universe, it does suggest that the value which God places on creation is related not to its information content, but to something else: an act of divine grace consistent with the continuing act of creation through love.[27] The second point is that if value is coupled with improbability within this creation, it follows that God should appear to us to be both of inestimable value, and also highly implausible. In God's apparent improbability, then, I agree, in the end, with Richard Dawkins.[28]

Notes

1. In a discussion on "Desire – a homing instinct for God", Alister McGrath cites what French philosopher Chantal Milon-Delsol called a "desire for eternity" (*Mere Apologetics – How to Help Seekers and Skeptics Find Faith*, Baker Books, 2012). I believe I felt this at a very young age.

2. "From the war of nature, from famine and death, the most exalted object of which we are capable of conceiving, namely the production of the higher animals directly follows. There is a grandeur in this view of life, with its several powers, having been originally breathed into a few forms or into one; and that, while this planet has gone cycling on according to the fixed law of gravity, from so simple a beginning endless forms most beautiful and most wonderful have been and are being evolved."

3. See Wilson, E. O. (2006), *The Creation: An Appeal to Save Life on Earth*, Norton, p. 7.

4. Norton, 1986.

5. Oxford University Press, 1976.

6. Noble, D. (2006), *The Music of Life*, Oxford University Press.

7. This adaptive "moulding" is referred to as optimization by biologists. The concept of optimality and its mathematical modelling, is important in modern evolutionary biology. In essence it says that organisms evolve *for the best* (towards the optimum) so as to maximize fitness within the physical, chemical, ecological, behavioural and genetic constraints in which the organism exists. All then is for the best in evolution.

8. On reflection I see also that there was something else, and it was personal. The attack on religion in general, and the Judeo-Christian narrative in particular, made by atheists was being made in the name of evolutionary biology. By implication then it was being made in my name also. Had I been asked if I wished to sign up to this slaying of my own cultural heritage? No, thank you, but no… and so I felt drawn into a battle that was not of my choosing, against an enemy towards whom I felt more sympathy than animosity, and aligning with modernist sentiments with which I was deeply uncomfortable because of my love of nature.

9. Oxford University Press, 1984.

10. Oxford University Press, 1985.

11. Sober, E. & Wilson, D. S. (1999), *Unto Others: Evolution and Psychology of Unselfish Behavior*, Harvard University Press; Ruse, M. (2004), *Can a Darwinian be a Christian?*, Cambridge University Press; Ruse, M. (2004), *Darwin and Design: Does Evolution Have a Purpose?*, Harvard University Press; Haught, J. F. (2004), *Deeper Than Darwin: The Prospect for Religion in the Age of Evolution*, Westview Press.

12. Miller, K. (1999), *Finding Darwin's God: A Scientist's Search for Common Ground Between God and Evolution*, Harper-Perennial; Jablonka, E. & Lamb, M. J. (2006), *Evolution in Four Dimensions: Genetic, Epigenetic, Behavioral and Symbolic Variation in the History of Life*, Bradford; Noble, D. (2006), *The Music of Life*, Oxford University Press; Tallis, R. (2012), *Aping Mankind: Neuromania, Darwinitis and the Misrepresentation of Humanity,* Acumen Publishing.

13. T&T Clark, 1996.

14. Ward, K. (1996), *God, Chance and Necessity*, Oneworld; Polkinghorne, J. (1996), *Scientists as Theologians*, SPCK; (1998), *Belief in God in an Age of Science*, Yale University Press; (1998), *Science and Theology: An Introduction*, SPCK; Jeeves, M. A. & Berry, R. J. (1998), *Science, Life and Christian Belief*, Apollos; McGrath, A. E. (1998), *The Foundations of Dialogue in Science and Religion*, Wiley-Blackwell; Clark, S. (1998), *God, Religion and Reality*, SPCK; Ruse, M. (2004), *Can a Darwinian be a Christian?*, Cambridge University Press.

15. The motto of Oxford University, *Dominus Illuminatio Mea*, translates as "The Lord is my Light". It is taken from Psalm 27: "The Lord is my light and my salvation": *Dominus illuminatio mea et salus mea*. What is this light? It is the light of reason in the darkness of ignorance, the light of order in the darkness of chaos, and the light of love in the darkness of indifference.

16. Gaston, K. and Spicer, J. (1998), *Biodiversity: An Introduction*, Wiley-Blackwell; Hambler, C. (2004), *Conservation*, Cambridge University Press; Norton, B. (2005), *Sustainability*, Chicago University Press.

17. Another such fruit, since faith and my engagement with Human Sciences led me to an interest in human relationships with nature, has been my discovery of ethno-biology, a field whose valuing of humans within nature aligns strongly with my own. Ethno-biology has shown me that the apparent cultural devaluing of nature often found in the West is not the default state of humans. It has therefore helped to heal my own perception of my species whilst also offering hope for conservation.

18. The information statistic from which ecologists derive the diversity index H-bar, is p.log$_2$p where p is the probability of an event (where $0 \leq p \leq 1$). In ecology, p_i is taken as the probability that an individual organism drawn at random from a community belongs to species "i", and the values are summed across species to give the statistic H-bar. This allows one to include in a single quantity both the number of species present in an ecological community and the distribution (or equitability) of individuals amongst those species.

19. Byl, J. (2004), *The Divine Challenge; on matter, mind, math and meaning*, Banner of Truth Trust.

20. Aleksander, I. (2002), "Understanding information, bit by bit: Shannon's equations", in Farmelo, G. (ed.), *It Must be Beautiful: Great Equations of Modern Science*, Granta Books, pp. 213–30.

21. Gaia: a theoretical global cybernetic system whereby living and non-living components interact via dynamic feedback which results, for example, in a stabilizing of the planet's atmospheric composition, marine salinity etc., and thus also climate, over millions of years to the benefit of life itself. Evidence for Gaia has grown steadily since James Lovelock first proposed its existence in the early 1970s, although it remains controversial. See Lovelock, J. (1995), *The Ages of Gaia: A Biography of Our Living Earth*, Norton.

22. Harvest, 1966.

23. Darton, Longman & Todd, 1996.

24. In Berry, R. J. (ed.) (1991), *Real Science, Real Faith*, Monarch.

25. SPCK, 2007.

26. Dawkins, R. (2006), *The God Delusion*, Houghton Mifflin.

27. MacKay, D. (1960), *Science and Christian Faith Today*, Falcon.

28. Dawkins (2006), *op. cit.*

Chapter 12

Inspired by the Heavens

Jennifer Wiseman is an astronomer, speaker, and author with a bachelor's degree in physics from MIT and a PhD in astronomy from Harvard. She studies star formation in our galaxy using radio, optical and infrared telescopes. She has served in several research and leadership positions at scientific institutions across the US, and has also taken a number of roles in science policy leadership. She enjoys speaking about the excitement of science and astronomy to academic, public, church, and civic groups.

I grew up in a rural community in the Ozark hills of Arkansas, surrounded by the beauty of nature and the love of God. I was very fortunate: it was a friendly place, and my family and church taught me in both word and example to live in love for God and for others. What a blessing. With hills, rivers, lakes, streams, meadows, and trees all around, the natural world surrounded me and was never far from our daily life, work, and recreation. We lived on a wooded farm with cattle, dogs, cats, gerbils, and wildlife close at hand. It was in this setting that I thrived, with a special love for animals, forests, and the dark night sky glistening with stars.

I also enjoyed academic study at our local school, and science was an intriguing part of that, helping me understand the natural world that I loved. I didn't know any scientists, so I could not easily envision being one. My parents had not had the chance to go to college, though they worked very hard to enable their four children to do so. My oldest brother and his wife often gave me science-related gifts at Christmas, which gave me a message of encouragement regarding science.

But other subjects also interested me: music, literature, and especially mathematics. Our small rural town was fortunate to have excellent, dedicated teachers, and owing to their good instruction and encouragement, I became fascinated by how mathematics could be used to solve the puzzles of physics. Through the confidence and interest they instilled in me, I sought higher education, even in faraway places.

In my family, and for many of my friends, church and faith in God were central to our lives. Growing up, we participated in church meetings and Sunday school classes every week, learning about God and especially about Jesus and his love for us. I was happily baptized at the age of around eleven, as a symbol of inward faith and of a forever bond with the church family. Mom and Dad both sought to live lives of integrity and faith, and prayer and Bible or devotional reading grew to become a regular part of our home life. Summer camps and teenage youth groups helped us siblings learn how to apply the lessons of God's love into practical choices we make in caring for others.

However, I was also growing up as a human being (!), with the ubiquitous human tendency toward self-centredness, independence, and pride, and, as the years went by, surrounded by the typical social pressures of teenage life, with everyone wanting to "fit in". At some point, maybe more than once, I was confronted by a stark reality as conveyed by fearless preachers: Jesus is Lord of all, and he wants full surrender of our lives to him. He loves with an all-encompassing desire to give us true, abundant and eternal life, and to live through us; without him there is no real life or joy or hope. He will return, and we will all stand before him someday, and all eternity is in his hands. Am I living for me, or am I living for him? I hadn't done many "bad" things in my life as far as others might take note of, but I did know that my heart needed to choose a first allegiance to God. I prayed and offered my life fully to him. Since those days, my life of faith has been centred on seeking how to know and follow Jesus Christ in all the situations and stages of life, with all its failures and joys and struggles.

Beginning in astronomy

So how did astronomy, my ultimate profession, come into this picture? A mixture of the natural and the unexpected joined together. First of all, growing up on that rural farm often included walks with my parents and dogs after dark, with the night sky filled with stars from horizon to horizon (light pollution had not yet tainted the skies, as it does for so many people today). It was natural for my eyes to be drawn upward toward the heavens, to be enthralled by the sheer number of stars, and to imagine being transported to visit these glowing lights in the sky. At about the same time, a popular television programme was showing us the first images of exotic moons around other planets, the fruits of the *Voyager* and *Pioneer* planetary probes that were the first to encounter closely these fascinating new worlds. As I was introduced to the fascinating surfaces of icy Enceladus and Ganymede, volcanic Io, and intriguing Europa, I dreamt of being there in person. But not for long – I soon realized that astronauts could not travel that far and for the foreseeable future at least, exploring these distant worlds required using telescopes.

So astronomy became a topic of consuming interest. One year, for our school science fair, I "built" a Black Hole. Thankfully, my cardboard invention did not have the same enormous gravitational pull as would a real astrophysical Black Hole! The real ones are formed from collapsed stars, with material becoming so dense that the gravitational field can even distort the path of light, pulling it in on a path that never escapes. As the time drew near for me to consider university studies, I was encouraged by my teachers and my brother to consider good science schools, and so, bolstered with that confidence, I applied for several schools, and my parents sacrificially enabled me to attend a good one. I did my undergraduate degree at MIT.

But then the unexpected came onto the scene. I didn't know that even as an undergraduate student I would be able to get involved in real scientific research. How thrilling it was to be able to dabble over the next few years in research ranging from astronaut space adaptation to studying the rings of the planet Uranus! I learned how messy it can be to work with real data. And I also had a very pleasant surprise. On a field camp in Arizona at Lowell Observatory, where we students were learning what "real astronomers" do, I noted an unexpected object on a photograph of the night sky that had recently been taken with a telescope. It didn't look like the asteroids I was supposed to be finding. It looked like a comet, though confirming that kind of identification was impossible with a single image. (In fact, the "comet-like" appearance was due to its motion during the exposure!) But with the help of the staff professionals there, we located the object again in the sky, and it was confirmed to be a newly discovered comet! At the time I did not know if comets were discovered once every year or once every day or once every thousand years. It turns out that about a dozen are found every year, although not all of them return regularly. Fortunately, this comet returns every six and a half years. I had nothing to do with naming it, but the authorities that name such objects called it Comet Wiseman-Skiff, after myself and Brian Skiff, the outstanding Lowell astronomer who took the discovery photograph in the first place.

At the time I had been praying for help to find a topic for a senior research paper I had to write in order to graduate with a physics degree. The comet discovery seemed to be the answer for this, and I continued to observe and study that comet with a university telescope for several months; it did indeed become the topic of my senior thesis. Now, my prayers are not usually answered with such "stellar" results (!), but for all the rest of the years of my life it has amused me that people remember the comet discovery more than any of the subsequent scientific research on other topics I have done over the years. It reminds me that, ultimately, it's not about our own efforts (though quality work is a good thing), but about God's provision (and even surprises!).

I had some hard times getting through difficult courses and situations as an undergraduate. And yet somehow the doors opened at just the right time for me to consider going on to graduate school, and I decided astronomy was the best way for me to apply my physics knowledge to what I loved: the study of space. So I entered graduate school at Harvard (after a blessed year off from school, including some time driving a tractor on the family farm!). I had no idea what sort of astronomy to pursue. I started off in the grandiose realm of cosmology, working with scientists who studied the arrangement of galaxies in the universe. But then I met a professor who was known to be a good mentor for students, and he introduced me to some very interesting research projects involving the study of the formation of stars in interstellar space, within very dense clouds of gas and dust. Peering into these hidden stellar nurseries meant we had to use radio telescopes such as the Very Large Array radio observatory in New Mexico. It was a great privilege to learn how to use facilities such as this, and I would never have known how to do this kind of work had it not been for being part of a congenial research group with a great professor-advisor. I studied in particular how new stars, currently "hidden" behind the Orion Nebula, are forming and affecting their surrounding environment. Such studies help us understand better how our own Sun and solar system, including planets, once formed. Currently we are discovering thousands of planetary systems around stars other than the Sun, so the study of star and planet formation is a hot topic. I have been able to continue in this interesting study of star formation ever since I finished my doctorate.

Astronomy research and Christian faith?

How does my faith interact with this research in astronomy? There are several answers to that. First, I have learned that "God is my help" (Psalm 54:4), however difficult the challenges I have had to face. I have learned to pray in every situation or concern, whether it be in preparation for an exam, looking for career direction, relationships or work with students and colleagues, family dynamics, government leaders, or even concerns for animals. I have learned that God *always* delivers and helps when we ask (Psalm 34 is a favourite of mine), sometimes in unexpected ways (and sometimes as part of a painful but fruitful lesson) – and that includes the help we need in our professional work. Since believers do everything as service to Christ and in his name, it is fitting to receive his grace to help us. A consequence of this is that others will see the Lord through us – not because of our own strengths but because of God's power working through us weak and fallible vessels. "Whatever you do, whether in word or deed, do it all in the name of the Lord Jesus, giving thanks to God the Father through him" (Colossians 3:17).

Grace is another wonderful aspect of this ongoing relationship with God. It means first and foremost that we can indeed have that relationship: grace means "unmerited favour", the forgiveness of our sins and reconciliation with God. It also means the ongoing kindness of God throughout life, including the redemption and transformation of gloomy situations into positive outcomes. I have experienced this in personal and professional situations that I and my fellow believers have bathed in prayer.

I try to remember to pray about my professional work. At first it seemed strange to pray about which kind of astronomy research to pursue, what jobs to seek, for help when research runs into a snag, or for preparation for professional meetings and decisions. And yet that is exactly what we should do. I believe that studying the heavens is something that glorifies God (as does, I believe, all scientific research done with integrity with good motives).

Fellowship and testing

I also have been greatly blessed by finding other believers for fellowship and friendship. As a student, I found student Christian fellowship groups helpful, but perhaps even more important were the fellow pilgrims I came to know as a graduate student when I joined a graduate Christian fellowship group. Some of these brothers and sisters are still friends decades later. In my present life, I find organizations of professional scientists who are Christians to be extremely valuable; we share the same love of our discipline, the same curiosity about the universe, the same desire to seek the Lord, and some of the same challenges that we can help each other with.[1] There is even a group of Christian astronomers that gets together regularly to encourage one another over meals at professional meetings. The value of realizing and experiencing our "connectedness" to other believers, especially those in similar professions facing similar challenges, is beyond measure. I have also found blessing in being in a prayer group with several women from my church and neighbourhood who are not astronomers or scientists. We lead very different lives, and yet we learn from one another, pray for one another, and love one another. One particular period of time when a telescope project I was working with had great problems, I timidly brought up the enormous challenges we were facing to my prayer group. Looking back, I have to chuckle:

while the others in the group were used to hearing what one might call "normal" prayer requests (such as healing for sick loved ones, or guidance for a church ministry to the poor, or help for someone needing a job), they nevertheless earnestly listened to me and prayed for this "observatory in distress" and the people involved, including my role, though I'm quite certain they didn't understand all the intricacies of the problems. Sure enough, over time the situation with the observatory was transformed into a wonderful outcome. I praise God for his deliverance, and I am thankful for these dear prayer sisters!

Working with non-Christian scientists from many cultures and nations has also been a great blessing to me. I have had the privilege of collaborating with bright experts from nearly every continent, as we strive to understand better the physical processes in the universe through astronomical observation and analysis. Contrary to the "science versus religion" motif routinely promoted in popular media, I have found that most scientists I work with are humble, curious and, whether they are religious believers or not, quite respectful and interested in the beliefs of their friends and colleagues; I feel the same way. In practice, something personal like religious belief rarely comes up during scientific work, because we are focusing on the technical scientific observations and analysis of our research. But over time personal friendships can develop between professional colleagues, and it is during off-times, sometimes years in the making, that we start to get to know each other better on a personal level, including sharing about our families, cultures, and thoughts and beliefs. At its best, I have experienced science as a real uniting force, bringing people from diverse backgrounds and countries together in a unified goal of understanding the physical truths of the universe. If the scientific approach is "working" properly, we as scientists will hopefully reach consensus on the scientific results of our studies, driven by curiosity and the search for physical truths.

Yet in the larger sphere of reality, purpose, and meaning, issues beyond the realm of what science alone can address, we may span a wide breadth of beliefs and philosophy. I treasure these rich relationships with such a variety of scientist colleagues.

Some may ask whether I ever sensed any discord between what is taught in the Bible and what I have learned in my science classes and research. The usual question regards the opening verses of Genesis in the Bible, which seem to depict a universe and all life coming into being in a matter of a few days, as compared to the scientific consensus of a universe developing over billions of years, with life on earth taking millions of years to evolve into its current diverse complexity. I know that many have struggled with these concepts, but honestly for me this has never really posed any major problem. While I'm sure that in my church, growing up, we all imagined the components of creation popping into being suddenly in each miraculous day, at God's command, we were also taught to be "humble" about Scripture, recognizing that God may not have revealed to us all the details of his workings in Scripture alone. Also we were cautioned to understand and respect the original audiences and purposes for different parts of the Bible, endeavouring to get the relevant and enduring messages God wants for us in our own time. That kind of humility leaves room and blessing for exploration, science, and even a thankful sense of awe as we begin to discover the mind-blowing size, age, and majesty of the universe. With such an approach to Scripture, nothing we discover in science can ever ultimately be in discord with faith in the God responsible for it all, though we may face some interesting questions along the way. In fact, hearing about a universe that may have taken a very long time to develop was not out of line with what I was noticing in my own childhood observations of nature. One of my favourite places on the planet, nestled deep in the Ozark Mountains of Arkansas, is "Blanchard Springs Caverns" (I encourage you to visit this beautiful area; it is worth the pilgrimage!). In these enormous underground caves, you can see huge majestic white columns of stalactites hanging from a rocky ceiling, and stalagmites building up from below. What is also striking about these caverns is that the system is "alive", meaning that water is still present in the caverns and dripping down the stalactites. Slowly, drip by drip by drip, the water falls from each stalactite down to the growing stalagmite below. Both are gradually growing from mineral deposits in the water droplets. The formation of these majestic structures can take many thousands or even millions of years. Even as a child I remember recognizing the quiet, slow pace of creation taking place right there in this underground palace, and feeling a sense of great humility towards nature and ultimately towards God.

All this means that I have never personally needed to "reconcile" science and faith (in fact, in my life science and faith enhance one another!). However, that doesn't mean I never had any spiritual struggles. For one thing, as a student I noticed that some prominent scientists would talk about science, in the classroom or on television, in such a way that religious belief seemed to be denigrated. Certainly there have been times in history when religious belief and authorities have indeed caused great trouble for science and other components of society, as have other philosophies and authorities. But some comments and implications seemed to deride or dismiss all current religious beliefs; I can well see why some religious believers feel alienated by science. Fortunately, in my own case I have known enough excellent scientists and colleagues who were either religious themselves or at least not anti-religious to give me a more balanced perspective. My own hardest struggle regarding the Bible and faith was not from science but rather from classes and professors who proclaimed that the words and even existence of Jesus were in great doubt. For me, this was much more serious. The words of Jesus proclaim the way of eternal life ("For God so loved the world that He gave His one and only Son, that whoever believes in Him shall not perish, but have eternal life", John 3:16). His teachings give wisdom, reveal God's incredible love (think of the prodigal son), and challenge us to follow him. His death and resurrection are central to all hope and meaning to all of us who follow him. So to hear from respected professors that we might not be able to trust any of this, in terms of New Testament scriptural integrity, was a very difficult blow for me. The implication was that no one really knows anything that Jesus ever actually said. Looking back, I think the Lord allowed this rug to be pulled out from under me for a while, to show me things that strengthened my faith. During this difficult period of time, I reflected and realized that I had witnessed the power of God in my own life and that I had seen God's love operating through other faithful, though imperfect, believers throughout my whole life. I could not deny this. Later I discovered other highly respected biblical scholars, both Christian and non-Christian, who restored my confidence in the New Testament (even with the interesting interpretative challenges it brings), and the life, death, and resurrection of Jesus. I think I had to go through this period to realize that my faith is ultimately in Jesus, not the Bible alone, though the Bible points us to Jesus.

In fact, the Bible reveals the nature of Jesus in a more profound way than most Christians even recognize. The opening of John's Gospel points to him as the "Word" who "became flesh". The world was created through this Word. The book of Hebrews (1:3) declares him as the one who "upholds the universe by His all-powerful word". Somehow this Person, of God's very Being, not only lived in the world, but is also responsible for the very existence of the universe.

An incredible universe

So what do we see when we look at the universe today? Thanks to improvements in technology, our telescopes are more sensitive than ever. We see beautiful gaseous nebulae filling space between stars. These gas clouds are often the nurseries where new stars continue to form. Hundreds of billions of stars, and the gas and dust between them, can comprise a galaxy held together by gravity. Our own Milky Way galaxy hosts not only our Sun and solar system, but also vast numbers of planets orbiting other stars, as indicated by the thousands of these "exoplanets" we have detected already. Someday we may even be able to detect signs of life on these external worlds, if it exists. How exciting!

We are also imaging vast numbers of other galaxies: there are hundreds of billions of them flung across the visible universe. For decades now we have realized that these galaxies appear to be moving away from each other, though they are actually caught up in the fabric of space that itself is stretching apart. The recent surprise is that this cosmic expansion seems to be speeding up, rather than the expected slow-down that gravity would cause. What would push the universe apart this way? Astronomers call this mystery "dark energy" as we study the nature of this unexpected discovery. Perhaps gravity itself has aspects we didn't know about until we could observe the universe at its largest scales.

For me the most fascinating part of astronomy is comparing the most distant galaxies with the ones closer to home; even our own Milky Way. Why? Because by looking carefully at galaxies, we can discern not only their sizes and masses, but also what they are made of. And it turns out that the earliest galaxies, the small conglomerations of gas and initial stars that formed not long after the beginning of the universe, were composed almost entirely of hydrogen, and a little helium. No surprise, because that's all that was around then. But now, in galaxies like our own, we also detect other elements such as carbon, oxygen, and nitrogen: things needed for solid planets, never mind life. Stars produce heavier elements like this as they shine. They are a product of the fusion process going on inside the highly pressurized cores of stars, and also of the gas emissions stars go through when they start to run out of "fuel" in their cores and get unstable. The biggest stars actually explode in a supernova when they get old. As these heavier elements get dispersed into interstellar space, they can get caught up in the next generation of stars. So over billions of years, a galaxy can support several generations of stars, each generation having more of the heavier elements than the previous one. Our own Milky Way galaxy has had several prior generations of some stars, making available heavier elements to our Sun when it formed. We are the happy recipients of these previous "stellar factories", enabling planets like our own Earth to form. What could be more spectacular than stars as a way to produce what we need for life?

I love the way that looking at these deep distances into space, viewing galaxies billions of light-years away, is literally a time machine enabling us to see things as they were so long ago (because it has taken light that long to get to us). Several facets of astronomical research all point to an incredible beginning of this universe about 13.8 billion years ago, and a majestic development of the universe in space and time ever since, leading to life on at least one planet. Does this point to God? Science doesn't answer that kind of question. However, looking through the "lens of faith", when I look at the universe I see amazing evidence of God's power, love of beauty, patience, and ultimate desire for life. Of course it's hard to fathom what God was doing all those years before we humans arrived! And there are the ever-present hard questions of why God would allow natural processes that sometimes cause such suffering on planet Earth (earthquakes, etc.). But the bottom line for believers is that the God responsible for the universe has also lived within it, in Jesus, and has experienced suffering, shared love, and now offers redemption and ultimate hope.

Astronomy can be a great vessel of uplift to people. Everyone I talk to, regardless of religious belief, education, culture, or economic status, is fascinated and amazed by the incredible and beautiful images of the heavens we can now obtain. Almost inevitably, they are drawn to ask, "Where did we come from?" and "Where do we fit into this incredible universe?" and "Could there be life on other planets?" and "What is our planet's future?" I feel one of the best gifts I can give to others, stemming from the opportunities in science the Lord has given to me, is to share with others the great discoveries we are making in science, instilling a sense of wonder, curiosity, and awe, and hopefully a desire to explore the natural world, with joy.

Notes

1. Such organizations are the American Scientific Affiliation and Christians in Science.

Chapter 13

Genes, Genesis and Greens

Professor R. J. (Sam) Berry, MA, PhD, DSc, FSB, FRSE. Educated at Kirkham Grammar School, Shrewsbury School, Gonville and Caius College, Cambridge, and University College London. Professor of Genetics in the University of London, 1974–2000. Member, Natural Environment Research Council, 1981–87. President, Linnean Society, 1982–85, British Ecological Society, 1987–89, European Ecological Federation, 1990–92. Chairman, Research Scientists' Christian Fellowship (now Christians in Science), 1968–88, President, 1993–95. Member, General Synod of the Church of England, 1970–90. Trustee, National Museums and Galleries on Merseyside, 1985–94; Governor, Monkton Combe School, Bath, 1979–92, Walthamstow Hall School, Sevenoaks, 2001–2005.

My father committed suicide when I was in the sixth form at school, working for A levels. I had been sent to boarding school because my mother was incapacitated with multiple sclerosis. As an only child, my father had thought it better for me to be away from home.

Because of my mother's illness, my father and I were particularly close, and his action was proportionately more difficult for me to understand. My memory is of coming home for the inquest and funeral, and going for long walks by myself, asking why? why? why? I don't know if I was a real Christian at that time. When I joined the Boy Scouts, I had been told that I ought to go to church because my Scout's promise included a commitment to "honour God". I used to haul my father along on most Sundays to a dreary and incomprehensible ritual at our local parish church. I took my confirmation (at boarding school) seriously, and later learned that the school chaplain had preached the Sunday before the confirmation service on the text, "Behold, I [Jesus] stand at the door and knock; if any man hear my voice, and open the door, I will come in" (Revelation 3:20, KJV). I remember the occasion, and know that I followed the steps in his exposition. But three years later, I could discern no meaning in life nor understand why my father decided "to take his life while the balance of his mind was temporarily disturbed".

The summer after my father's death I went to a house-party run by the Scripture Union. There I heard that the death of Jesus Christ at Calvary was not simply the end of an inspired teacher or the defeat of a promising liberation movement, but was God's intervention to provide a way back into his purpose for all who accepted him at his word, including me. In hackneyed words, "everything fell into place". The explanation of the New Testament events was intellectually satisfying and blindingly obvious. Like Thomas Henry Huxley a century earlier, who commented on reading Darwin's *Origin of Species*, "how stupid not to have thought of that oneself", I was rationally convinced of what I later discovered was the Christian gospel of "salvation through grace alone".

My acceptance of Christ as my Saviour is relevant because it was to me at the time (indeed, looking back, ever since that August day in 1952) a completely logical response to a reasoned argument on a par with the rigour expected in my A level science studies. I had planned to be a doctor and already had a provisional offer of a place in the medical school at Cambridge. A few months later, I realized that I would not be happy spending my life coping with other people at first hand, and, in the first event which, in retrospect, showed me God's nudging Spirit, I changed from a medical to a biology course.

As a Christian at university, I was faced with a hierarchy of possibilities. The really holy people became missionaries, the rather holy people were ordained, and the fairly holy people became teachers; the "also rans" did all the other jobs in the world. I hope I was prepared to serve abroad if God wanted me there, but I felt no particular call. I was tempted to train for the Church of England ministry, but two weeks of "testing my vocation" proved to me that God did not want me in that job; just as I would have been a terrible doctor, I would also have been a disastrous parson. So I started applying for school teaching posts – but no one offered me a job. I assumed God had a purpose for my life, but it wasn't very clear. The line of least resistance was to do the minimum; I stayed in the university world, working for a PhD in genetics at University College London. And, despite having pushed a few doors, I have remained in the university world; from 1974 until retiring in 2000, I was Professor of Genetics in the University of London.

Linked to the false assumption about the sanctity of various jobs that was around in my Cambridge days was a parallel belief that all Christians were supposed to be evangelists. My problem was that I had none of the gifts possessed by some of getting alongside people and proclaiming Christ. It was a great relief when I realized that we have all been given different talents and callings, and that there is not (and should not) be such a thing as a typical or normal Christian. This is not an excuse to avoid living and speaking for Christ at every appropriate opportunity; rather, it is a recognition that "the chief end of man is to glorify God and to enjoy him for ever" (as stated in the *Westminster Catechism*), which I interpret to mean that we are not all supposed primarily to operate as more or less full-time evangelists.

Looking back, it took me some time to accept that I was in a place that God had prepared for me. After all, making microscopical preparations of mouse embryos (which was the main practical work in my PhD studies), or catching radioactive rats in India, or melanic moths in Shetland, or limpets in the Antarctic, are not usually considered to be spiritual activities. But, like most of the other contributors in this volume, I have no doubts that God has wanted me as a scientist, and that he has given me work to do for him because I was in the place he had prepared for me.

Evolutionary biology

When I first began to learn biology at school, it appeared to be a hotchpotch of facts and ideas – interesting but disconnected. Only when we were introduced to evolution did everything start to make sense; it became possible to recognize patterns in classification, distribution, development and biological history. It was the same at university. By then I was vaguely aware of the nineteenth-century debates about Genesis and evolution, but they remained shadowy until a medical student friend whom I had taken to hear a number of evangelistic sermons informed me that it would be intellectually dishonest for him to become a Christian because he "would not be allowed to believe in evolution". Of course I told him that was nonsense, that neither belief nor disbelief in evolution had anything to do with his relationship with the crucified Christ, but he would not be swayed.

I suspect that my friend's views about evolution were really an excuse to avoid commitment – although they were real to him at the time. But they made me go back both to the Bible creation stories and to the history of the evolution–creation controversy. It rapidly became clear to me that much of the argument was about interpretation rather than basic doctrine. The Genesis account of creation is of a progress from nothing (or more accurately, God only) through geological and biological change to mankind. Nowhere in the Bible are we told the mechanisms

God used to carry out his work; indeed, we only know by faith that God is involved (Hebrews 11:3). The normal Hebrew term used for God's creating activity in Genesis is *asah*, which is the word for shaping existing material, like a potter moulding clay. Another word (*bara*) is used for God's creation of matter and mankind, implying a different and specifically divine act. This should not be taken to mean that God necessarily made our body from scratch, as it were; we are distinguished from the rest of creation by God's image in us (Genesis 1:26–27), not genetically or anatomically. In other words, there is no biblical reason why we should not be descended from animal ancestors; the important element is that we are subject and responsible to God in a qualitatively different way to the rest of creation.

There are, of course, other superficial conflicts between the scientific understanding of evolution and the biblical record, but none are serious. For example, the "day" framework of creation in Genesis 1 can be interpreted in a number of ways other than as a series of literal twenty-four-hour periods. Indeed, the statement that "God rested" on the seventh day (Exodus 20:11) cannot be taken literally, because our God never sleeps (Psalm 121:4); this suggests that the week of creation should not be regarded as a calendar week; but it does indicate that one of the many lessons we can learn from God's establishment of the natural order is the importance of a regular rhythm of work and rest.

As a professional scientist, I am often asked to speak about my faith to Christian groups. At a meeting for Christian doctors in Australia (whither I had gone on my way to trap mice on the sub-Antarctic Macquarie Island), I was urged to write down my understanding of the creation events, because it seemed both scriptural and helpful to that audience of educated men and women. This led to a book first published as *Adam and the Ape* in 1975, and revised as *God and Evolution* in 1988. I often meet people who thank me for publishing my ideas, since they are more convincing to them than the traditional understanding of God as the Divine Watchmaker who made the world in a six-day period 6,000 years ago. I frequently wonder why the old view persists as stubbornly as it does. My provisional belief is that "creationists"[1] are frightened of the challenge of a God who is Lord of change as well as of changelessness, and who may surprise by his demands and unexpectedness; in other words, "creationism" can be a wall against God himself. The irony is that Charles Darwin destroyed the intellectual legitimacy of a God who is separated from his world, and forced us to recognize that he is also present in processes and mechanisms. In theological language, God is both transcendent and immanent.

Miracles

At the same time that I was working out the positive lessons to be drawn from the evolution–creation controversy, I was moving in my research from developmental to ecological genetics (I wanted to study how developmental processes influenced population processes), which in effect means the study of evolutionary mechanisms operating in living populations. In other words, I became an evolutionary biologist. I acquired various responsibilities outside my university duties. From 1982 to 1985 I was President of the Linnean Society, the oldest biological society in the world, and the one to which the original papers of Darwin and Wallace on evolution by natural selection were read in 1858. I was aware of how careful I had to be. Thomas Bell, who was President of the Society in 1858, summed up at the end of the year, saying it "has not been marked by any of the striking discoveries which revolutionise the department of science on which they bear..." I will not comment!

Involvement at the national level widens one's horizons and make one aware of the responsibilities and opportunities to attempt positive contributions. In 1984, there was a debate in Britain about the beliefs of church leaders, and in particular whether miracles are still credible in a "scientific age". It seemed right to criticize the sloppy thinking being bandied about, and I co-ordinated a letter to the London *Times* about miracles. Fourteen of us signed the letter; all of us were professors of science. We asserted that it is:

> not logically valid to use science as an argument against miracles. To believe that miracles cannot happen is as much an act of faith as to believe that they can happen. We gladly accept the virgin birth, the Gospel miracles, and the resurrection of Christ as historical events... Miracles are unprecedented events. Whatever the current fashion in philosophy or the revelations of opinion polls may suggest, it is important to affirm that science (based as it is upon the observation of precedents) can have nothing to say on the subject. Its "laws" are only generalizations of our experience... (*The Times*, 13 July 1984)

The following week, a leading article appeared in the scientific journal *Nature*, agreeing with our statement on the nature of scientific laws, but dissenting from our conclusion about miracles, calling them

> inexplicable and irreproducible phenomena [which] do not occur – a definition by exclusion of the concept... the publication of Berry et al. provides a licence not merely for religious belief (which on other grounds is unexceptionable), but for mischievous reports of all things paranormal, from ghosts to flying saucers.

The editor of *Nature* received a number of letters dissenting from his argument, and, to his credit, he published them. One correspondent objected that "your concern not to license 'mischievous reports of all things paranormal' is no doubt motivated in the interest of scientific truth, but your strategy of defining away what you find unpalatable is the antithesis of scientific."[2] A letter from Donald MacKay in the same issue emphasized that

> *for the Christian believer, baseless credulity is a*
> *sin – a disservice to the God of truth. His belief*
> *in the resurrection does not stem from softness*
> *in his standards of evidence, but rather from the*
> *coherence with which (as he sees it) that particular*
> *unprecedented event fits into and make sense of a*
> *great mass of data… There is clearly no inconsistency*
> *in believing (with astonishment) in a unique event*
> *so well-attested, while remaining unconvinced by*
> *spectacular stories of "paranormal" occurrences that*
> *lack any comparable support.*

I was then invited to reply to the correspondence; my response was published in *Nature* in 1986.[3] I concluded my article:

> *The conventional view of miracles is that they depend*
> *on supernatural intervention in, or suspension of,*
> *the natural order. Some theologians have been over-*
> *impressed with scientific determinism, and have*
> *attempted a demythologized (miracle-free) religion.*
> *This endeavour is now unfashionable, but it is worse*
> *than that; Harold Nebelsick (a Scottish theologian)*
> *called it "a speculative device imposed on unsuspecting*
> *persons… based on false presuppositions about both*

*science and the scientific world view". This is no help
to scientists, and an interventionist God will always be
an embarrassment to us.*

*I believe the interpretation that miracles are a
necessary but unpredictable consequence of a God
who holds the world in being is more plausible and
more scriptural than deist interventionism (i.e. the
nineteenth-century distortion of the doctrine of
God, who was assumed to be nothing more than
a Divine Watchmaker). This does not mean that
apparent miracles should be approached with any less
objectivity than we would employ for any scientific
observation; our standards of evidence should be just
as rigorous. Those who deny the possibility of miracles
are exercising their own brand of faith; this is based
on a questionable assumption, and one which creates
problems with its implications. Miracles in the New
Testament are described as unusual events which
are wonders due to God's power, intended as signs.
Confining oneself wholly to this category (leaving aside
the question of whether other sorts of miracles occur),
this makes at least some miracles acceptable and non-
capricious, and independent of our knowledge of their
mechanism.*

The appearance of a long article on miracles in a journal such as
Nature inevitably caused a stir. The President of the American
Statistical Association devoted his presidential address to
a discussion of the implication of miracles for probability
theory.[4] It produced some adverse reaction. But it established
clearly that we have a rationally defensible faith. Obviously not
everyone will agree with our interpretation, but a faith based on
the Scriptures cannot be dismissed as woolly wishful thinking.
Like the psalmist, in words carved on the doors of the old

Cavendish Laboratory in Cambridge (where Lord Rutherford directed much of the early research on atomic structure), we can affirm, "Great are the works of the Lord, studied by all who have pleasure therein" (Psalm 111:2).[5]

Conservation and stewardship

One of the sadnesses of the evolution–creation debate is that it has delayed the proper understanding of God's entrusting his creation to us. Christians have been so busy defending their personal interpretation of Scripture that they have neglected to work out the implications of the creation narratives. We face increasing problems with pollution, over-population, poverty, and climate change. All these make ever more urgent the need to define a proper attitude to nature. This is a problem for everyone, but Christians have a special responsibility if they believe in a creating and sustaining God who holds mankind accountable for the gifts and privileges given to them.

In 1980, the International Union for the Conservation of Nature and the United Nations Environmental Programme issued a World Conservation Strategy (WCS), arguing that we misuse the resources of the planet to our own detriment. Good environmental behaviour was, according to the WCS, simply self-interest. All member nations of the United Nations Environmental Programme were required to respond to the WCS. The United Kingdom's response was in several parts (urban, rural, industrial, etc.) and included an ethics section, which I was asked to write. I pointed out a deficiency in the WCS: our attitude to the environment is determined by four valuations – to ourselves, our community, future generations, and nature itself; from the secular point of view the first three can be justified on utilitarian grounds, but nature's own interest is understandable from this standpoint only if we identify ourselves as inseparable from nature. This option is the route taken by the "deep greens" and by the New Age (the two are not necessarily the same). However, to a Christian, nature is valuable because it is God's – created by him and declared to be good. A scriptural view thus gives weight to all four interests, and should be proclaimed positively by all Christians.[6]

Unfortunately, Christians are often attacked because (it is said) the Bible teaches that humankind has an obligation to use the world's resources for itself ("have dominion" as a ruler), and to reproduce unrestrainably (Genesis 1:28). Both assumptions are wrong. God's command to "have dominion" is given explicitly to mankind made in God's image. His concern is that we are responsible to him for his world; in other words, we are stewards of the world's resources, answerable to God as the owner (see Luke 12:13–48; 19:12–27; 20:9–18). And family size is a part of our responsibility; the command to reproduce without limit applied to the chosen people of the Old Testament, but physical continuity has now been replaced by spiritual spread in Christ's regime. The creation ordinance to "fill the earth" with our physical children should now be interpreted as an obligation to spread Christ's rule on earth by making disciples of every nation (Matthew 28:19–20). (The idea that contraception is "unnatural" is based on the notion that God works through largely immutable laws; it diminishes in importance once we accept that God is active – and sovereign – in natural processes.)

My involvement with the World Conservation Strategy had a sequel when, in 1989, I was asked to help prepare a Code of Environmental Practice for the Economic Summit Nations (Canada, France, Germany, Italy, Japan, Britain and the United States). The Code we produced was based on an environmental ethic, involving "Stewardship of the living and non-living systems of the earth in order to maintain their sustainability for present and future, allowing development with equity". Acceptance of this ethic involves responsibility, freedom, justice, truthfulness, sensitivity and awareness; and leads to a series of obligations, some of which are difficult for politicians to accept (impact assessment, monitoring and publication of results, full accounting, easing of technological transfer, polluter pays, transnational recompensation, etc.).[7]

The Code is, of course, not a Christian document, but the three elements of the ethic (stewardship, sustainability, and quality of life produced by development with equity) are scriptural notions, and the Code can be regarded as a statement of biblical principles. God cares for the whole world; not a sparrow dies without him knowing; he causes the rain to fall on the just and the unjust alike. I believe the preparation of the Code was as religious an activity as almost any we carry out in the name of the church. Just as God calls scientists as well as pastors, so he abhors us erecting barriers between different parts of our life. The evolution–creation debates have made us face the fact that God is both immanent and transcendent; the environmental debate has forced us to recognize anew that we are all stewards – not merely of time, money or talents, but of all the resources of God's creation. The challenge that Christians who are scientists should be presenting to the church and the world alike is to recognize the greatness of the Lord – Creator, Redeemer and Sustainer.

Humpty Dumpty

We often speak of someone's world crashing in pieces or their "life falling apart", with the implication that "all the king's men couldn't put it together again". I suppose my future appeared like that to me when my father died. My testimony from that time and on many subsequent occasions has been completely different. I can testify unreservedly of the wholeness which the Lord gives. This should not be surprising to a believer; the Greek word *soteria* which we translate as "salvation" literally means "wholeness". Such wholeness (or "healing") should pervade all parts of our life, uniting body, mind and soul. It links evolution and creation, law and miracle, environmental care and stewardship.

Charles Darwin was buried in Westminster Abbey (after some jiggery-pokery by T. H. Huxley and Francis Galton, who wanted to make a political point about science triumphing over superstition). An anthem was composed specially for the funeral by Frederick Bridge, the abbey organist, based on Proverbs 3:13: "Blessed is the man who finds wisdom, the man who gains understanding". I don't know whether Darwin actually achieved understanding but I am utterly persuaded that the inclusive wisdom which begins with the fear and wonder of God and which was granted to Solomon (1 Kings 3:9–12) is necessary and, through God's Spirit, available to all of us who are open to it.

If I draw one lesson from my experiences as a scientist and a Christian, it is that compartmentalization of life, thought or worship is damaging and potentially dangerous. The gospel involves reconciliation between God and humankind. In my own research, I have repeatedly had to straddle the boundaries between traditional disciplines – ranging between ecology, genetics, geography, pathology, history, physiology, behaviour and others. In my spiritual life, I have similarly tried to worship my God in laboratory, field and church alike – not as a vague influence, but as a personal Lord, Saviour, Guide, Comforter.

One of the few poems I have managed to learn since leaving school is a sonnet by Robert Rendall, an Orkney draper and naturalist, and a devoted member of his local Brethren Assembly. It is perhaps especially real to me because I have been involved in many scientific studies in Rendall's native islands. It is not an overtly Christian poem, but it incorporates the wholeness and balance of attitude which is the fruit of life in Christ.

Scant are the few green acres I till,
But arched above them spreads the boundless sky,
Ripening their crops; and round them lie
Long miles of moorland hill.

Beyond the cliff-top glimmers in the sun
The far horizon's bright infinity;
And I can gaze across the sea
When my day's work is done.

The solitudes of land and sea assuage
My quenchless thirst for freedom unconfined;
With independent heart and mind
Hold I my heritage.

Of course, we are called to speak of Christ and his saving grace whenever possible, but it must be in the context of a life and attitude which demonstrates the saving ("making whole") and transforming work which the Lord Christ has and is doing in individuals and communities alike. Science and faith have different methodologies, but they are complementary, not contradictory; a faith without reason is as stultifying as a reason without faith.

Notes

1. I put the word in inverted commas. All those who believe in a Creator God are creationists, whether they believe God made the world more or less instantaneously, or through the evolutionary process. It is just as real for an evolutionist to affirm "I believe in God, Maker of heaven and earth", as it is for a literal six-day "creationist".

2. Clarke, P. G. H. (1984), *Nature*, 311: 502.

3. 1986, 322: 321–22. My title for the reply was "Miracles: scepticism, credulity or reality?" The Editor changed it to "What to believe about miracles". It was reprinted as an appendix to my book, *God and Evolution* (Hodder & Stoughton, 1988), and also (in a slightly changed

form) in a book edited by Andrew Walker, *Different Gospels* (Hodder & Stoughton, 1988).

4. Kruksal, William (1988), "Miracles and statistics: the causal assumption of independence", *Journal of the American Statistical Association*, 83: 929–40.

5. Berry, R. J. (2008), "The research scientist's psalm", *Science & Christian Belief*, 20:147–161.

6. An excellent exposition of this is by Richard Bauckham (2010), *Bible and Ecology*, Darton, Longman, Todd.

7. The basis of the Code and its relationship to the United Nations "Earth Charter" are set out in my book *Ecology and the Environment: The Mechanisms, Marring and Maintenance of Nature*, Templeton Press, 2011, pp. 174–83.

Chapter 14

No Easy Answers

John Wyatt is Emeritus Professor of Ethics and Perinatology, and former Consultant Neonatologist at University College London Hospital. He is a Fellow of the Royal College of Physicians and of the Royal College of Paediatrics and Child Health. He chairs the Christian Medical Fellowship Study Group. He is the author of *Matters of Life and Death* (IVP, 1998).

At high school my abiding passion was physics and I had a rather romanticized ideal of becoming a research scientist. I gained a place to read physics at Oxford University and started the course with great enthusiasm. But my first year of university was a time of spiritual crisis and challenge. Although I had been raised in a Christian home, I had profound doubts about the intellectual credibility of orthodox biblical Christianity. At university I was able for the first time to test the truth claims of Christianity and the rational evidence for belief in the God of the Bible. Over that first year I had a steadily increasing conviction that the Christian faith did stand up to the most fundamental questions I could come up with. And if this faith was true, then it had radical implications for the way I should live. My decision to change direction and study medicine was bound up with my growing Christian commitment. I sensed a new vocation – to use the scientific abilities I had been given for the benefit of people whom God loved.

After medical training and junior hospital posts in London, I was increasingly drawn into paediatrics and then into neonatology, the medical care of newborn infants. In the

1980s this was a new and rapidly growing medical speciality. It combined the human challenge of caring for the most vulnerable of human beings with the technical and scientific demands of novel intensive care methodologies.

Clinical care: problems with newborn babies

Intensive care for newborn babies had made great strides since its first experimental introduction in the 1960s and 1970s. Survival rates had improved markedly, but the great unsolved problem of neonatology was (and remains) that of brain damage leading to long-term disability such as cerebral palsy or learning difficulties. I had the remarkable opportunity of joining a multidisciplinary research team at University College London (UCL) which was developing sophisticated new brain imaging techniques (magnetic resonance and near infrared spectroscopy) to investigate the mechanisms underlying brain damage and search for preventative strategies.

As part of the clinical team we were caring for babies and their families whose lives were devastated by the consequences of brain damage. This gave a powerful drive to our research efforts. There must be something we could do to find how to prevent or treat this terrible problem. Over a period spanning more than twenty years we made slow but steady progress. The sequence of metabolic events in the infant brain following exposure to damaging oxygen lack was elucidated. Then we demonstrated that moderate brain cooling had a powerful protective effect, provided it was started within a few hours of the start of the oxygen deprivation. This was highly controversial, since the ruling orthodoxy had always been that it was essential to keep all newborn babies warm! However, other research groups around the world were coming to similar conclusions. To my surprise, I found myself acting as co-Principal Investigator for the first international randomized trial of neonatal hypothermia treatment, involving major centres in the UK, the USA, Canada and New Zealand. Although much work still needs to be done, it seems that hypothermia treatment when used appropriately does lead to a significant reduction in death and long-term disability and that it will find a role in treating vulnerable babies across the world.

My personal experience, like that of so many other research scientists, is that the fundamental Christian understanding of the cosmos, the Christian worldview, supports and motivates scientific exploration. The profound conviction that the universe is built on rational principles, and even more remarkably, that it is possible for the human brain to uncover and understand those principles, lies at the heart of the research enterprise. It is the Christian understanding of creation order, and of human beings made in God's image, which underpins and illuminates these convictions. In addition, in the search for new and effective medical therapies, the Christian understanding of creation supports the idea of the remarkable healing potential locked within the human body and of the fundamental link between the natural world and humanity itself.

As a practising doctor caring for newborn babies and confronting the painful realities of disease, disability and suffering, there is the constant challenge of building a bridge between my Christian faith and the highly technological and scientific world of modern neonatology. At the heart is the need to develop a more profound understanding of what it means to be a human being. Christian ethics (understanding what is right and wrong) comes from Christian anthropology (understanding how we are made).

Precious dust

In biblical thinking human beings are made out of dust, like the rest of the natural creation. This is seen both in Hebrew, where the name Adam is derived from *adamah*, "the ground", and also in English where the word "human" is derived from *humus*, "the soil". We have a profound solidarity with the rest of creation. Biblical Christians should not be surprised at the recent findings of remarkable similarities between the human genome and that of other species on the planet. We are made out of the same stuff as everything else. It seems to me that this ancient understanding illuminates the amazing ability of molecular and genetic research in rodent and other animal models to be translated into medical applications for humans. We belong together. We share the vulnerability, dependence and contingency of the biological world.

But at the same time biblical thinking stresses that human beings are unique amongst all the living organisms on the planet. We alone are made as God's image. In some mysterious way we reflect the profundities of God's character and nature. It has been well said that "A human life is not just a gift of God's grace, it is a reflection of his being." The dignity of our humanity is fundamentally derivative; it comes from him whose image we bear.

This implies that human beings are not self-explanatory. We derive our meaning from outside ourselves. Much scientific research on human beings is driven by an understandable desire to achieve an ultimate explanation of what it means to be human. It is the desire to understand ourselves – to achieve self-transcendence. There has been a great deal of interest in comparisons between the human and chimpanzee genomes. If we can understand the role of the comparatively small amount of DNA which is unique to human beings, perhaps we will finally understand what makes us different from the great apes. But it seems to me that the quest for self-transcendence is doomed to failure. Indeed from a Christian perspective it can be seen as a form of idolatry – to make the human form itself the ultimate source of meaning in the cosmos. We will never understand what it means to be a human being by advances in human genomics or by neuroscientific breakthroughs. In part this is because the quest is self-referential and ultimately circular. Can the human brain ever fully understand the workings of the human brain? Can an evolved being fully understand the mechanisms and consequences of its evolution? But more importantly the quest for self-transcendence is doomed to failure because the ultimate nature of human beings is derived from outside ourselves, from a different order of reality completely, from the nature of God himself.

Imagine a super-intelligent alien civilization in the Andromeda galaxy. They have picked up a distorted image which appears to have been transmitted from a small planet in an outer arm of the Milky Way. The image consists of coloured lines in a mysterious pattern. The alien intelligences analyse every aspect of the image. Each pixel is dissected in terms of frequency, intensity, saturation, relationship to neighbouring pixels, and so on. However detailed the analysis, the aliens will never understand what they are looking at, unless they realize that the image is a map. In fact it is a distorted image of the London underground map. The collection of coloured pixels represents another sort of reality completely, a series of metal tubes set into the ground in a particular location in a particular planet.

The analogy is obviously limited, but perhaps it illustrates the way in which the unique and multifaceted structure of our humanity represents, maps onto, another reality – the mysterious being and character of God.

The challenge for biblical Christians is to keep these twin understandings together, without emphasizing one at the expense of the other. Human beings are made out of the same stuff as everything else. We are simply an unlikely combination of trace elements, genomic transcription, biochemical engineering, and neuronal processing. And yet at the same time each one of us is a mysterious and unique reflection of God's unseen reality – each one is a being of infinite value and eternal significance. In the literal Hebrew of Psalm 8 each human life is described as "lacking a very little of God…"

The materialist says that human beings are *really* sophisticated self-replicating survival machines who happen to have achieved self- consciousness. On the other hand, the philosophical dualist says that human beings are *really* spiritual beings who happen to be attached to a body for a period of their existence. Biblical anthropology has to resist both of these alternatives. Human beings are, at one and the same time, fully physical and fully spiritual beings. We hold the physical and immaterial realities in tension, a tension which is familiar to biblical theology. We see it in the doctrine of the incarnation – Jesus was at one and the same time completely human and completely divine. We see it in the doctrine of inspiration – the words of the Bible are at one and the same time the words of human writers and the words of God. We see it in the doctrine of God's providence in history – events in history are contingent, dependent on multiple causal factors and yet they are the outworking of God's hidden purposes.

This twin perspective on human life can illuminate the mysterious process of the development of a human person from an embryo, a single totipotent cell. At one level this is "just" a cell. It has all the usual components of a mammalian cell: a bilipid membrane, nucleus, mitochondria, organelles. The cells of the embryo multiply in an ordered and predictable fashion. And yet at the same time as the embryo develops, God is calling into existence a unique and wonderful being, At one level the embryo is just biology, a collection of genetic information and cellular machinery. But at the same time it is a physical sign of an immaterial or spiritual reality, even a sacrament of a hidden covenant of creation. A sign that God is bringing forth a new being, a god-like being, a unique reflection of his character, a being to whom he is locked in covenant commitment. At the same time that the biological mechanisms are ticking away, the divine artist is creating a unique masterpiece. So we cannot treat the human embryo with contempt because it is "just" a minute blob of jelly, any more than we can treat the written words of the Bible with contempt because they are "just" human words. These particular physical words are special, they have a unique spiritual significance; this particular physical blob is special, it is a sign of God's creative covenant.

In my view the way of thinking that stresses the distinction between the embryo and the later person, tends towards a form of philosophical dualism. It implies that the embryo or foetus is merely a physical entity and of little consequence until the spiritual bit, the soul, or the responsive mind enters. Since it is the spiritual bit of humanity that really matters, the argument is that the purely physical stuff of which the embryo is constructed may be regarded as disposable or used for research. To me, this way of thinking splits the indissoluble biblical link between the physical and immaterial realities of human existence.

Of course we have to recognize that not every embryo is destined to develop into a person. More than 50 per cent of all human embryos fail to implant in the uterus or miscarry at an early stage of pregnancy. Studies indicate that the majority of these embryos have major chromosomal anomalies which are incompatible with life. We cannot always know in advance what the future of an individual embryo will be. But it is equally true that as we trace our own personal history back into our mother's womb, we recognize that there is no stage in human development at which we can confidently say "I was not there." When you were a one-cell embryo, God knew you and loved you and was calling the unique you into existence. Moreover, some people reading this will have been conceived by *in vitro* fertilization. If the embryologist who selected you for reimplantation into the uterus when you were an eight-cell bundle, had instead decided to use that particular embryo for research, you would not be here reading these words.

Limits

This form of reflection leads me to the somewhat controversial view that embryos should not be deliberately created or destroyed, even for the laudable purpose of developing new medical treatments, for instance in the creation of embryonic stem cells. Of course I understand and respect the position of other Christians who have come to a different conclusion, believing that the unique value and significance of a human life commences at some stage after fertilization, at the development of the central nervous system, for example. But my own belief is that it is a mistake to use biology to determine the point at which God's unique covenant with an individual person commences. You cannot use electron microscopy or DNA probes to meet people. It is what philosophers call a "category mistake". You discover the personhood of the other when you reach out to them in love, protection and commitment. So it seems to me that we should reach out to embryonic humans, with protection, care and commitment, in the hope that their personhood will subsequently become revealed to us.

A Christian understanding of humanity has particular implications for those caring for newborn babies, because the philosophical status and value of the newborn has become an increasingly controversial and difficult area. A number of influential philosophers and ethicists have even raised the question as to whether newborn babies, especially those who are premature or malformed, should be regarded as full members of the human community. Some have argued that a newborn baby, like a foetus, should be regarded as just a "potential person", without the full human rights and privileges of older children and adults.

This is based on the argument that some form of self-awareness is central to what we understand by our "personhood". Closely related to this is the concept of autonomy – a person is a being who is able to determine their own path, to make choices; the word "autonomy" literally means self-rule or self-governance.

The philosopher Peter Singer puts it like this: "When I think of myself as the person I now am, I realise that I did not come into existence until some time *after* birth."[1] Since the newborn baby shows no sign of awareness of its own existence, then it can't be said to have any interests in its own life or future, unlike you and me. This means that to end the life of a newborn baby because it is severely malformed or suffering from brain injury, or indeed for any reason, cannot be said to be ending the life of a person. It is merely preventing a potential person from coming into existence. In fact some have argued that there is a moral equivalence between contraception, abortion and infanticide. All are acts intended to prevent a potential person from coming into existence!

It has also been argued that there are non-human beings who meet the criteria of persons, including at least chimpanzees, gorillas, monkeys and dolphins. In fact it has even been proposed that within the foreseeable future some supercomputers may have the essential properties to be regarded as persons. Some years ago I had a public debate with a distinguished professor of medical ethics who argued that if a computer became self-aware, it would be a greater moral evil to switch off its power supply, than to kill a newborn baby which was unwanted. (I subsequently learnt that the wife of the said professor was less than enamoured with his views on newborn babies – describing them as "the ethics of Herod"!)

It is tempting to dismiss this kind of argument as self-evident nonsense, but I think that Peter Singer and similar thinkers are both insightful and helpful, since they illustrate the logical consequences of their materialist and utilitarian presuppositions. If conscious self-awareness and autonomous choice are the ultimate values, then some members of the human species must be regarded as having less value and significance than others. The most fragile and vulnerable members of the species should give way and serve the needs of the more fully developed and valuable members of society.

But the biblical perspective turns this way of thinking on its head. In the Deuteronomic law, the mighty Yahweh describes himself in striking terms:

> *[Yahweh] your God is God of gods and Lord of lords,*
> *the great God, mighty and awesome, who shows no*
> *partiality and accepts no bribes. He defends the cause*
> *of the fatherless and the widow, and loves the alien,*
> *giving him food and clothing. And you are to love*
> *those who are aliens, for you yourselves were aliens in*
> *Egypt.* (Deuteronomy 10:17–18)

There is a striking contrast in this passage between the person of Yahweh in his absolute power, and his gracious concern to defend the nobodies of society. The significant triad of widows, orphans and aliens recurs many times throughout the scriptures. They symbolize those who were most *vulnerable* in the social structures of ancient Israel. The widow had no husband to defend her from abuse and hardship, the orphan had no parent, the alien or immigrant had no community, no religious or family structures to fall back on. Yahweh's people had a responsibility to act according to his character and to develop social structures which protected the most vulnerable.

So I see that a central aspect of my role as a neonatologist is to defend the interests and concerns of these most vulnerable members of society. Paradoxically, it is precisely because of their vulnerability and dependence, that newborn babies deserve the greatest level of protection from abuse and manipulation.

This is especially important when planning medical

research which involves the newborn. Some have argued that because newborn babies cannot give valid consent to research, then no experimental research procedures should be carried out in this age group. But this policy would mean that no progress was possible in medical care at the beginning of life. So it has become generally accepted that research in newborns can be carried out under stringently controlled circumstances: that parents are fully informed and involved if research is contemplated, and that it is only carried out with their free consent. In addition clinical research in newborn babies must ensure that any possible risk or adverse outcome is minimized. It is for this reason that our research group at UCL, in collaboration with colleagues in the Department of Medical Physics, decided to employ methods of newborn brain imaging which did not involve ionizing radiation and hence avoided tissue damage. Cranial ultrasound, magnetic resonance spectroscopy and imaging, near infrared spectroscopy and electrical impedance tomography are all methods of interrogating the newborn brain without any identifiable risk, and these methods have the potential to provide new information about the mechanisms and prevention of brain injury.

To a neonatologist, the Christian doctrine of the incarnation has special resonance. When God broke into human history as an actor in the human drama, how did he come? What character did he adopt? He came not as the imperial Caesar, the world president, the Olympic athlete. He came as a pathetic, vulnerable and totally defenceless newborn baby. A baby who can do absolutely nothing for himself, who depends on human breasts for milk and human hands to wipe his bottom. No wonder this was the aspect of Christian theology which the Greek philosophers found most scandalous and frankly laughable.

I have come to realize that I am called to treat every newborn baby in my care, even the pathetic little scrap in the corner with tubes coming out of every orifice, with the same sense of wonder, tenderness and respect that Mary and Joseph had towards their little bundle all those years ago. Because Jesus was a baby, all babies are special. Because Jesus was a dying man, all dying people are special. And in this strange and wonderful story of the incarnation we discover that dependence does not demean or diminish our human dignity. In fact it seems to me that we are designed to be dependent on others, we are designed to be a burden to one another. Truly, human existence is one of "mutual burdensomeness".

To the secular philosopher dependence is a terrible threat because it robs us of autonomy – the essential defining characteristic of personhood. But in Christian thinking dependence is part of the narrative of a human life. You came into the world totally dependent on the love and care of others. The very fact that you are reading this is only because someone loved you, fed you, and protected you when you were a defenceless newborn baby. After this we go through a phase of life when others depend on us. And most of us will end our life totally dependent on the love and care of others. But this does not rob us of our humanity. No, it is part of the common narrative of human life. It is an essential aspect of the human nature which God in Christ has vindicated and authenticated.

Treating babies with respect and protection does not mean that we have a duty to provide every possible medical treatment in every possible circumstance. There are tragic situations in which intensive medical care can become abusive and damaging. It is possible for modern technological medicine to change from a source of healing and restoration and instead become a strange monster, even an institutionalized form of child abuse. Treating babies with respect means that sometimes we must learn to let go, to recognize the point where medical treatment becomes futile and abusive, where the burdens of treatment exceed any possible benefit. But this is not because we estimate one life as less valuable or less morally significant than another. Each human being deserves our wonder, respect and compassionate care. I believe our role as clinicians is not to make "value of life" judgments, to evaluate one life as fundamentally more worthwhile, more significant when compared with another. But we can and must make "value of *treatment*" judgments, to evaluate the relative benefits and burdens of treatments and to stop treatment if it is excessively burdensome, futile or abusive.

It has been my painful privilege over the years to care for many dying babies, and to try to support parents and families devastated by the loss of a precious and irreplaceable life. Strangely, as I look back it is often the dying babies and their parents which stand out in my memory. Despite the emotional trauma and intensity of the experience, there is a genuine sense of privilege in providing respectful and loving care to a dying person. To a doctor who is a consistent materialist, death must always represent a form of failure – the triumph of disease and disorder over technological solutions. I know that feeling. I have held the body of a dead baby in my arms and wept together with the parents at an overwhelming sense of helplessness, of failure, of outrage, at this cruel, untimely death. But to a Christian believer, although death is an evil against which we struggle with all our skill and courage, it is also a mysterious reality which can become by God's grace even a strange form of healing, or in C. S. Lewis's words, "a severe mercy". There are some medical situations which are so intractable, the problems so profound, that only death can provide a form of healing, a gateway into a new reality.

Isaiah described the coming age:

> *Be glad and rejoice for ever in what I will create, for*
> *I will create Jerusalem to be a delight... I will rejoice*
> *over Jerusalem and take delight in my people; the*

> *sound of weeping and of crying will be heard in it no*
> *more. Never again will there be in it an infant who*
> *lives but a few days, or an old man who does not live*
> *out his years. (Isaiah 65:18–20)*

God himself recognizes the peculiar outrage of an infant death. That is the Christian hope, and it is what this particular neonatologist longs for. The day that is coming. The day when never again will there be an infant who lives but a few days.

Notes

1. Kuhse, H. & Singer, P. (1985), *Should the Baby Live?*, Oxford University Press, p. 133

Chapter 15

Earthquakes, Volcanoes, and Other Catastrophes[1]

Robert (Bob) White graduated in Geology from the University of Cambridge in 1974 and was awarded a PhD in Marine Geophysics in 1977. After spells as a postdoc, he was appointed to the academic staff at Cambridge in 1981 and to the Chair of Geophysics in 1989. He was elected a Fellow of the Royal Society in 1994. He runs a research group in the university investigating the dynamic earth and has published over 300 academic papers and seven books. In 2006 he founded with Denis Alexander, and is now Director of The Faraday Institute for Science and Religion at St Edmund's College, Cambridge (where he has also been a Fellow since 1988). He is married to Helen and has two (now adult) children.

All children are born scientists. Any parent knows the perpetual refrain of "why does this happen, why that, why the other; why, why, why?" Though many distractions and what is laughingly called "growing up" tend to submerge those childish enquiries, some of us are fortunate enough to have spent our lives indulging our natural curiosity and able to make a living out of it to boot. A life as a scientist is in some ways to live out a protracted childhood – fifteen minutes listening to a group discussing the latest controversial ideas at a conference might well reinforce that impression.

How does Christian faith affect one's scientific endeavours and vice-versa? To a first order (as a physicist might say), a Christian faith has no greater and no lesser influence on how one behaves as a scientist than any other activity. I was asked recently what advice I would give to a Christian politician about how to deal (in this case) with the prospect of global climate change. My answer was that it would be much the same whether they were a politician or a policeman, an office cleaner or a managing director, a parent bringing up children at home or a professor in the academy: it would be along the lines that they continually remind themselves before speaking or acting that one day they will have to account to God for everything they have done, and for their use of the opportunities and talents they have been given (Luke 8:17–18). Are there things we should have done, but didn't? Would we be ashamed to say those words or to do those things if Jesus were standing beside us in the room watching? Because, of course, in reality he is.

Our work, the attitudes we bring to it and the way we do it should be as much part of our worship of God as is the hour or two we spend in church on a Sunday. Of course, as fallen humans we continually fail to reach the standards of behaviour towards God and to others that Christ sets before us. Certainly I do. But as Christians we are a "work in progress", a work which will only be perfected in the new creation. In the meantime we are called to be salt and light in a fallen and lost world, a task in which we can take the first faltering steps only by the grace given us by God and through the promptings of the Holy Spirit.

There are some activities which are beyond the pale: quite clearly we should not knowingly do anything immoral or illegal. Nor, in the same light, can the ends ever justify the means. As an academic, I have the luxury of freedom to choose what research I do, so I do not often find myself in a position where I am asked by my employer to do something I don't think I should do. Nor is the pursuit of excessive monetary gain normally the main temptation faced by academics.

For academics there are perhaps rather different but equally insidious temptations. One of them is the pursuit of a "reputation": the wish to be recognized above others as a pre-eminent authority. This is not to say that you shouldn't do your work as well as possible, and publish cutting-edge papers in the best international journals if that is within your reach. But if it segues into doing others down in an attempt to enhance yourself, then it has undoubtedly crossed a line. If it turns from healthy competition about better understanding how the world works to unseemly rivalry with others, then how can that be worthy of God's calling? How would that square with the fact that all people are created in God's image? Speaking to a Christian community, the apostle Paul wrote: *"Do nothing from rivalry or conceit, but in humility count others more significant than yourselves. Let each of you look not only to his own interests, but also to the interests of others"* (Philippians 2:3–4, ESV).

Another temptation faced by academic scientists is that the pursuit of new ideas, of new experiments can be so exciting, so heady that it unbalances one's priorities. That temptation is not, of course, unique to scientists: artists, businessmen, city traders, all face the same pressures. But for academics the temptations are perhaps more easily indulged: there are few constraints on how you spend your time, no specified working hours (and usually no specified holidays), and often implicit praise for spending long hours at the laboratory bench, for publishing more papers. Yet if this leads us to neglect our families, our responsibilities to the communities in which we live, our friends, and indeed our God, then it is at root selfishness, which, to call a spade a spade, is no less than sinfulness.

What follows is my personal story as a scientist and a Christian believer, and how these have interacted in my own life.

School and university

My memories of school in the 1960s are of spending a lot of time outdoors: in those days bicycles were our passport to freedom and I spent many happy hours cycling around the quintessentially English countryside of Leicestershire and Nottinghamshire where I grew up. The Scout movement gave me an enduring love for the outdoors. Together with the Duke of Edinburgh's Award scheme, the confidence and self-reliance we developed from many camping and hiking expeditions opened up vistas for travel into remote places. A lightweight hiking tent was one of the first things I bought with money I earned during a gap year before going to university. It is still going strong today, though at nine kilograms (twenty pounds), "lightweight" is a strictly relative term...

The other thing I remember was continually making things: from a huge box of Meccano parts, from old cardboard boxes, scraps of wood and the like. Jumble sales were a great source of old radios and gramophones which could be cannibalized for their motors and electronic components. I built crystal radios and amplifiers, aeroplanes, biscuit-tin ovens and a rather wonky go-cart. All this stood me in good stead when I eventually started doing scientific research, because many of the instruments we used for marine geophysical studies were home built. And once you are on a research ship at sea for four or five weeks, if something goes wrong you have to fix it with whatever you have available.

My father worked for the Ordnance Survey making maps. Strangely I ended up making maps too, though of the seafloor rather than the land, and in areas that no one had mapped before. I loved science at school, and applied to do physics at university. My application to Cambridge University was initially turned down and I accepted a place at Imperial College London. But my A Level results led to me being accepted at

Cambridge, and I have never properly left since.

My parents were regular churchgoers, and I progressed through all the years of Sunday school. I remember being fascinated by the formulae in the Book of Common Prayer which enable you to calculate the date of Easter for decades – indeed for centuries – ahead. Many a sermon was spent trying to fathom it out. I suppose that was my first introduction to science and religion, because the date of Easter is based on astronomical calculations of the phase of the moon.

At Cambridge I automatically and without much thought joined the two organizations in which I had already been involved for much of my youth. But this time they both changed the course of my life. In the Scout & Guide club I met Helen, who is now my wife of nearly forty years; and in the Christian Union I met Jesus, whom I have also followed for well over forty years.

On the academic front, I discovered geology. One of the unique features of Cambridge is that in the sciences you are accepted for a general course in natural sciences. Though I had come expecting to do physics, it was necessary to take at least one new subject in the first year. Geology had field trips, and because it was a smaller subject with trips led by academic staff, it had a camaraderie missing in the huge undergraduate classes of the subjects like physics and chemistry. And it rapidly became clear to me that whereas in geology we were (and undergraduates still are) learning about and critiquing current research papers and ideas (and not infrequently learning about them from the very people who had developed the theories), in physics you never got much past work done in the 1950s. So I switched to geology and eventually ended up working in geophysics, effectively getting the best of both worlds. Geology of course offered plenty of opportunities for outdoor work. One year I estimated that I probably spent more time under canvas than sleeping indoors – not as difficult as it might sound, since Cambridge terms only occupy twenty-four weeks of the year.

All the time I was growing as a Christian on a wonderful diet of teaching in the Christian Union at central meetings and in small groups, and through membership of the Round Church. The central churches of Cambridge do an amazing work with students – year after year they have to start afresh from the beginning, yet generations of students leave with a sound Christian grounding to all corners of the world. They often go on to positions of influence in both secular and Christian work. It wasn't until my wife and I spent sabbaticals away from Cambridge that we fully appreciated what a privilege it is to sit under such consistent, godly teaching week in, week out.

Research

I moved into PhD research under the supervision of Drum Matthews, who with his student Fred Vine had postulated the theory of seafloor spreading, which led directly to plate tectonics. He was an inspiring leader, and much of what I have learnt about how to do research came from him.[2] My research was in marine geophysics, seeking to understand the earth from observations made at sea. Since over 70 per cent of the world is covered by water and the structure and development of the seafloor is much simpler than that of the continents (because it is much younger and therefore not complicated by hundreds or thousands of millions of years of geological history), it was to prove a fruitful endeavour.

In the mid 1970s, much of the seafloor was completely unknown and unexplored. So I had the privilege of investigating hitherto unknown areas and discovering many new features and indeed a new plate boundary. They were heady times and scientific progress was rapid. I went to sea on research cruises most years. The flip-side to this was leaving my wife and two children for five weeks or more at a time, usually out of contact in those days before emails and satellite phones. As is often the case, during these periods my wife bore a heavy load in supporting me in my work.

In my department at Cambridge there was a small group of extremely able and committed technicians who built amazingly innovative and effective seabed instruments which enabled us to measure things that no one had measured before: a sure way to make progress. They were matched by a succession of outstanding research students who used new analytical techniques as computer power burgeoned, and applied new theories to move scientific understanding forward. One of the joys of my career has been working with such talented young people doing PhDs – fifty to date – and seeing them develop skills far in advance of my own. They have moved on to professional positions in industry, government, academia and indeed some in full-time Christian work.

During all this time, it never crossed my mind that there was any conflict between what I was learning scientifically and my Christian faith. Nor do I remember there being any particular problems in this area in the minds of my Christian friends who were scientists. We were busy simply getting on with the job of doing science and living out Christian lives. I don't want to give the impression that this was without difficulty. Wresting information scientifically is long, often tedious and frequently hard, grinding work – in my case I struggled with equipment failures or losses, with weather that sometimes curtailed our work at sea, with computer programs that never quite behaved as one wanted, with continually raising grants for what is very expensive research, and retaining enthusiasm and commitment in the light of the almost inevitable grant rejections and delays along the way.

Yet the long days and nights, the blind alleys and disappointments are forgotten in those (rare) moments of finally understanding something new, of seeing how a range of disparate data fits into place. Living a consistent Christian life is a continual battle in a not dissimilar way, as any veteran Christian will testify. Yet I can say with certainty that over the years, as my Christian understanding has grown, it has done nothing but fill me with greater certainty that the Christian gospel is truth, truth that all the world needs desperately to hear, and that I am completely unworthy of the grace God has shown me. The more I learn, the more I see of the consistency and depth of what the Bible says about the human condition, and of the relations between the creator God, his creation and ourselves, his created people.

Geology and Christian belief

Science is a secular activity insofar as its very strength lies in not appealing to any external causes (such as divine activity). So scientific theories can be understood in the same way by atheists, Buddhists or Christians and work equally well in Beijing, Birmingham or Budapest. This is not to claim that some cultures may not be more conducive to the development of science than others, or that science cannot offer any insights that colour and give added depth to one's religious beliefs. All life's experiences bear on one's beliefs and vice-versa. Indeed, I have often thought that scientists are particularly privileged in their studies because their underlying beliefs are so consonant with Christian tenets: both scientists and Christians believe that there is an underlying reality to be found; that some things are true and others palpably untrue; and that we can distinguish between them in statements that apply to all people and for all time. Scientists, and most particularly geologists, have the added bonus of studying God's creation directly in a way which is not the case for our arts and humanities colleagues: in a milieu of relativism and post-modernism where things mean what you want them to mean, the latter have fewer and less-certain anchors. It does not surprise me that the city centre churches in Cambridge consistently have many more students studying science than humanities.

One of the insights of geology for me is the amazing providence of God in creating a home just right for humans to inhabit. Geologists get used to thinking in terms of timescales of millions of years. The earth, for example, has been here for 4,567 million years, give or take a few million years. The best estimate of the age of the universe is that it is about three times older, around 13,700 million years. Life has been present on Earth since almost as soon as it was possible. Isotopic evidence for life dates from 3,800 million years ago, and the oldest known fossils are about 3,500 million years old. One of the amazing facts about the earth is that throughout that time it has maintained a temperature between 0°C (when water would freeze) and 100°C (when all the water would evaporate), despite the sun getting 30 per cent hotter over the same period and the earth's rotation having slowed four- or five-fold. Without that consistency of surface temperature, life as we know it could not have survived. Furthermore, over the past 50 million years the earth's average surface temperature hasn't changed by more than 10°C from the present, making it possible for mammals, and eventually for humans to flourish in a stable environment.

These immense timescales are sometimes difficult to comprehend. A helpful way to get them into perspective is to think of the age of the earth as one year. On that scale, the oldest known microbial fossils date from around Easter, the first multicellular animals from mid November, the dinosaurs went extinct on Boxing Day, early *Homo sapiens* appeared on the scene less than half an hour before midnight on New Year's Eve, Adam and Eve a minute before midnight; and Jesus was born just fourteen seconds before midnight.

All this could be taken as meaning that humans have occupied such an infinitesimal part of the history of the universe that we really aren't anything special; that we are just an accidental happenstance. That is the view of reductionist atheists. There is no question that we are animals and share through our evolutionary history our genetic fabric with all other living organisms on earth. But another way of looking at the evidence is that God has made an immensely fertile universe in which those 13,700 million years preceding our appearance were used in getting conditions just right for humans. This has involved progress from the evolution of stars where the very atoms of which our bodies are constructed were synthesized in nuclear reactions, through the growth of our solar system, and finally to the development of an oxygenated atmosphere in which mammals could survive on earth. The biblical view is that humans are special – we are made in the image of God, which means, amongst other things, that we can relate to God and he to us in an interpersonal way (Genesis 1:26–31; Psalm 8).

It is almost inevitable that I repeatedly have to spend time responding to Young Earth Creationists (YEC), whose unwavering confidence in their own interpretations of the early chapters of Genesis is that the earth cannot be more than about 10,000 years old. My respect for the Bible as the word of God is as high as theirs, but we part company over the exegesis of the early chapters of Genesis and over scientific evidence for the age of the earth. The scientific evidence for an old earth is overwhelming and is based on numerous independent lines of evidence.[3] Indeed, the evidence that Adam and Eve, the first hominids into whom God breathed spiritual life so as to make them humans in his image rather than just animals, lived about 8,000–10,000 years ago is consistent with both biblical evidence and archaeological findings. The only part of the timescale on which I part company from YECs is in the extent of the pre-human period, when of course there were no human observers anyway. There is not space here to discuss the reasons why the YEC claims for a young earth lack scientific credibility, but well-argued secular and Christian point-by-point rebuttals are widely available.[4]

The most fruitful approaches take seriously both the scientific evidence and the literary genre of the Genesis passages dealing with the six days of creation. Since specialized scientific writing did not emerge until the founding of the first scientific journals in the seventeenth century, it is anachronistic to press scientific meanings on to Genesis. In any case Augustine, Origen and other early Church Fathers were already interpreting Genesis figuratively in the early centuries AD.[5] The central aim of the Genesis text is theological: to explain God's purposes in his creation and his own relationship to it. The early Genesis narratives proclaim that the universe was created by a loving, personal God in an orderly fashion, that he was pleased with it, and that one of his main objectives was to make it a place in which humans could live fruitful lives and have loving relationships with himself. The biblical evidence of a purposely created universe, taken together with the scientific evidence for its evolution over billions of years into a place fit for human habitation, reinforce the message that humankind is not the accidental product of a meaningless universe.

My sadness about the debate within Christian circles over the age of the earth is that it is sometimes elevated by the YEC community almost to an article of faith. It can also provide a barrier to reaching out to other scientists if they are told that they need to accept something so obviously contrary to scientific understanding of the world. The age of the earth is not a salvation issue. That it need not be divisive is illustrated by my own experience: our home group in Cambridge included for many years one of the most prominent YEC proponents in Britain and his wife. We agreed to differ on the age of the earth but were one in fellowship and friendship as we studied the Bible together and sought to apply its teachings to our lives.

Education and outreach

Although science and Christian faith have never presented any major intellectual conflicts for me, it is clear that in our culture there is an often unspoken assumption that they are in fact opposed to each other. This is certainly proclaimed stridently by atheists such as Richard Dawkins, and fostered by a media which prefers conflict to consensus. Sometimes Christians contribute to this distrust of science and retreat into statements that the Bible as interpreted literally is the only truth. The implication is that the science must be wrong – or worse, that some of its theories, such as those dealing with evolution or conclusions regarding the age of the earth, are part of an anti-religion conspiracy. This generally creates more heat than light as well as being a rather poor evangelistic strategy, with scientists at least.

If our worship of God is to be meaningful and authentic it has to embrace *all* of our endeavours, including insights from science. Anyone receiving a British government grant to do research now is required to explain the results to the wider public as part of accepting that funding. This seems quite proper, since the public paid for the research in the first place. It seems to me that scientists who are Christians have a similar duty to explain their science to fellow believers and to educate them so that they are equipped to grapple with some of the hard ethical and practical issues that face folk in the world today. It is for that reason that Denis Alexander and I wrote a book together "for the thinking person in the pew" to discuss scientific understanding of the world and how that impacts on Christian faith.[6] Denis is a biological scientist and I am a physical scientist, so we reckon we cover much of the range of science between us.

The collaboration between Denis and me expanded when we gained funding to set up The Faraday Institute for

Science and Religion in Cambridge at the beginning of 2006. Our objective was to reach working scientists via weekend and week-long courses in science and religion, and to do high-quality academic research in science and religion. We organize regular seminars and lectures and produce material at both an academic and a popular level. Most science–religion enterprises are based in theological departments. So as not to put off scientists, we purposely located The Faraday Institute in a neutral setting at St Edmund's College, Cambridge University. Our lectures and seminars are posted on a web site (www. faraday-institute.org) and have become an extremely well-used resource internationally. Another important aspect of our work is to show the reasonableness of the Christian faith to those who are not Christians, by allowing them to engage at lectures and dinners (easy to arrange in a Cambridge College!) with well-known scientists at the peak of their particular disciplines who are also Christians.

There is no shortage of ways for Christians to bring their faith to bear upon current issues in the world. In my case, this is largely in the environmental arena, where global climate change is one of the great uncertainties and challenges facing humankind.[7] This is a particularly apposite issue for Christians because it is the poor and marginalized living in low-income parts of the world such as sub-Saharan Africa and parts of Asia and South America who will suffer most from climate change, whereas it is the largely Christianized high-income countries of Europe and North America who have created the problem. Because our high standards of living have been purchased through the selfish and unsustainable use of natural resources, we have a particular responsibility to care for those affected by global climate change.

Another area in which my academic expertise and my Christian faith converge is in the study of so-called "natural" disasters.[8] The name itself is misleading, because God is sovereign over all of the cosmos, including what we call "nature", so there should be no sense in which a massive earthquake, tsunami, flood or volcanic eruption is outside God's purview. But it remains the case that such catastrophes cause great loss of life in a world that has an exponentially growing population (three times more people are alive today than when I started school), with an increasing proportion living in mega-cities in locations particularly susceptible to natural disasters. It is likely that sooner rather than later there will be a catastrophe that causes over a million deaths. Historically floods are the world's main killer; by 2020 it is estimated that half the world's population will be at risk from this cause. And again, it is the poor in low-income countries who invariably suffer by far the most in natural disasters.

Although the secular world wrings its hands about the problems and consequences of natural disasters and global climate change (and often enough shies away from the hard decisions required to address them because they usually entail changes in lifestyles), Christianity brings a radical new approach. The Christian perspective is that the resources of this earth are only on loan from God, and that they are to be used for the worship of God and the good of all. Christians are called to live counter-culturally.[9] It is a profoundly Christian response to be prepared to give up some privileges for the sake of others, modelling in a small way Christ's ultimate sacrifice for us (Philippians 2:1–11). Christians should care for the stranger and the foreigner even if they live out of sight on the other side of the world. And where the secular world has no answer to the evident injustices and suffering in the world, the Christian has the assurance that sin and injustice have already been dealt with for all time on the cross, and the certain hope for the future that in due course the whole cosmos will be renewed in the new heavens and new earth.[10]

God has created an orderly, consistent universe where it is possible not only to do science, but also to use understanding from it to help others. Medical advances such as the eradication of smallpox and improved healthcare are obvious examples, but there are myriads of others. In my own area of research they include understanding better the causes of natural disasters and global climate change. This provides the means to educate people about them and to facilitate suitable mitigation and adaptation policies – part of what it means to fulfil God's very first commandment to humankind to have dominion and to rule over the world. The commandment was linked to blessing in Genesis 1:28. I consider myself fortunate to have been able to spend my career in science, playing a very small part in that process.

Notes

1. My title is taken from the epithet with which my friend and colleague Denis Alexander often introduces me when I give talks at the Faraday Institute.

2. White, Robert S. (1999), "Drummond Hoyle Matthews", *Biographical Memoirs of Fellows of the Royal Society*, 45: 275–94.

3. For a summary, see White, Robert S. (2007), "The Age of the Earth", *Faraday Paper No. 8*, available for download from www.faraday-institute.org

4. Wiens, R. C. (2002), "Radiometric dating: A Christian perspective", available at www.asa3.org/ASA/resources/Wiens.html; see also the comprehensive website www.answersincreation.org

5. Kidner, D. (1967), *Genesis, Tyndale Old Testament Commentaries*, IVP; Lucas, E. (2001), *Can we Believe Genesis Today?*, IVP; Wilkinson, D. (2002), *The Message of Creation*, IVP.

6. Alexander, D. & White, R. S. (2004), *Beyond Belief: Science, Faith and Ethical Challenges*, Lion

7. Spencer, N. & White, R. (2007), *Christianity, Climate Change and Sustainable Living*, SPCK; White, Robert S. (ed.) (2009), *Creation in Crisis: Christian Perspectives on Sustainability*, SPCK; Bell, Colin, Caplin, Jonathan & White, Robert (eds.) (2013), *Living Lightly, Living Faithfully: Religious faiths and the future of sustainability*, The Faraday Institute for Science and Religion.

8. White, Robert S. (2014), *Who is to Blame? Nature, Disasters and Acts of God*, Monarch

9. John Stott's volume on *The Message of the Sermon on the Mount* in *The Bible Speaks Today* series was originally entitled *Christian Counter-Culture: the Message of the Sermon on the Mount* (IVP, 1978).

10. Jonathan A. Moo & Robert S. White (2013), *Hope in an Age of Despair: The Gospel and the Future of Life on Earth*, IVP.

Chapter 16

One Impossible Thing Before Breakfast: Evolution and Christianity

Simon Conway Morris is Professor in Evolutionary Palaeobiology at the University of Cambridge. He is a fellow of St John's College and of the Royal Society. He took his first degree at the University of Bristol, and apart from four years at the Open University, his career has been spent in Cambridge. His research interests include the study of Burgess Shale-type faunas and the Cambrian "explosion". Some of this work was reported in *The Crucible of Creation* (1998), while more recently his *Life's Solution: Inevitable Humans in a Lonely Universe* (2003) addressed the importance of evolutionary convergence. His interests extend to the science/religion debate and the public understanding of science. He gave the Royal Institution Christmas Lectures in 1996 and the Gifford Lectures in Edinburgh in 2007. If undisturbed he can often be found reading G. K. Chesterton, with a glass of wine (or something stronger) nearby.

One doesn't have to look very far (dear me, I almost wrote "lift a stone") to find colleagues who regard any religious perspective as grievously skewed, a terrible distortion of reality, of interest only to those involved with the most arcane areas of anthropology. And should one meet somebody who professes, well, *actually believes*, that can only point to a lamentable softness of mind. Nor is this an area of murmured regrets, of quiet condolences, in shadowy rooms with heavy curtains blocking the outside sunshine. On the contrary, the disagreement is strident, often vitriolic. Let me give you two examples. Here is what an Australian, David Oldroyd, wrote in the opening paragraph of his chapter in a collection of essays on *Darwinism & Philosophy*: "I should first state my metaphysical position. I am an atheist. The arguments for theism appear so preposterous that their finding any favor can be accounted for, in my view, only by sociological means."[1] The merits of his chapter as a whole I will leave for others to judge, but what I found intriguing is that his dramatic, no-prisoners-taken proclamation has no obvious bearing on the rest of his thesis which broadly addresses the question of stratigraphy and evolutionary trends. Why the outburst?

Nearer home and nearer the bone: alluding to my own views on directionality in evolution (to which I return below), Jürgen Brosius in an article in the journal *Paleobiology* has a footnote in the form of what can only charitably be called an "amplification". Its reference was to a section broadly addressing the role of contingency in the history of life. He wrote:

> *Although it is highly beneficial to occasionally challenge entrenched concepts* [and here Brosius is referring to Conway Morris, 1998[2] and 2003[3]], *I wonder whether this is a poorly disguised attempt to let religion participate in evolutionary thought: if you can't fight evolution – join it? Instead of catering to the ultra-naïve creationists, Conway Morris (2003) appeared to target a more intelligent segment of our non-rationalist population, perhaps those who should know better but cannot liberate themselves from infantile imprinting and religious indoctrination.*[4]

The relevance of the attack is more obvious than Oldroyd's, but once again one wonders what this little barb is meant to achieve. We can pass by the presumed tacit compliance of the editors, who are charged with the control of a scientific article as against mere polemic in a very well-respected journal. All one can say is that it certainly takes a very strange view of religious belief. It is perhaps regrettable that Brosius did not care to enquire of me what my own view of "ultra-naïve creationists" might be, let alone bother to quote me on this issue, but that I suspect was hardly the point.

Well, no matter. We all know that when it comes to religious belief the world is as sharply divided as it ever was, yet now it seems as if there is something new in the air. The belligerence, contempt, loathing, derision, condescension, arrogance and sheer bad manners of some exponents are stifling. Not, of course, that these traits are unknown elsewhere. Plenty of Christians, for example, are belligerent and so on, but one hopes that on reflection they would be deeply ashamed of such behaviour, however recurrent. But secularists' anger seems to be something different. Their point is not that gods are anthropological manikins, but that religious types are manifestations of extreme wickedness, engaging in activities that are almost indistinguishable from, for example, child abuse. Indeed, in extreme circumstances their warped and bizarre beliefs may well require the imposition of drastic remedies. Clearly we have touched a rather raw nerve.

It certainly is not my intention to attempt any "dialogue". If the aforementioned Brosius chooses to regard my stance as being no more than "infantile imprinting and religious indoctrination", then it is difficult to see how any sensible exchange of views will be possible, given that my opponent's mental image seems to be one of nurseries full of cooing babies patrolled by crafty priests. But it is noteworthy that despite torrents of diatribe, remarkably little emerges in any concrete way. Indeed, my sense is that the secular agents have run out of things to say; why else the shrillness and (more interestingly) a reluctance to familiarize themselves with the subject area? In their oxymoronic attempt at novelty they seldom refer to their predecessors, perhaps because the comparisons are telling. Think of Thomas Carlyle's existential horror of a "Universe all void of Life, of Purpose, of Volition, even of Hostility… one huge immeasurable Steam engine rolling on in dead indifference", or in some ways even more terrible when George Eliot spoke of "God, Immortality, Duty, [so she] pronounced with terrible earnestness how inconceivable was the *first*, how unbelievable the *second* and yet how peremptory and absolute the *third*."[5]

Ironically, Victorian perspectives of deep, existential despair are much closer than imagined to some religious belief. While we admire the pillars of faith, their interior world is often far less rosy and secure than popularly supposed. Indeed, if a lifetime commitment hinges on a moment of insight about the numinous revelation that unrolls as the abysses of creation reveal their infinite depth, the fact remains that for many of a religious inclination (if not conviction) their faith is hedged by doubt and uncertainty. This should not be regarded as a confession of weakness: it is because of the unknowability of God, the paradox of being involved in an intimate engagement but still remaining a straw tossed in a howling maelstrom.

Sticking to the truth

So am I about to abandon Christianity? Will I finally have my limpet-like attachment to utter absurdities prised from my pathetic grasp? Will I finally submit my letter of resignation to Brosius' "non-rationalist population", assuming of course I can find an address? No, not at all. Of course, I will continue to doubt, but I trust I will also continue to learn. I will not try to persuade you that Christianity is true; others can to do that much more effectively, although like me they will ask for the courtesy of an open mind. Rather, I will propose that the gibe of "non-rationalism" comprehensively misses the point and reflects the very closing of the scientific mind. Indeed you may discover that there is rather more to reality than meets the eye if you want to follow this path.

To help to explain how I got to where I am, and more importantly why I now sense that our adventure has scarcely begun, I begin with myself.

I was born in London and decided to become a palaeontologist at the age most children are still determined to succeed as train drivers. My parents were Christian to a degree, but my father only returned fully to the fold not long before his untimely death from cancer. I studied geology at Bristol and was fortunate with both my teachers (especially an irascible Scot, one Crosbie Matthews) and small classes. Thence I went to Cambridge with more than a hunch that the Burgess Shale in western Canada were special. I was exceedingly lucky to be supervised by Harry Whittington. It was he who also encouraged me subsequently to apply for research fellowships at various Colleges; by a whisker I was accepted by St John's in 1975. The electors were probably baffled by the title of my essay that began, "Interesting fossil worms...", based of course on the rich assemblages from the Burgess Shale. This deposit is located near to the small town of Field, in the Canadian Rockies of British Columbia and hosts a quite remarkable fossil biota, approximately 505 million years old. The diversity and exquisite preservation give us a privileged glimpse into one of the most important evolutionary events, the Cambrian "explosion". In a relatively short period of geological time, perhaps 40 million years, evolution shifted from an exceedingly lethargic mode to pell-mell; animal evolution greatly accelerated and body-plans were spewed out of a Darwinian furnace. Unsurprisingly, this extraordinary explosion has attracted attention; indeed Darwin himself was puzzled by it. Attempts have been made to explain it away, most commonly by treating it as an artefact that simply represents the earliest possibility for fossils to form abundantly. However, the general view now is that the Cambrian "explosion" is real, although the trigger is still hotly debated. A rise in atmospheric oxygen is perhaps the most plausible explanation.

As it happens, I am writing these words in China, where for a number of years I have had a very fruitful collaboration with Professor Degan Shu on the Chengjiang deposits in Yunnan province. The fossils there beautifully complement those of the Burgess Shale, but are somewhat older. They have yielded a number of new forms, including the earliest known fish. On this visit I have just had what appears to be a lucky escape: some very rare fossils, which I had studied earlier, seemed to throw new light on a particular evolutionary question. But only two specimens were known. A third specimen turned up, and some niggling doubts that had been carefully swept under my researcher's carpet suddenly became relevant. A brilliant idea is brilliantly wrong. Fortunately, there is no publication and so no chasing of wild hares. There is still an interesting story to be told, but it is less dramatic and certainly these fossils have not revealed all their secrets.

So it was too with my work on the Burgess Shale: it had some glorious mistakes, glaringly obvious in hindsight. They mostly involved the minutiae of interpretation of unfamiliar forms, preserved like "squashéd slugges", as a French colleague called them. There was, however, a more pervasive error which was less forgivable, but here's my excuse. Imagine you have an ocean trawler that also conveniently is capable of time travel. Off we go, but owing to the Manton Conjecture ("Surely you remember? You know, when the zeta function intrudes on the third derivative, that's right..."), only a very short visit is possible. So working like a maniac, you grab everything in sight, sometimes in shoals, sometimes as a handful of slithering worms, at times perhaps only a unique specimen. Time to depart! But as the time-travelling trawler climbs upwards and through the cloud bank, before temporarily de-materializing (here, happily, the Manton Conjecture has never been shown to fail), you know that your fleeting visit has hardly scraped the surface of the Cambrian ocean. So too with the Burgess Shale: it is a remarkable sample, but still only one small scoop into the past.

In that period of geological time evolution was moving at such a rate that changes were rapid. As a result, you quite often find a fossil that is quite clearly some sort of animal but one with only a vague similarity to any known group. It's bizarre, it's a "weird wonder". One option is to say, "Well, here's a new body-plan, a new phylum", an experiment in evolution that evidently failed. Why? Because it is extinct. One can then speculate what might have happened if this design had survived and others that ultimately populated the world around us (including, of course, ourselves) had gone to the wall. For all we know, the choice was on a knife-edge. This idea, which I mentioned in passing in a technical monograph[6] and more fully in a popular article,[7] was seized upon by the late Stephen Jay Gould and turned into a best-seller *Wonderful Life*.[8] Gould was generous in his praise of the work carried out in Cambridge, but it is clear that his enthusiasm was because he saw it as another nail in the coffin that evolution was either directional or, in his view even worse, shows progress. This interpretation was central to his ideology – that the emergence of humans was evolutionarily entirely fortuitous.

Gould certainly had a number of heterodox strands in his evolutionary thinking, but the view that humans (or indeed any other species) are effectively accidental is a belief that is almost universal amongst neo-Darwinians. Such luminaries as George Gaylord Simpson[9] and Jared Diamond[10] have been equally insistent that humans are fortuitous, with an important corollary that any extra-terrestrial analogue to ourselves is exceedingly unlikely. Simpson and Diamond are both, of course, outstanding exponents of Darwinian evolution, but it seems fair to say that so far as popularization is concerned they are outclassed by Gould. Indeed, his effectiveness as a communicator was because he constantly strayed beyond the science itself, but repeatedly dragged in evolution as a chorus. He argued that since humans are a product of chance, we are unconstrained by outmoded moral systems embedded in credulous, pre-scientific minds by non-existent agencies. Consequently we are at liberty to make the world the best of all possible places, free of mythical hocus-pocus, including undeniably malign influences such as racism. Ironically, many of Gould's scientific opponents also subscribe to similar scientistic utopias, where science will transport us to the heights of unparalleled happiness and beauty, leaving the stagnant marshes of religious obscurantism behind, emptying the nurseries of the cooing babies and leaving those crafty priests to their fiendishly futile devices.

The manifest failure of this scientistic agenda hardly needs emphasis, nor, if Richard Dawkins' utterly lamentable "Ten Commandments" are any indication, can we expect any insights into our existential predicament to be other than childish.[11] But for Gould the work on the Burgess Shale came (so to speak) as a godsend: real facts, real conclusions and a firm mandate to de-throne man and thus liberate him. Unfortunately, things began to unravel rather quickly so far as the fossils which underpinned the thesis of *Wonderful Life* were concerned: supposedly bizarre animals turned out to be misinterpreted or, as importantly, new forms turned up that suddenly began to fill in the jig-saw of evolution. A more coherent story started to emerge, with the net result that the wonderful fossils of the Burgess Shale, Chengjiang, and other localities including some in Greenland turned out to be instrumental in allowing us to see how body-plans are actually constructed. The discussion is redolent with unfamiliar names like halwaxiids and vetulicolians, and there is still very active debate, but the idea that the Cambrian was awash with failed body-plans can now be abandoned.

Evolution and convergence

Around the same time that I was re-assessing the Burgess Shale, I became interested in the evolutionary phenomenon known as convergence. This is actually an unremarkable observation that certain biological "designs" work very well, so unsurprisingly are arrived at independently. In other words, different starting points end up with much the same solution. Perhaps the best-known examples are the camera-eyes of ourselves (and other vertebrates) and the octopus (and other cephalopods, a group of molluscs) or the sabre-tooth carnivores, which evolved at least three times in the cats and independently in the marsupials (thylacosmilids). My interest was surely provoked by Gould's famous metaphorical articulation of the re-running of the tape of life. If, as he insisted, the Burgess Shale animal *Pikaia* (our putative ancestor) had been knocked on its tiny head, then our lineage would have been forever denied its place in the sun. True but trivial, because evolutionary convergence demonstrates that the same solution would emerge, come what may. When did I stumble to this view? Certainly by the time I reviewed Gould's set of essays bound together as *Bully for Brontosaurus*, I was busy pointing out that Gould's own examples supported the thesis for convergence.[12]

Since then my interest has blossomed and I am quite happy to bore any passer-by for hours with tales of convergence in enzymes (e.g. carbonic anhydrase), echo-location (as in birds), or response to death (in elephants). To find convergence in molecular systems might be unexpected; to find it in sensory systems is a clue to the universality of mental states; whilst to find it in an awareness of death touches on the unknown.

Perhaps convergence has a wider implication than often thought? Moreover, there are intriguing insights even in the classic cases. Take the case of the camera-eye. Whilst there is no doubt that cephalopods such as the octopus and squid have excellent vision, the received wisdom is that the vertebrate eye is superior because a degree of visual processing takes place in the retina before the signal goes to the optic lobes. This does not happen in the cephalopods. However, less well known is that immediately behind the retina of (at least) the octopus an area of nervous tissue achieves the same processing. The reason for the differences are because the respective retinas have different embryological origins, and thus the footprints of evolutionary history are readily discernible; the crucial point is, it doesn't make any difference. Consider now the thylacosmilids, the extinct marsupials that lived in South America and are strikingly similar to the sabre-tooth cats. Again, an important point is sometimes overlooked. The thylacosmilids belong to a group known as the borhyaenids, which as the name hints are mostly rather dog-like. The thylacosmilid is an extraordinary morphological excursion, quite unlike any other borhyaenid.[13] It is as if there is a sabre-tooth "space", waiting to be occupied. Not only that, but amongst the placental sabre-tooth cats, the method of hunting is broadly divisible into runners and ambush predators, and each type has its own characteristic adaptations. The thylacosmilids fall into the ambush variety.

Convergence is, of course, widely acknowledged and uncontroversial in itself. So what else is there to say? It is all very well giving examples, however fascinating they might be. I suggest some things that may point to some more interesting general principles. First, convergence is ubiquitous: insect milk, lizard placentas, fish agriculture, elastic proteins; I'll be happy to supply the details. Second, and tellingly, the adjectives employed in describing convergence are nearly always ones of surprise: "remarkable", "unexpected", "astonishing", "stunning", even "uncanny". For descriptions of what is Darwinian adaptation, this seems a little odd. Third, given the combinatorial immensity of biological hyperspace (typically the number of possible alternatives is c. 10^{50} to 10^{250}), then it is self-evident that only an infinitesimally tiny fraction of this "space" can ever be occupied; a far, far smaller "space" than is, for example, represented by the size of an atom in proportion to that of the visible universe (these are separated by approximately thirty-seven orders of magnitude). Doubtless, this is why it is generally thought that any other fraction of biological hyperspace can be as easily occupied, and presumably at an entirely different point. The ubiquity of convergence, however, suggests that our point of occupation may be specially favoured. Contrary to the received opinion that most things in evolution will work, the reality may be that practically nothing works.

There are several metaphors that try to capture this idea. One is to extrapolate the argument just given, and to think of stable positions – attractors, if you will – that act as irresistible "magnets". An alternative metaphor, which I prefer, is to imagine a map across which life must navigate. The landscape, however, is extremely precipitous and it is only by the narrowest of roads that life can thread its way through inaccessible mountains and past impossible chasms. However, both descriptions beg the question of what defines the "attractors" or the "map". There are two other aspects that I find intriguing. For the first time we can begin to confer a predictability to evolution because stable solutions must recur, not only here, but everywhere. Second, and in a way related, we might start to identify some general biological properties, much as physicists and chemists do. The adaptive immune system (which incidentally is convergent) is one example. It employs a remarkable versatile molecular system to respond to almost any pathogenic challenge. "Decisions" have to be made extremely rapidly, the appropriate antigen identified and then massively produced before the bacteria "wins". Now think of the brain. It is far too complex to be encoded directly by the genes. A key process in its early development is an immense number of "decisions", effectively how to wire the brain. If the brain is to function effectively, there is no time for hesitation. Obviously there is an analogy to the immune system, but much more interestingly some of the same molecules are used. Indeed it is most likely that these molecules first evolved for brain development and were only later co-opted for the immune system.[14] Here we have stumbled on a similar design system. And whilst speaking of nervous systems, it is interesting that the proliferation of nerves finds striking parallels to the growth of blood vessels.[15]

Mention of the brain is doubly relevant because it is evident that advanced cognition is convergent and has evolved independently at least three times (apes, crows and octopus), and more likely at least three more times (dolphins, elephants, parrots, and maybe bees).[16] If this is true, then it is not just mammals *per se* but at least three groups (apes, dolphins, elephants, and actually a fourth instance with the New World monkeys) have each arrived at the same solution. The contrast, however, between birds and mammals, and even more so octopus, is particularly intriguing because the structure of their respective brains is markedly different. So how does the same cognitive map emerge? At what level of brain organization should we look? Cellular? Chemical? Atomic?

Consciousness

We are actually touching here on one of the only two real scientific mysteries: how was the Universe instantiated and how are we conscious? So far as consciousness is concerned, no matter how much convergence we identify within and between sensory systems and no matter what is the structure of the brain, we seem not a whit closer to explaining how it is that my neural porridge is gripped by sounds of the Good Friday music from Wagner's *Parsifal*, the sight of a new moon, or the remembered taste of a Madeleine cake. And I would suggest that the materialist perspective on these questions of qualia has not so much broken down but was never particularly relevant. Of course, claims for the former (that somehow consciousness has been "explained") appear with monotonous regularity, but strangely none convince. Nowhere do I read in neurobiology, "Well, that's that, chaps, all solved, consciousness is simply due to x; time to shut up shop, what?"

In trying, oxymoronically, to think through this area, a vital clue for me came from a stimulating essay on music, especially animal music, written by Patricia Gray and colleagues.[17] They point out that this music is patently convergent, but to explain it simply in terms of vibrating columns of air seems inadequate. We are talking about music we can not only listen to but enjoy, with its harmonies, melody and invention. Moreover, there are plenty of anecdotes of musicians and birds combining instrument and song. So this similarity can be approached in quite a different way, not by denying the physics of sound production, but by transcending it. Let us suppose, they argue, that there is a universal music "out there", so the reason the music is the same is because it is discovering the same source. This is familiar as a Platonic argument but it casts evolution in quite a different light. It is in marked contrast to the received orthodoxy and looks to "emergence": from simple starting points things become successively more complex. Quite why this emergence occurs is obscure; while much is made of the mantra of self-organizing systems, their relevance to biological systems remains rather tenuous.

This is not to deny that emergence is real and evolution is very largely a reflection of this process. The point I am making is somewhat different and more general. Thus, the properties of emergence may well be built into the universe, but one senses that there are still more fundamental principles at work. When it comes to consciousness, if one adheres to a notion of bottom-up causation then of course mind can only be the result of chemistry and aggregating neurons. Whilst this is the standard evolutionary response, it seems incoherent to me: the sheer intractability of how matter comes to understand anything remains insoluble. Materialists will insist, of course, that the senses somehow guarantee mind. But unless the world is deeply rational, which they must deny because of their belief (*sic*) that all is the product of blind and meaningless forces, then we can find no explanation for the is-ness, the "hiccity", of the world, its qualia of experience, let alone the chariots of thought that allow us to formulate extraordinary abstractions. An alternative view that has, I think, rather more to recommend it is to propose that evolution is more like a search engine, so that the universe does not become conscious, does not boot-strap mind, but like the universal music discovers mind as a pre-existent reality. This is, of course, a familiar trope, captured by Eddington's remark as to how in his view the universe was looking more and more like a great thought.

And this applies with equal force to the "origin" of language. A colleague once said in my hearing that in the last billion years only two things of any importance had happened: the Cambrian "explosion" and language. In their different ways, both transformed the world. Here too the usual appeal is to an emergence, as is evident in the fascination for purported genes for language. This is not to say that with either language or the mind, the material world is, well, immaterial, but simply to insist that a materialist explanation *in toto* will fail. Now a particular curiosity about language, in contrast to the evolutionary convergence of intelligence and cognitive maps, is that many animals elaborately vocalize and have learnt to do so independently. In the case of vervet monkeys at least, they convey specific information, whilst dolphins are semantically and syntactically competent to decipher different human messages. But neither they nor any other animal asks their friend to pass the gin and adds, "No, thank you, quite enough tonic, indeed a splash more if you'd be so kind…" If evolution is a search-engine, then maybe language is also "out there", like music and mind, even though we articulate it by material means.

Here I am greatly influenced by the thinking of Owen Barfield,[18] an extraordinarily underestimated man, although not by his close friends C. S. Lewis and J. R. R. Tolkien. His ideas are heterodox and wide-ranging, but so far as language is concerned he made two related claims. First, in earlier stages of human development a particular word could have an immense burden of meanings, so that apparently mundane words like "wind" or "iron" actually carried a whole series of deep and abstract concepts. Subsequently, language almost literally splintered, to the benefit of ever more precise meanings in highly specific circumstances (most notably in the sciences), but with the loss of a unique grasp of reality.[19] Second, words that were once literal have tended to become metaphorical (think of the term "scruple": it is used today to imply moral hesitation but was once an obstruction in a shoe). The specific becomes rather vaguely abstract, while as mentioned the abstract disintegrates. There is more than an echo here of both the *logos*, the transcendent Word, but also the naming of animals in the Garden of Eden followed by the Fall and more particularly the Tower of Babel – a sense that what was once whole and mythopoeic has now become hopelessly fractured.

Obviously, this discussion is merely superficial in the case of consciousness and language, but I am struck by the deep theological resonances such possibilities may present. In a way familiar to philosophers and mathematicians, the suspicion is that the world is considerably more interesting and complex than meets the mundane eye. I find it decidedly odd that many scientists declare that the only route to understanding anything is *via* their method alone. How on earth can they be so sure? Certainly science tells us much, but in this context it is also paradoxical that there is a pervasive sense that before very long there won't be any scientists because there will be nothing for them to do. Here too, I fail to understand the logic. It seems just as likely that we know almost nothing, our "triumphs" are merely a small hill projecting from a vast ocean of ignorance.

Unseen worlds

We should not feel embarrassed by calling upon metaphysical arguments; even a nihilist must do so. Moreover, it is necessary to remind ourselves that material instruments can only inform us about the material world, but if mind is indeed different – impinging on the material world, but not of it – then a decidedly different perspective opens up. I can see no reason why there should not be worlds invisible as well as visible. And there are plenty of indications. Think of out-of-body experiences, where clinically dead people see things they cannot. Or to take just one of innumerable such cases, the one of Harold Owen sitting in his cabin on a ship off the African coast in 1918. His brother Wilfred, soldier and poet, joins him. Harold understood at once what had happened. Now if you choose to be a materialist it cannot be too strongly emphasized that you *must* categorically reject all such stories. For your material (*sic*) well-being they simply *must* be false, and under no circumstances at all are you allowed what otherwise appear to be perfectly sane witnesses on the witness stand. If, for a moment, you even grant the possibility of out of body experiences or that the recently killed Wilfred visited his brother, then your entire materialistic world is in danger is in danger of crumbling around you.

But why should one choose Christianity, even if one accepts the transcendental world? The village atheists derive much merriment in pointing out that there are umpteen religions and the one you are born into is most likely the one that will also arrange your last rites. True enough – but self-evidently there were no Christians before Sunday, 9 April AD 33 (or 5 April AD 30, if you plump for the only other realistic date for the Resurrection,[20] and just as a bunch of scared women and deeply sceptical men were persuaded, so can you if you so choose. This is not to make the ridiculous claim that all non-Christian religions lack insights and wisdom; very much the reverse. But one needs to opt for one that is coherent, has historical veracity and offers more than a lifetime's pilgrimage. Even if one is born to one religion there is nothing to stop you investigating and weighing the alternatives (at least in principle).

For many when first meeting the Christian faith, the apostle to the sceptics, C. S. Lewis, remains the initial port of call. It was his literary, poetic, philological and intellectual skills that told him that the Gospels not only ring true, but are true. The aforementioned Brosius might, at some point, care to investigate Lewis' life to discover his "infantilism and indoctrination". In my journey, it was (and remains) the strong meat offered by Dorothy L. Sayers, and that other apostle of sanity, G. K. Chesterton which was (and is) instrumental. Dip into Chesterton's *What's Wrong with the World*, or consume *Orthodoxy* and the *Everlasting Man*. If the scales still remain firmly attached to your eyes, find another doctor. But there are many, many others: Peter Kreeft, Ben Witherington, Tom Wright, Stanley Jaki, Austin Farrer, Gerald O'Collins, Charles Williams, Martin Hengel – all offer sustenance and hope in a parched world. Collectively, and in many different ways, these authors speak to a common theme. With respect to the Gospels they are deeply doubtful of the hermeneutic of suspicion, the pervasive distrust of the text, the insistence that the narratives have evolved and been edited beyond almost all recognition. In reality the evidence points in the opposite direction. Of course one keeps one's critical faculties, but several lines of evidence suggest that the Gospel reports possess veracity and what happened actually happened: in the reliability of oral tradition, of internal consistencies, and perhaps most intriguingly implications that can too easily escape notice.

Think, for example, of John's account of the miracle at Cana. His mother would not have told the servants to follow the instructions given by Jesus unless she already knew his powers were a bit out of the ordinary. And why is this miracle not mentioned in the synoptic Gospels? The village atheist will insist because it is a fairy tale, but one can take the view that John was interested in narrating what had not been reported previously. So too it is quite likely that the raising of Lazarus could only be safely reported after he had died, a second time. People were after his blood, literally; in post-Resurrection Palestine such witnesses were dangerous.

The central fact is that if Jesus was (and is) who he clearly said he was (and in passing we can notice that Dawkins' view that he might have been "honestly mistaken" reveals depths of naïvety that are difficult to plumb[21]), then for many the reality (so to speak) of the Gospels still seems unattainable. So dry can be the analyses, so thick the layers of piety, so scoffing the opposition (epitomized by the Bloomsbury trick of ending a debate by finally holding one's head in one's hand and shaking slowly from side to side) that it takes more than an average effort to project yourself back to AD 33. Forget the libel of the first Christians being credulous peasants and hysterical women; these were hard-nosed individuals far more familiar with the realities of life than most of us. Death, disease, foreign occupation and manifest injustice were all around; these people had neither the time nor inclination to engage in New Age fantasies. What was happening was simply incredible; you hardly have to read between the lines.

All this crystallized in the resurrection. In those few years of Jesus' ministry and its aftermath not only can a reliable history be reconstructed, but again it is the indirect evidence that oddly enough is the more compelling. We know the resurrection was proclaimed from the earliest days, simply, forcibly and unequivocally, with no ifs and buts. Paul was almost certainly converted within five years of the resurrection, and he insists the central dogma was not his invention, but crucially (so to speak) handed down to him. If we believe the chum of Caesar, the Jewish historian Josephus, in due course James, the brother of Jesus, was murdered by orders of the Sanhedrin. Now that is a bit of a strange fate for a most pious Jew. Except, of course, after Jesus was executed by the Romans, James had suddenly changed his mind about his brother, and Paul mentions that he saw (and almost certainly talked to) the resurrected Christ. Disillusioned people who have seen their estranged brother die in the most degrading circumstances are not in the habit of suddenly entertaining a *volte-face*. So too in the list of resurrection appearances Paul mentions 500 people; rather a lot, one might think. But that is the point; to organize such a gathering would require both logistics and secrecy; there were people in Jerusalem who were already rattled by the stories doing the rounds. Of course, like James this might be a fairy story, but it has the ring of truth.[22]

All these accounts also insist that in some way the resurrected body was material, although in other ways it was completely baffling. But if we think again of worlds visible and invisible, of realties orthogonal to our mundane world, then perhaps there is a glimpse of why the witnesses constantly struggled to articulate what in their eyes, and ours, should be impossible. The scientistic agenda will, of course, have none of this. As we have already seen, for them to be a Christian one requires the idiocy of children and the whips of indoctrination. But both scientistic belief and Christianity have their metaphysics. Both paradoxically claim there will be a truly glorious future. For those of a scientistic bent the vision lacks self-doubt: superstition banished, freedom restored, rationality triumphant. Strange, is it not, how repeatedly those hopes wither, how radical evil re-asserts its malign grip with each passing generation and with the advances of science the temptations of enforcement, discipline, control, manipulation and monopolization are the more easily achieved? "All most regrettable," they murmur, "but at least we scientists remain pure and detached from the sordid behaviour of our masters. Let us, in freedom and optimism, continue to probe the great secrets of nature." Let us do so indeed, but unless we take careful heed we will certainly find that at best, like Gollum, those supposed secrets are ultimately worthless and have lost all meaning. And at worst we may find we have opened the door to loathsome worlds from which there is no return.

Acknowledgments

I warmly thank Vivien Brown for typing various versions of this manuscript.

Notes

1. Oldroyd, D. (2005), "Evolution, paleontology and metaphysics", in *Darwinism and Philosophy*, 30–57, Hösle, V. & Illies, C. (eds.), University of Notre Dame Press, p. 30

2. Conway Morris, S. (1998), *The Crucible of Creation,* Oxford University Press.

3. Conway Morris, S. (2003), *Life's Solution: Inevitable Humans in a Lonely Universe*, Cambridge University Press.

4. Brosius, J. (2005). "Disparity, adaptation, exaptation, bookkeeping, and contingency at the genome level", *Paleobiology*, 31 (Supplement to part 2): 1–16, p. 11.

5. Quoted by Haynes, R. (1982), *The Society for Psychical Research 1882–1982: A History*, Macdonald, p. 2

6. "The Middle Cambrian metazoan *Wiwaxia corrugata* (Matthew) from

the Burgess Shale and *Ogygopsis* Shale, British Columbia, Canada", *Philosophical Transactions of the Royal Society of London B, 307:507–86*, 1985.

7. "Cambrian enigmas", *Geology Today*, 3: 88–92, 1987

8. Gould, S. J. (1989), *Wonderful Life: The Burgess Shale and the Nature of History*, Norton.

9. Simpson, G. G. (1964), "The nonprevalence of humanoids", *Science*, 143: 769–75

10. Diamond, J. (1995), "Alone in a crowded universe", in *Extraterrestrials: Where are They?*, Zuckerman, B. & Hart, M. H. (eds.), pp. 157–64, Cambridge University Press.

11. Dawkins, R. (2006), *The God Delusion*, Houghton Mifflin, pp. 263–64

12. Conway Morris, S. (1991), review in *Times Literary Supplement*, no. 4628, p. 6

13. Argot, C. (2004), "Evolution of South American mammalian predators (Borhyaenoidea): anatomical and palaeobiological implications", *Zoological Journal of the Linnean Society*, 140, 487–521.

14. Blalock, J. E. (1994), "The syntax of immune-neuroendocrine communication", *Immunology Today*, 15: 504–11.

15. Carmeliet, P. & Tessier-Lavigne, M. (2005), "Common mechanisms of nerve and blood vessel wiring", *Nature*, 436: 193–200.

16. Conway Morris, S. (2003), *op. cit.*

17. Gray, P. M., Krause, B., Atema, J., Payne, R., Krumhansl, C. & Baptista, L. (2001), "The music of nature and the nature of music", *Science*, 291: 52–54.

18. For example, *Poetic diction: A study in meaning*, Faber & Faber, 1952.

19. Flieger, V. (2002), *Splintered Light: Logos and Language in Tolkien's World*, Kent State University Press.

20. Brown, R. E. (1998), *The Death of the Messiah: From Gethsemene to the Grave*, Doubleday, pp. 1350–78.

21. Dawkins, R. (2006), *The God Delusion*, Houghton Mifflin.

22. Wenham, J. (1984), *Easter Enigma: Do the Resurrection Stories Contradict One Another?*, Paternoster Press.

Chapter 17
Inconvenient Truths

Dave Raffaelli is Professor of Environmental Science at the University of York. He grew up in Kilburn, North London, read Zoology at the University of Leeds, followed by a PhD in Marine Biology at Bangor University, post-docs in Otago and Essex, a lectureship at Aberdeen University in 1980, and finally appointment to York in 2001. He has been director of the UK office of the International Biodiversity Programme DIVERSITAS and of the Natural Environment Research Council Programmes concerned with biodiversity and sustainability, UKPOPNET and BESS. He has been a Vice-President of the British Ecological Society and in 2013 was awarded the BES President's Medal; he was editor of the *Journal of Animal Ecology* for many years.

I became a Christian at the age of thirty-eight, for reasons I explain in this essay. Before that I was an atheist. I expected that as a Christian in an academic science environment I might be floating all alone on a sea of atheism. It has been immensely comforting to know about other scientists who are Christians, some of whose testimonies are set out in these pages, even though my own journey to Christianity and living a Christian life whilst practising my science, seems quite different from the experience of others. I have had an easy ride compared to many others – so far at least!

Several years ago, Al Gore challenged our views and beliefs on the reality of climate change through his film and book *An Inconvenient Truth*, three words that have come to define our scepticism and hostility towards the blindingly obvious because of our reluctance to change the way we live our lives. In fact

– and somewhat scaringly – scientists like myself who have become Christians late in life face similar issues. Inconvenient truths are revealed that force us to confront our lifestyles and fundamental worldviews. I don't claim to have come to terms with all of those inconvenient truths, but I am definite that they need to be brought into the light so that they can be debated, however challenging and scary that might be. Such inconveniences are a repeated theme in my own faith journey and I hope that what I have penned here may encourage others struggling with how to deal with them.

My challenge is to reflect on the *difference that my science* (mainstream academic population, community and ecosystem ecology) – *if any – has made to my faith.* I should say up front that my scientific atheism was well formed and I was a card-carrying non-believer whom the New Atheists would certainly have embraced as a brother before I made the leap to become a Christian at the age of thirty-eight. That leap exposed many inconvenient truths for both my new-found faith as well as my science. Paradoxically and probably unbelievably as far as my atheist brotherhood are concerned, dealing with any science–faith tensions was surprisingly easy. I knew for certain that the science was basically sound, and I also knew that my conversion was utterly real. In other words, it was inconceivable that I could reject one because of the other. I would have to somehow live with both, whatever the inconvenient truths. That was a blessing!

The converse question of *what difference my faith has made to my science* is less easy to answer. This is in part because both questions are two sides of the same coin, but also because I can now see that my life took a number of startling turns before my conversion which laid the ground for what I hope is a faith-based approach to my science. In other words, what limited skills, insights and talents I seemingly picked up at random over the years have allowed me to use those talents for what I believe is a contribution to God's work through my science. Constructing narratives from half-remembered events and processes over a period of more than sixty years is likely to be fraught with difficulties of self-deception, but I don't believe that the broad outline of the journey so far is contrived. Anyway, here is my version of events.

Born-again scientist

My early upbringing was definitely secular and agnostic. As a child, I was not aware that I received any religious education, even though I attended a Church of England primary school in the 1950s. I have a hazy memory of sitting in front of an enormous loudspeaker listening to a squeaky BBC voice delivering sessions on morning worship, music and nature study, but I can honestly say I developed no interest or knowledge in either religion or nature at that age. Sports and playing adventurous games with friends were more to my liking. That is not to say I wasn't interested in learning about the world. I used to browse in an unstructured way old pre-war encyclopaedias, as well as that wonderful weekly magazine *Knowledge*, which so many children must have benefited from at the time. Who can tell exactly what actually stuck and what buried itself deep in the subconscious to re-emerge later? But there was certainly no obvious fervour for either nature or religion.

My interest in nature came rather late and in a quite startling way. I was sent to the local grammar school in the early 1960s, where I performed poorly and by the age of fifteen, I managed to scrape four O levels. I was set to leave to become a trainee GPO telephone engineer, but was asked to stay on because I was the full back in the school First-15 rugby team. I was told to fill my time in the Fifth Form by attending Physics, Maths, Chemistry and Zoology A Level lessons, because they timetabled neatly together, although I had no real interest in any of them. Presumably, my betters thought that such learning would later come in handy when I took up my career fixing wires at the top of a telegraph pole.

What changed was the arrival that year of a new teacher for the Zoology lessons, a young chap who had worked with the British Council in the West Indies, Bryan Hornett. I saw all new staff as an opportunity to play up in class, and it was just retribution that he sent me packing to sit in isolation, provided with a newspaper weekend supplement – improving literature to keep me quiet. I grudgingly opened this at random. In the next few seconds, I knew how I would spend the rest of my life.

It was indeed a blazing epiphany, but I can assure the atheists that God did not put in an appearance. There were no angelic choirs or blinding lights; rather I felt as if I had been hit by a lorry. The newspaper supplement article was on the Galapagos, a group of islands off the coast of South America of which I had never heard, but it was the pictures that transfixed me. I can still see the image of a marine iguana and other wildlife. I knew that, however inconvenient this might be, I had no choice but to take up a career in this "wildlife stuff".[1] But how to begin? Bryan, bless him, pointed out that I would need a degree. The problem was, I had few qualifications and an even poorer academic outlook. Inconvenient truths, and my chances were not great, although I now had the zeal of the recent convert. Amazingly, and despite my previously awful behaviour, Bryan stepped up to the plate and assured me that he would get me there by taking me through not only Zoology A Level but Botany A Level as well, a miracle which he would perform by coming in before school every morning for an extra hour or so. I still reel when I consider that generous and spontaneous act for which I cannot thank him enough. Bryan also deserves to be honoured for keeping the GPO telephone network safe from me.

Thanks to Bryan, I did well enough to get into the University of Leeds to read Zoology in 1969, then onto a PhD in Marine

Biology at Bangor, then post-docs in Otago, New Zealand and at Essex, and I managed to get a lectureship in Zoology at Aberdeen University in 1980. I was still very much in love with the natural world and the wonders of ecology. At Aberdeen, I was able to reinvent myself as a food web ecologist, which allowed me to work on just about every major animal group. I worked at the Zoology Department's Culterty Field Station for the next twenty years, the most formative periods in my life for my understanding of both nature and religion.

Since my Galapagos epiphany, I realized that evolutionary ecology, especially adaptation and natural selection, would be the framework for most aspects of my science. I was seduced by the adaptation paradigm that held sway at that time in just about every area of ecology, and where every feature of the structure and dynamics of life would be explained as adaptation through natural selection. My colleagues at Culterty soon disabused me of this uncritical way of thinking into which I had lapsed and they exposed many inconvenient truths about the way science should really be done. One person deserves especial mention: John Ollason,[2] famed for his diatribes against optimal foraging theory which had become distinctly Panglossian in its assumptions.[3] John was a fierce and unrelenting critic who never let me get away with anything remotely loose and instilled in me the need to always search out alternative and competing hypotheses that could be rigorously tested (falsified) in the laboratory and the field. The design, execution and interpretation of field experiments on species interactions in food webs became and have remained the bread-and-butter of my career. Culterty was an uncompromising intellectual environment where nothing was taken for granted and everything was tested. The weekly research seminars were always challenging for the speaker, occasionally a bloodbath, and consistently cathartic. Not everyone enjoyed being hammered on an anvil, but most speakers were sufficiently brave or masochistic to come back again and again. One might have thought that such a crucible would militate against spiritual ideas, but, ironically, that challenging approach to my science helped to bring me to Christ.

Born-again Christian

Aberdeen was one of the few universities that still ran a Zoology degree (as distinct from a more general Biology one). One of the modules I really enjoyed teaching was a waltz through the Invertebrate Kingdom, taking an evolutionary approach to show how all of the major invertebrate body-plans could be derived through natural selection and simple physics. One year, two students approached me after a lecture and asked if I really believed all that rubbish. Somewhat taken aback, I asked for clarification and they patiently explained that evolution was impossible because the Bible told them so. No amount of polite discussion could dissuade them from this view and I got quite angry with them. I asked them how they thought they would perform in the examination, to which they obscurely replied, "Go and read *Mere Christianity* by C. S. Lewis." I was furious and stormed off in a splendidly Dawkinsesque manner.

As fate would have it, C. S. Lewis's book almost literally dropped into my lap whilst I was granny-sitting for my cousin. I read it, just for fun, you understand, and for the devilment of being able to counter those students when I next met them. This turned out to be a serious miscalculation. Instead, I ended up dedicating my life to Christ that night. (A word of warning: if you think that Lewis' book is the fast-track to conversion, then you may be disappointed. I have gone back to *Mere Christianity* several times and whilst it is a cracking good read full of fundamental truths, I cannot for the life of me explain why it had such an effect at that precise moment.) But I do recall approaching the "problem" of this person Jesus in the same way that I would have done for any competing hypotheses in science: was Jesus just a fairy tale, albeit an enduring one, sucking millions into a huge deceit? Even if Jesus was real, was he truly the incarnation of God come down to earth, or was he a delusional madman, a Walter Mitty type? I decided that on balance it was probably all true, and he was the Son of God; so I made that leap from non-belief to faith and have never looked back.

The influence of science on my faith

Beyond my fateful evening with C. S. Lewis, I knew very little of the Bible and the foundations of Christian belief at that stage. It was only over the next few months that various inconvenient truths emerged. As a born-again Christian very shaky in his faith credentials, I was lucky enough to be picked up and nurtured by a wonderful minister and church in my parish, Pitmedden and Udny, Aberdeenshire, where I was later to be made an Elder in the Church of Scotland. They provided rock-solid support for me to come to terms with those inconvenient truths, the most difficult one for me being the whole issue of Creation and evolution.

I do not believe that the Creation narrative in Genesis can be a literal account of how life on Earth came about in seven days. The evidence for evolution and the mechanisms that underpin it are so compelling that they cannot be dismissed. So, here is an inconvenient truth: the opening passages of the Bible cannot be taken literally, and this has intellectual implications for interpreting the remainder of the Bible. Yet I know that Genesis is God's inspired word to us, so it must somehow be true in another sense that I did not yet understand and possibly never will. I have read all the theories and arguments that attempt to square that particular circle and have found none of them really convincing.

I decided just to park that one for a while and then a few years later I discovered the book of Job, Chapter 38, and this has been a great comfort. That text is too long to set out here, so here is a verse or two that seem to sum up how scientists should not approach biblical accounts: *"Where were you when I laid the earth's foundation? Tell me, if you understand. Who marked off its dimensions? Surely you know!"* And especially for the food web ecologist: *"Do you hunt the prey for the lioness and satisfy the hunger of the lions when they crouch in their dens or lie in wait in a thicket? Who provides food for the raven when its young cry out to God and wander about for lack of food?"*

The message is clear – scientists are pretty arrogant if they think they have all the answers to the big questions and there will be many things which may never be revealed to us.

For me, Genesis holds far more inconvenient truths about evolution than trying to square seven days of Creation with the known 4.5 billion years of earth's history. Fundamental to the idea of evolution by natural selection is the death of individuals, without which evolution cannot take place. Drawing on various parts of Genesis, some Christian commentators have suggested that death was not a feature of life until the fall. That is, until after the evolution of humans. For instance, Genesis 1:30 tells us that: *"To all the beasts of the earth and all the birds in the sky and all the creatures that move along the ground – everything that has the breath of life in it – I give every green plant for food."* Note, everything, not just the herbivores. So much for predator–prey interactions shaping evolution! In fact, it is not until after the flood (Genesis 9:3) that God expressly gives humans permission to eat meat: "Everything that lives and moves about will be food for you. Just as I gave you the green plants, I now give you everything." Again, in that terrible passage where God condemns Adam and Eve, there is even the suggestion that their actions have only then brought death into the world: "since from it you were taken; for dust you are and to dust you will return." It is also reported that Adam lived 930 years, Seth lived 912 years, and Methuselah lived 969 years, whilst Noah and his sons were a mere 500 years or so on this earth.

In Genesis a disturbing pattern emerges about life and death which simply doesn't make sense in terms of evolution and natural selection or of what we know of the scientific basis of ageing in humans (the Bible is silent on other species). Are these inconvenient truths for our reading of Genesis or for our understanding of science? Either way, they are inconvenient and force us to re-examine our ideas. Prior to 1988 and in the best traditions of atheism, I would have dismissed all of the above as a fanciful story, but I am now certain that God speaks through his written word, even though it doesn't seem to make sense at present.

Given those inconvenient truths that lurk like bear traps within Genesis, I would be amazed if any evolutionary scientist already well established in their discipline could possibly come to faith simply by reading the Old Testament books of the Bible. There are just too many apparent contradictions and tensions to deal with. On the other hand, I could imagine the same person coming to faith through reading the New Testament. Yet its message of hope cannot be fully understood without reference to the Old Testament. Genesis explains that we failed God by our disobedience and sin, which in turn ushered in pain, suffering and death. The New Testament is the good news that God has been gracious enough to forgive us by offering himself as the ultimate payment for those sins and in the process conquering death. I was brought to faith in a simple yet powerful conversion at the ripe old age of thirty-eight when I knew little of the Bible, so that the Genesis narrative was never a stumbling block, more of a puzzle to spend the rest of my life trying to sort out. Wish me luck.

The influence of faith on my science

My early scientific career dealt with the population and community ecology of marine species, but has since broadened into the study of whole ecosystems and how people depend on the services that ecosystems provide. My research shifted from pure science to socio-economics, so I clearly needed to learn about those disciplines. This was a natural progression: the estuarine food webs I worked on at Aberdeen were becoming dysfunctional due to nutrient enrichment and I was naturally curious to find out where the nutrients were coming from. I soon discovered that the high levels of nutrients were due to the way the river catchment was being farmed, in turn driven by that most perverse of instruments, the Common Agricultural Policy. The CAP encouraged excess application of fertilizers (cheap) to produce more crop yield (highly profitable), much of which was subsidized. The Ythan Catchment became the first Nitrogen Vulnerable Zone (NVZ) to be declared in the UK. Our local enrichment issue on the River Ythan and its estuary became a test-bed for European policy and a political football for a conservation *versus* farming battle. I hated being involved. It became a real trial of my relationships with local farmers, some of whom served with me as church elders and others were bosom friends of long standing; unhappily, many saw me as the villain of the piece. I had exposed an inconvenient truth, that their practices were messing up what was not only a beautiful area but also a National Nature Reserve. That period was painful and a test of my faith and my understanding of our role as stewards of God's Creation.

Looking back on it now, that Ythan NVZ period had a profound effect on my future research career after I moved to York in 2001. I understood much better our personal responsibility for Creation and that my own academic journey had given me skills and talents that might enable me to make a small contribution to the stewardship entrusted to us. At York, I was fully immersed in a university department that included many of those socio-economists whose ways I had so struggled with back in Aberdeen. Also, I was formally asked to work with the York Diocese on developing an environmental policy, which meant that I was forced to better articulate and refine my ideas on stewardship in a Christian, specifically Anglican, context. I'm not sure how well I performed, but at least the diocese has an environmental policy now and I have been given an opportunity to speak to many church groups and organizations about the environment, from conclaves of Catholic bishops to individual congregations.

At the start of my faith journey, I tried hard to keep my faith activities, my family life and my scientific work in quite separate boxes. I convinced myself that this was the best way to manage my time across the competing demands of each, but in retrospect I suspect that I was unsure as to how they might interact and what the consequences would be. Keeping them apart seemed a much safer strategy. I had imagined that becoming a Christian in an academic environment such as that which prevailed at Culterty would be a huge issue, but I need not have worried. I'm sure that some of my colleagues thought I had lost the plot but were too polite or embarrassed to mention it, whilst others were simply not interested, perhaps because it might have challenged their own secure secular worldview. I have met much the same at York, but here at least I have a public profile in the diocese, I am known as the churchwarden of our village church and, as I have tried to outline above, much of my scientific research seems completely consistent with my faith. I often have young Christians approaching me at conferences, which is good. Those separate boxes seem to have collapsed into one. There still remain many paradoxes and inconvenient truths about faith and science that I will continue to try and sort out, but I don't see that as an issue, rather an exciting opportunity. I used to think that when I finally meet my Creator, I could ask him about all those inconvenient truths, but I somehow suspect they won't seem important at all then.

Notes

1. I have yet to realize my dream of visiting the Galapagos, often called the "Enchanted Isles".

2. Pierce, G. J. & Ollason, J. G. (1987), "Eight Reasons Why Optimal Foraging Theory Is a Complete Waste of Time", *Oikos*, 49: 111–17.

3. Do read Stephen J. Gould's magnificent 1979 essay, "The Spandrels of San Marco and the Panglossian Paradigm: A critique of the adaptationist programme" in the *Proceedings of the Royal Society of London* B, 205: 581–98.

Chapter 18

A Different Drum-beat

Denis Alexander read biochemistry at Oxford University and then a PhD in neurochemistry at the Institute of Psychiatry in London. Following this, he spent fifteen years in academic positions in the Middle East, in Turkey (1971–80) and as Associate Professor of Biochemistry at the American University of Beirut, Lebanon (1981–86). From 1989 until retiring he was at the Babraham Institute, Cambridge, for many years as Chairman of the Molecular Immunology Department. He is a Fellow of St Edmund's College, Cambridge and founder Director of the Faraday Institute for Science and Religion, based at the College. His first book on science and faith was *Beyond Science* (1972). More recently he has written the critically acclaimed *Rebuilding the Matrix – Science and Faith in the 21st Century* (2001) and co-authored *Beyond Belief – Science, Faith and Ethical Challenges* (2004). His most recent books are *Creation or Evolution – Do We Have to Choose?* (2008) and *The Language of Genetics* (2011). Dr Alexander was Editor of the journal *Science & Christian Belief* (1992–2013).

My lab assistant carried on calmly with her experiment, set up temporarily in the corridor, while the explosions of incoming shells boomed from just up the street. Having a lab at the American University Hospital in West Beirut with windows facing toward the opposing side during the civil war of the early 1980s was not, I sometimes reflected, a smart move. There are not many parts of the world where scientists have to move their experiments into the corridor to avoid shrapnel.

This was not really what I had in mind when I embarked on a career in biochemistry. The influences that tipped my interests in the direction of the biological sciences were a mother who had been one of the rare women to read physiology at Oxford in the late 1920s; a GP grandfather whom I never met because he died in the closing days of the First World War, but whose inherited microscope opened my young eyes to the fascination of all things creepy-crawly; and a brilliant biology teacher at school who made the subject interesting. But history was an attractive alternative. It was an era when my historian uncle, the late A. J. P. Taylor, was delivering popular TV history lectures (without notes) at a time when the idea was quite novel. History looked cool. Writing was an early passion and my eldest brother had chosen to study history. But as my mother wisely advised, one can read history as a hobby, whereas science as a part-time interest is more difficult, not least because the specialized language makes it less accessible. Her argument tipped the balance: I chose science, later finding that her advice was entirely correct.

The central importance of the Christian faith was as much a part of my upbringing as an appreciation for the arts and the sciences. Faith and science were always together, never pitted against each other. Darwinian evolution was simply assumed as background knowledge for any budding biologist. Creationism had not yet been invented or, if it had, remained unknown and unmentioned. When, at the age of thirteen, I put my personal trust in Christ as Saviour and Lord and became a Christian, it was a natural maturing of a faith already nurtured by example. I have always thought that the deepest influence on any growing child is not their parents' overt exhortations and teaching, but the implicit understanding of what, deep down, really matters most to them.

By the time I went on a gap year to Canada before taking up my place as an open scholar at Oxford to read biochemistry, a standard type of academic research career seemed to lie ahead. A conveniently placed uncle, at that time General Manager of Schweppes, arranged by a piece of pure nepotism that I should work in a factory that made Welch's grape-juice, and there I laboured in the early months of 1964. We were told that we could drink as much grape-juice as we liked. It was very refreshing for the first week, but the attraction soon palled. The time in the factory was followed by some months of travelling in the USA and Canada.

Periods away from home during one's formative years can provide opportunity for reflection. I was not expecting that my gap year would radically affect my life's direction, but it was then that I gained the clear conviction that God wanted me overseas in a cross-cultural context, using my science in the service of others. Some words of Jesus spoke to me very powerfully during this time: "From everyone who has been given much, much will be demanded; and from the one who has been entrusted with much, much more will be asked" (Luke 12:48). I had been given much: the benefits of a secure, loving Christian home; financial security; a good education; the fruits of science; the prospects of an Oxford degree. What was I going to give in return? At the time I had no idea what this might involve.

Oxford and London

I was at Oxford from 1964 to 1968. My tutor at St Peter's College was Arthur Peacocke, later to gain a high profile in the area of science and religion, but at that time known principally for his work on the structure of DNA. Weekly tutorials with Arthur and one other undergraduate were always stretching. My grasp of irreversible thermodynamics, a topic dear to Arthur's heart, was never strong, and discussing the topic with a world expert must have been tedious for the expert on occasion. But Arthur was very focused, arriving in a whirl of papers and departing in a cloud of dust for the next appointment. His output was prodigious; by the end of his academic career he had published 12 books and more than 200 papers.

During this period, Arthur organized a College group with the aim of introducing students to systematic theology. Every week we discussed a chapter of *Christian Doctrine* by J. S. Whale, but science was never far from theology in our discussions. Arthur provided a role model, someone who regarded science and theology with equal seriousness, combining both worlds in one career.

There were plenty of other role models around for those who knew where to look. I became involved with the Oxford Inter-Collegiate Christian Union (OICCU), later to become its President, and it was a time when the OICCU often invited scientists as speakers. One of these whose influence was perhaps the greatest on my own thinking was Donald MacKay, at that time Professor of Communications at Keele University, a Chair not of IT, as the title might suggest, but of cognitive science – the way the brain interprets and perceives the world around us. Donald MacKay was without doubt one of the major pioneers in building an effective dialogue between science and faith during the latter half of the twentieth century. There have not been many scientists in recent times who have published, as MacKay did, papers on philosophy in the journal *Mind* in parallel with his neuroscience papers in *Nature*.

I listened to Professor MacKay several times in my student years, but one occasion stands out above all the others. He had been invited to give a seminar to the Humanist Society, at that time the biggest society in the university and aggressively anti-Christian. Professor MacKay had laryngitis and could only speak in a whisper; we had to strain to hear what he was saying. As was his wont, MacKay gave a very clear and accessible account of how to relate scientific and religious types of explanation, showing how they provided complementary rather than rival accounts of the same reality. Both accounts were needed to do justice to the world around us. After the talk was over I was chatting with the student Secretary of the Society. "If I ever become a Christian, it will be because of that man," he said, pointing to Professor MacKay. I don't know if he ever did, but I do know that the Treasurer of the Humanist Society around that period became a Christian a year after leaving Oxford, later to write a book critiquing atheism.

One of the many stimulating aspects of the 1960s was the intellectual, political and social turmoil that swept across the campuses of the Western world during that period. Fuelled by the anti-Vietnam war movement, radical left-wing groups proliferated. I well remember a lecture room full of Oxford undergraduates waving their "little red books" of the thoughts of Mao in the air. I doubt many had actually read it, but this was an era of left-wing icons and sloganeering. There were protests about almost everything. At the same time there were sea-changes going on in music and the arts. For all its extremes and its posing, the sixties post-War bulge generation was destined to make a lasting impact on the cultural milieu of this country.

Into this heady mix came Francis Schaeffer, at first sight an unlikely candidate as a commentator on the sixties counter-culture. He had been pastor of a rather conservative church in the USA, but a series of events brought him to Europe to set up a centre in Switzerland called L'Abri where people could stay and investigate the intellectual case for Christianity. Schaeffer encouraged Christians to leave their cultural ghettoes and engage with secular culture, immersing themselves in books, art and films. His printed and taped messages spread across the Christian world of the time, encouraging us to grapple with our faith and its intellectual underpinning. It was through Schaeffer that I learnt how people's worldviews are shaped by a few key underlying presuppositions. Though not himself strong in the sciences, it was Schaeffer who got us narrowly focused scientists into reading Sartre and Camus, and to take a greater interest in the arts.

The main intellectual challenges thrown at the Christian faith in 1960s Oxford were moral and political. Christianity was on the side of the bourgeoisie, not the masses. Religion supported the *status quo*; it was the opium of the people. On the other hand, I don't think Christians reading science were in any doubt that religion and science were harmonious first cousins. Occasionally humanists might try and attack Christian faith using varying forms of naïve reductionism, but there was nothing of the concerted attempt to hijack the prestige of science to promote atheism of the kind popularized by Richard Dawkins in later decades. Out of the many OICCU meetings that I attended during those four years, I cannot remember a single one where evolution was discussed as a topic that might be of concern to Christians. The background assumption was simply that evolution was God's chosen method for bringing biological diversity into being. Of creationism there was no sign.

I was a voracious reader as a student, but the only book that gave me any pause for thought as far as the roots of my own faith were concerned, was *Battle for the Mind – a Physiology of Conversion and Brainwashing* by William Sargant. In the book Sargant argued that the ways in which POWs are forced to confess and people are religiously converted are pretty much the same. I remember wondering whether I had simply been "brainwashed" into faith by my family upbringing? Journalistically it would be of more interest if I could recount some "crisis of faith" that arose from this new insight but, boringly, I simply chewed on the problem when I had time, and it gradually dissolved for what now seem very obvious reasons.

For a start, most religious conversions, certainly the ones I knew about (including mine), were simply nothing like the dramatic brain-washing episodes that Sargent recounted in his book, but instead very ho-hum mundane affairs. Second, the whole point about the brain-washing techniques recounted by Sargent is that they don't work in the long run. For sure, the POW confesses under duress, but at home after the war he reverts to his previous beliefs. The very term "brain-washing" is a misnomer because long-term memory is remarkably resistant to change, whatever short-term changes may be effected by psychological manipulation. Third, in any case, all beliefs have to be justified rationally by appeals to evidence, so the fact of having been raised either with or without a certain belief provided no support *per se* for or against its truth status. Fourth, a related reflection, had I been brought up in Saudi Arabia it was much less likely that I would have become a biochemist; nevertheless I would still be able to give grounds for believing that biochemistry was a well-justified way of spending one's time, despite the fact that my environmental and cultural milieu had clearly been influential in guiding me towards such a belief. In the end there has to be, by definition, a psychological account for the holding of any or all beliefs, but this insight, important as it is, does little to tell you whether those beliefs are well-justified beliefs.

London and the Institute of Psychiatry

A fascination with the workings of the brain led to a PhD in neurochemistry. There were several reasons for this choice of research area. Since the resolution of the structure of DNA had provided a mechanistic basis for genetics, the last great frontiers of ignorance seemed to be in the neurosciences. Nearer home, my eldest brother, nearly a decade my senior, had been an open scholar at Trinity College, but had there suffered a mental breakdown, diagnosed as manic-depressive psychosis. I think the knowledge of that fact at a young age, coupled with the ensuing realization that so little was known about the causes of such pathology, was a significant influence in choosing the path of the neurosciences.

When I think of the efforts nowadays to select the most promising PhD students, the way my own PhD place was secured seems remarkably casual. My tutor wrote to an acquaintance of his running a neurochemistry laboratory at the Institute of Psychiatry in Camberwell Green, London. A letter came back saying, "Fine, I've got two MRC [Medical Research Council] bursaries next academic year, he can have one of them", which is how I came to do my PhD studies with Dick Rodnight, later to become Professor of Neurochemistry. The MRC bursary paid about £500 a year, plenty enough to live on in the London of the late 1960s.

After Finals at Oxford, I went travelling, then showed up at the Institute of Psychiatry at roughly the right time. It turned out that the holder of the other MRC Bursary had arrived a week earlier, so had the opportunity of first pick on the two research projects on offer. He had chosen what seemed at the time a much more interesting project: the electrical stimulation of brain slices to investigate the turnover of protein phosphorylation, the addition of phosphate groups to proteins being a key modifier of their function. I was left with what seemed a less interesting goal: to work out how the sodium-potassium pump works at the biochemical level. This is the vital pump found in the membranes of all nerve cells that "recharges" the electrical difference across the membrane, thereby making possible the next nerve impulse. In the event the other person's project turned out to be technically challenging and it took him four years, whereas my project was relatively easy, and took only two years (plus a few months to write up). There are sometimes unexpected benefits that result from being late for things.

My research involved scraping the cerebral cortex off frozen ox brains and using it to make purified synaptic plasma membranes, rich in my precious sodium-potassium pump. Obtaining ox brains was a non-trivial exercise. They needed to be undamaged, so I collected them from a Jewish slaughter house in east London where the animals were killed by cutting the throat rather than by the more normal method of a steel bolt into the brain. Since, unlike most nationalities, the British do not fancy brain salad, it was then just a question of tipping the worker ten bob (50p in "new" money) to carefully cut out the brain. Double-wrapped in plastic bags, the brains were quick-frozen in dry-ice and transported back to the lab strapped to my Honda 49cc motorbike. Although I did come off my Honda twice during my sojourn in London (once in the middle of Trafalgar Square), my real concern was having an accident when the brains were on board. Fortunately this never happened; people rushing to help might have become somewhat alarmed.

I mention all this to illustrate the fact that PhD projects in biological subjects might sound straightforward at first, but are rarely that simple in practice. But we neurochemists certainly considered ourselves a cut above the less reductionist work carried out on the floor below. There we volunteered for the researchers working with Hans Eysenck, the Professor of Psychology. It was all great fun and involved performing fairground-type games, like moving a coil along a wire without touching it, at the same time being blasted (or not) with loud noises through earphones, all the time being watched through mirrors, supposedly secretly. The real game was to try and persuade the experimenter that you were introvert when you were really extrovert, and vice-versa. I never really believed Eysenck's models of introversion–extraversion because of such mean intractability in his human subjects.

The general attitude towards religion in the Institute of Psychiatry at that time can best be described as "frosty". Religious beliefs were generally equated with some kind of obsessional neurosis, possibly to be patronized, but certainly not to be taken seriously as claims to reality. Today there is a wealth of published data that support a positive role for religious belief in mental health, but those data came later. Although the Institute generally had a hard-nosed reductionist attitude towards psychiatry and little time for the psychoanalytical schools that were popular in the US, Freud's antipathy towards religion still filtered down through the ranks. Having said that, there were also some Christian psychiatrists in the adjacent Maudsley Hospital and I met with them regularly for prayer and Bible study. Then and since I have always felt that it is important for Christians to get together for fellowship in their work context, not least to avoid the idea that faith and work are in any way divorced.

Two important extracurricular events took place around this time. First, whilst showing a coach load of overseas students from London round Cambridge, I met my future wife; studying in London, but with a home in Cambridge, she happened to be helping out on the same trip. Our courtship involved many trips on the Honda, now nicknamed *Bucephalus* (the name of Alexander the Great's horse), with many cries from the back seat of "Mind my legs!" as the driver weaved his way through the London traffic. Sadly, *Bucephalus* was eventually stolen one night, wheeled away from outside the Institute, as it had no lock. More happily, courtship led to marriage soon after my PhD was finished.

The second significant event was an approach by my elder brother, David, to write a book on science and faith. David had worked for eight years for IVP, a publisher specializing in Christian books, before branching out to start his own publishing house called "Lion" with the aim of publishing Christian books for a broader, more secular readership. There were indeed very few sensible books on science and faith available at the time. Donald MacKay had not yet published much, Arthur Peacocke nothing, and there were just a few other authors in the field. In any event I was told to write something "popular" and, typical for an elder brother, David sent me a one-page summary outline of what should be in the book.

But first the thesis had to be finished, a task I completed at home on my father's old and cumbersome office typewriter. This involved making five carbon-copies using my one-finger typing; every time I made an error, this had to be corrected with Tippex, blowing on each page to dry it before being able to correct the one below. I like to tell this story to PhD students today, when they complain that the printer jammed once whilst printing from their laptop.

With the thesis out of the way, it was time to give attention to the book, eventually called *Beyond Science*, one of the very first books to be published by the fledgling Lion in 1972. I wrote it in the latter half of 1971 when I had just turned twenty-six. I now shudder at the arrogance of youth in thinking to write such a book, but at least it was fresh and spoke to my contemporaries, and it sold well. In fact I still come across people today who say how useful they found it in developing their own thinking: that science and faith were friends not foes, and that scientific advances were throwing up a host of questions that science itself was quite unable to address, but for which Christian faith had the answers. When it comes to writing, we're never too young to at least get started.

Science, faith and life in Turkey

During my student days, I had never lost the sense of God's call to work overseas. With *Beyond Science* nearly complete, I was verbally offered a teaching position at the Middle Eastern Technical University (METU) in the capital city of Turkey, Ankara. We waited eagerly for written confirmation in the last months of 1971, but nothing came. What did come was a telegram from our friends in Ankara saying, "Flat rented, come now". We went.

Loading a Ford Transit van with wedding presents and other paraphernalia we thought might be useful for a new home in Turkey, we set off for Ankara. I had visited Turkey once before, my new bride never. Unlike today, it was not then a well-established holiday destination and could best be described as "developing".

A week's drive brought us to Ankara, only to find that there was no job at METU; the hoped-for budget had never materialized. So I went back to Haceteppe University, where the Biochemistry Department had previously said that they had no openings, but where there was now a new Chairperson with new ideas. She was only too delighted to offer me a position as a *Yabanci Uzman* ("Foreign Expert" – in reality a glorified post-doc position). So began a pattern that continued throughout life, of God opening some doors and closing others at the appropriate moment. I have always taken very seriously the promise of Jesus given in Matthew 6:33: "But seek first his kingdom and his righteousness, and all these things will be given to you as well" – "these things" referring to the daily necessities of life.

Eventually we spent fifteen years in the Middle East. People often ask what it was like to teach science and carry out research in the Muslim world. The answer I always give is, "It depends which bit you mean", for in truth there is no such entity as "the Muslim world", as if it represented some homogeneous geographical area. There are countries where Muslims are either a majority or a significant minority, but these in turn vary enormously.

Turkey is and was a Muslim country in the sense that 99 per cent of its inhabitants have "Muslim" stamped in their identity cards as their religion. On the other hand, it is a more secular country than Britain, having a legal separation between religion and state. When Kemal Ataturk established the modern republic of Turkey back in the 1920s, he carried out a radical westernizing programme of reform in which the political power of Muslim leadership was destroyed, the Arabic alphabet of Ottoman Turkish was replaced by the Latin alphabet, and the population were forced to adopt surnames to make them more like their European neighbours. In the 1970s, just as today, Turkey was continually pulled between East and West, with Ataturk's reforms under continued threat from those wishing to impose either fundamentalist Islam or ultra-nationalist agendas upon the Turkish state.

The most visible impact of Ataturk's reforms for me was that when I started work at Haceteppe, I was the only male in the Biochemistry Department. Turkey indeed has a good record of sexual equality in the scientific workplace, and today in the country's best universities, one third of the mathematicians and physicists, two thirds of the chemists and one fifth of the engineers are women. Proportionally there are higher percentages of women in different scientific disciplines in Turkey than in many non-Muslim countries.

After two years my contract at Haceteppe came to an end, but by that time a lecturing position had opened up down the road at METU, the very department to which I had originally intended to come. The university was and is operated totally in English, and my job involved setting up for the first time a neurochemistry lab and establishing a number of new courses, both undergraduate and graduate. One of the stimulating experiences of working in other countries is the way that you can be plunged into responsibilities at a much younger age than might otherwise be the case.

The equipment was not bad, but the shortage of consumables was chronic. I spent a lot of time scrounging consumables and radioisotopes from my old lab in London, who were very kind in sending out items. Somehow we managed. My very first Masters student now has her own lab in the USA; I discovered that another was now head of department when I went back to give a seminar in Ankara recently. But this also illustrates the challenge of much development work – to see trained people staying on in their own country to pass on the fruits of their experience to others.

At METU I found the Turkish version of secularism was based more on the French pattern of radical exclusion of religion from all state and official affairs (hence no headscarves on French campuses), as compared to the more British relaxed version (do what you want as long as no one is upset by it). The METU campus was entirely left-wing; the student body would not allow any right-wing students on campus, irrespective of whether they had a right to be there or not. Many faculty had been imprisoned and tortured by the military after the previous coup that took place shortly before we arrived in the country. There were frequent clashes between different leftist factions on campus, especially as the 1970s progressed and Turkish politics became increasingly fraught. The Maoists fought the Trotskyites, and the Trotskyites fought the Marxist-Leninists. Actually half the time I don't think even the students really knew who was fighting whom. The Biological Sciences Department where I worked was right in the middle of the campus opposite the Rector's building, a favoured spot for confrontations, and on more than one occasion I was thankful for the large desk in my office, which I hid behind as shoot-outs took place outside. Nevertheless, despite endless chanting of "death to America", the students were studiously polite and friendly when they came in for their biochemistry lectures afterwards: there was no personal antagonism involved.

A key element lacking in Turkey to a significant degree, is tolerance. Ataturk may have launched important reforms, but the idea intrinsic to the Western liberal tradition that you can hold individual beliefs quite different from those of others, yet still be valued as a citizen and even as a friend, seems quite alien to the Turkish psyche. What mattered is the *millet*, the nation, and what the nation wants. We in the West are so used to our individualistic freedoms that we forget the way in which communal thought and action is so much more valued in most parts of the world.

Certainly there was little tolerance shown towards the Christian faith during the years we were in Turkey. Leftist secularists were opposed to it because all religious beliefs for them were associated with backwardness. I have never heard such ready espousal of scientistic views as from my Turkish colleagues. This is the idea (quite fallacious, as it happens) that only science provides a reliable source of knowledge and that all other types of knowledge are unnecessary or based on "mere opinion". Right-wing nationalists, of whom there were many, opposed Christianity because they saw it as a "new crusade", a Western plot to subvert the nation. Islamists, of whom there are now more than in those days, viewed the Christian faith as a threat to Islamic hegemony. The idea that you could choose your own faith, yet at the same time remain a good Turk and loyal citizen, was not even countenanced.

All these factors eventually impinged on our own future. The late 1970s were years of increasing economic and political turmoil. The country ran out of money and could no longer pay for oil. Queues formed for everything, so that we started joining a queue as soon as we saw one, in the sure knowledge that some rare commodity (like margarine) was surely on offer. On one occasion I queued for twelve hours to buy sufficient petrol to take the family to the south coast for a weekend break. Inflation soared. Clashes between left and right increased in different parts of the country, until ten to thirty people were being killed each day. Civil war loomed.

There was no church building in Ankara where Protestant Turkish Christians could meet, so we routinely welcomed the nascent Turkish church of a small handful of students and others coming together for regular worship and Bible teaching into our home during this period. In a secular state, where the legal right of religious assembly is protected by law, there was nothing illegal about such meetings. But the state thought otherwise, and in 1979 we received a deportation order. We duly tried to have this reversed and had some temporary success, but we were finally forced to leave the country in 1980 just weeks, as it turned out, before the next army coup.

Life, science and faith in West Beirut

During a year back in the UK I was offered a position in the Medical Faculty of the American University of Beirut, to set up a laboratory of biochemical genetics as part of the National Unit of Human Genetics. Our three children were still young. If we were going to spend more time overseas, now was the time to do it. There was a major snag: I didn't know anything about the kind of genetic diseases that I was being asked to work on, nor the specific techniques involved. Never mind, came the reply, we have good links with the Paediatric Research Unit at Guy's Hospital in London, and we'll fund you there for two months whilst you learn your new field. Human genetics, in a land where up to 42 per cent of some communities (the Druze) married their first cousin, certainly seemed much more relevant than neurochemistry from a practical point of view. I accepted the offer.

When we arrived in West Beirut it was still ruled by the Palestinian Liberation Organization (PLO), run like a slightly disorganized Scout camp by Yassar Arafat. The city had never fully recovered from the civil war of 1975–76. But an uneasy equilibrium of a kind had been achieved, although the power of the state was rudimentary, most areas being controlled by different militias, of which the PLO was deemed the most powerful. The balcony of our apartment faced the Arab Bank where the PLO gold was stored, one benefit being that in the space in between, our car was well guarded.

The American University Hospital was modern, effective and well funded, the University being registered in the State of New York, with an American President (sadly assassinated during our time there). The University operated entirely in English. Our Genetics Unit represented just about every one of Lebanon's diverse communities: Armenian, Druze, Sunni Muslim, Shiite Muslim, Maronite Christian, Protestant and Orthodox. We all got on extremely well, with a communal meal once a week, each member bringing a meal typical of their community. Sometimes these communities were fighting each other bitterly outside, but at least peace reigned in the hospital.

It was in the Genetics Unit that I encountered the first moral dilemmas arising out of my science. Working on ox brains had raised no pressing ethical concerns. Genetics was something quite different. It gradually dawned on me that I was being asked to set up prenatal diagnosis on as many lethal genetic diseases as I thought appropriate. In fact we established the first prenatal diagnostic clinic anywhere in the Arab world. There was no ethics committee to give advice: I *was* the ethics committee. The techniques of the time involved therapeutic abortions at 12–14 weeks in the case of an affected foetus. Families of 8–12 children or more were not uncommon. Sometimes we had parents coming for genetic counselling who had seen 3 or more of their young children die slowly and painfully around 6–10 years old. Typically such couples were both carriers of defective genes for enzymes used in lysosomes, the waste-disposal organelles of the cell. That meant that each child had a 1 in 4 chance of being homozygous for the defect. They would be normal at birth, but then the gradual accumulation of waste-products would lead to an untreatable cell pathology that would kill them in early childhood. At the same time there was still a strong (and horrendous) belief in less educated families that giving birth to a child that was or became abnormal was a judgment from God. There were stories of such children being left to die, hidden from the community in dark cupboards.

I took the pragmatic decision that if a gene defect had a 100 per cent chance of killing a child at a very early age, then we would develop the biochemical assay needed to do the prenatal diagnosis, but any disease that developed later would not go on the list. This was based on the firm belief that all therapeutic abortions are evil, but on the equally firm belief that allowing a child into the world that was destined to die slowly and painfully at a very early age, with all the agony that involved for not just the child, but also the parents and wider family, was an even greater evil. Quite often medical interventions involve choosing the lesser of two evils.

Today technical advances have changed the picture considerably. Chorionic villi sampling has enabled prenatal diagnosis to be carried out earlier in pregnancy. The advent of preimplantation diagnosis, involving the genetic screening of embryos prior to implantation, has rendered discussion of abortion redundant for an ever-wider range of diseases. Such technologies have raised new questions about how far to go. But as far as the really lethal diseases are concerned, I have never seen any reason to change my ethical position from that worked out "on the hoof" in the maelstrom of early 1980s Beirut. Those holding to "absolutist" views on such matters are often not those who have to face a mother who has seen several of her children slowly die from a devastating disease.

Re-entry

Turkey had gradually dissolved into political chaos during our time there, and Lebanon did the same. We were evacuated three times. Twice we returned once things quietened down, but the third was our final exit. This took place because President Reagan decided to bomb Libya in a crazy plan to kill Colonel Ghaddafi (they missed him, but killed one of his adopted children). The planes took off from a US base near Cambridge.

Not surprisingly the Arab world seethed in anger. Three Western hostages were killed in retaliation in Beirut, one of whom was the Director of the Language School where my wife was teaching. Our Lebanese friends said: "We love you, please leave now." We left within forty-eight hours with experiments sitting unfinished on the lab bench and children wailing as they said farewell to the family cats. As we drove across from West to East Beirut under armed escort, the British Ambassador greeted us in his bullet-proof car and took us all off to experience that great British response to all emergencies: a nice cup of tea.

Re-entry to British life proved more problematic than readjusting to British tea (with milk – ugh!) and the terrible weather. A life of research in the UK had never been on my agenda. Fortunately I had never left active scientific research and teaching, and had managed to get a few papers published in decent genetics journals whilst in Beirut. Fortunately, also, no one had told me that getting one's first job in academic science in Britain at the age of forty-one is impossible. Remarkably a post as visiting researcher at what was then the Imperial Cancer Research Fund (ICRF, now Cancer Research UK) opened up. I was told very firmly that it could be for one year only, but in the end it continued for more than three years, giving a great opportunity to get a toehold back in the UK research community. The position necessitated shifting fields once again, this time to molecular immunology, but this returned me to my "first love": protein phosphorylation (and dephosphorylation, just as important). Again through some rather extraordinary "coincidences", the way then opened up for a position at the Babraham Institute in Cambridge, where later in the 1990s I became Chair of the Molecular Immunology Programme.

In January 2006 I established the Faraday Institute for Science and Religion at my College in Cambridge, St. Edmund's College, where I had previously been elected a Fellow; this was carried out in collaboration with Bob White FRS, Professor of

Geophysics at Cambridge. I finally closed my research group at Babraham in 2008, continuing on as Director of the Institute, now full-time, until handing over to Bob White as Director in 2012. Over the years the Institute has grown to exert a significant international influence on the discussion between science and faith.

Life in science for the Christian can indeed be an exciting adventure of faith. Sometimes it turned out for us a little more exciting than we had intended, but this can be useful in increasing one's dependency upon God. We have continually experienced the truth of Jesus' promise that if we seek first his kingdom, then the necessities of life will come along behind. Science and faith are not two different worlds, but different aspects of one world, God's world. All scientists have the privilege of uncovering just a little more of the wonders of God's creation, but scientists who are Christians have the added privilege of seeing this as part of their worship as they seek to use their science in the service of others.

Chapter 19

Building Technology with Emotion

Rosalind Picard was raised as an atheist, but became a Christian as a young adult. She earned degrees in electrical engineering and computer science from the Georgia Institute of Technology and from MIT, including a doctorate of science from MIT. She is now Professor of Media Arts & Sciences at MIT, where she founded and directs the Affective Computing Research Group in the MIT Media Lab. She co-founded two companies, Empatica Inc, creating wearable sensors and analytics to improve health, and Affectiva Inc., which provides technology to help people communicate facial expressions. She is best known for founding the field of Affective Computing. This work has led to many new areas where technology can help people, including in autism. She has a husband and three sons, and is a regular speaker at science and faith events.

Reason and faith

I am a scientist, and my work is based on reason, logic, and on observations – measurable and repeatable. My desire to focus on reason, logic, and science followed from my childhood as a proud atheist. I believed that rational scientific thinking was the only way an intelligent person would operate, and I assumed it was sufficient for all truth.

When I was twelve I volunteered to lead the evolution team in the "evolution versus creation" debate in our science class at school. To my sixth-grade brain, creation was clearly a myth along with belief in God, and evolution was very clearly the rational scientific view. I had pictures of monkeys evolving into people, and of course we believed what we saw in science books. My side argued, "Evolution is true; this is science." The other side said, "The Bible teaches creation, and I believe it." Their side was led by the most popular girl in the class with blonde pigtails, a great tan, and a house with a swimming pool. Everybody liked her (including me). In contrast, our side's leader was the last person picked for any sport on the playground. When the class voted the winners, I could not believe it; my side's defeat only made me more determined to seek reason, and to promote science.

Some neighbours whom I worked for kept inviting me to church. I didn't want to go because, first, I wasn't interested in having what I thought were fake beliefs, and second, I thought I had to wear a dress. I faked ailments every weekend when they'd ask if I was ready to join them. Finally my neighbours said, "It's not that important that you go to church. What's most important is that you know what you believe." They challenged me to read the Bible.

I wanted to be well educated, and the Bible was the best-selling book of all time. I decided I should read it, figuring I'd be even better at shooting it down. I started reading using a paraphrased version called *The Way*, ticking off three chapters in the Old Testament and two from the New Testament each day, which would get me through the Bible in a year. At my neighbour's suggestion, I started with the book of Proverbs. I thought it would just be fantastical stories of beings appearing in the middle of the air and things like that, but I was wrong.

Proverbs was full of wisdom. I often felt the need to pause and ponder what was written, not just rush through to check off the boxes in a record of what books and chapters I'd read. The content was powerful and profound.

I read the whole Bible. While I had been quite content and uninterested in change, things started to change in me as I read. I can describe it as an experience of "being spoken to". You know the feeling you have when you sense that something mentally is nudging you, trying to get your attention? It is persistent.

When you enter into a conversation with somebody, if you sincerely listen, then you open yourself to being changed. In this case I was not interested in changing, but I listened with sincerity. I began to question my beliefs. I saw that some aspects of what I thought were "faith" were "reason" and vice-versa.

I came to realize that a lot of what I was attributing to science was based on faith, on simply believing what some scientists declared, without deeply questioning what it was based on. Meanwhile a lot of what I had assumed was religious bunk was actually rooted in historical events complete with eyewitness testimony and repeated observations.

While I needed to think carefully about what to believe, I actually faced a much harder challenge: my pride. My pride didn't want to believe anything that could be associated with religion, no matter how reasonable or solid. I did not want to be known as somebody who was religious. Even to this day, I do not like "religiosity" and much of the trappings that go with religious behaviour are repulsive to me. I had to separate the pursuit of what was true from my conceptions of religion.

Most of what I had been exposed to about religion was from the media and passers-by and invited mocking. I had assumed that what I'd been exposed to was accurate and representative of religion. As I started to meet intelligent, thoughtful people who believed in God, and who did many good deeds that were not done for media viewing, I began to see how superficial and inaccurate the public face of religion was. I realized so much of what I believed about religion was associated with a false image and not with first-hand observations, historical evidence, or scholarly study. Most of what I believed came from pride associated with wanting to appear intelligent and reasonable, without doing the work required to actually be knowledgeable about faith or what scriptures say. The Bible said, "prove all things; hold fast that which is good". It urged me to "seek knowledge". This was good.

I didn't want to admit that my beliefs were changing and I still didn't want to go to church. On the other hand, I was gradually accepting the presence of God, and attracted to the amazing person of Jesus and his counter-cultural teachings.

Considering that the Bible might have overly influenced me because I lived in a supposedly Christian culture, I decided I should back off and get more perspective: I should read scriptures from all the other major religions. Perhaps they would have an equal or stronger influence. While my family had never gone to church or discussed religion, we did consume a chocolate bunny on Easter morning and we put up a Christmas tree, complete with bright lights, the kind where if one bulb burned out the entire strand went dark. Easter and Christmas in our home were secular; however, I reasoned that perhaps they made me more comfortable with Christianity. Maybe I just needed to get more comfortable with the other faiths and I would find them equally attractive.

I had lived as a child in Europe, Central America, and four different regions of the United States; I had unusual exposure to different ways of thinking. I was friends with Jews (including my favourite teacher) but I knew that the context around me was predominantly Christian. I thus began to make a focused study on Islam, Judaism, Buddhism, Hinduism, Confucianism, Taoism and more, still a bit puzzled that I, who hated religion, was choosing to study it. I wanted to make myself less biased, more knowledgeable, more objective. I also needed to know better how to handle a feeling of the existence of God that was starting to become increasingly present. I was keenly aware that I began my study to debunk religion, and chided myself that maybe this partial embrace, this momentary attraction to something religious, would pass like some episode of young love.

I forced myself to read many different scriptures and histories. I made time to visit mosques, synagogues and temples and meet with their believers. I opened myself to being even more persuaded by them than I had been by the Bible. I candidly disliked so many things about local Christian culture from the media that I truly hoped the other world religions would show me something better. I thought that perhaps I was cognitively biased toward a Christian worldview simply by having been raised in the West.

Of course, Christianity did not start in the West; it started in the Middle East and spread to the West. Today it is most swiftly growing in Asia, with countries like Korea and China having rapidly increasing Christian communities. But I believed the myth that Christianity was a Western way of thinking.

That year of study evolved into lifelong learning; it is important to always remain open to new evidence, to keep learning. To date I have found nothing at all like what is in the Judeo-Christian scriptures. The messages there, rooted in historical events, witnessed by writers both of books of the Bible and of external reference texts, and with a culturally transcending message, offered power that can bring love, hope, redemption and forgiveness to a world that lives in rebellion and denial.

When I went to college I met smart people who asked me not only, "What do you believe?" but also, "Are you committed?" I realized that there was more to do than just believe God existed, or that the historical biblical events happened. People are not only called to believe what happened, but also to live differently because of the events. We are called not only to believe that the historical Jesus lived, died, and showed power over death, but also to try to live the way he urged. We are challenged to treat others as greater than ourselves, to give expecting nothing in return, to seek peace and pursue it, to love even those who return hatred. We are called not to judge, but to show grace and mercy; after all, what makes us superior? Were we not given all that we have? The Bible flips upside down the messages that our world gives: "You are the best and the brightest; be all you can be, make yourself beautiful, promote your accomplishments, gain everything you can." Our world tells us to focus on self; Christ tells us we are not our own. The Bible says, "To the one who has been given much, much is expected."

Choosing to decide whether or not I was willing to take myself off my personal throne, and commit to a changed life was a significant challenge for me. Jesus said, "If you are not for me, then you are against me." How could I be against the greatest mind in the world, the very Word present in the Beginning, the author of time and space, of all knowledge, science, reason, and even our very ability to consciously wrestle with any of these concepts? Jesus' life showed more wisdom, generosity, self-sacrifice, and grace than any example throughout history. Is there any greater individual to follow? Not that I was looking for anyone to follow; I was quite content before I had opened Proverbs.

I ran an experiment: "OK Jesus, I'm no longer going to be lord of my life. I hand that over to you." The change in my life was tremendous: Profound Peace. The way I began to see the world was as if I had been living anxiously inside a black-and-white photograph and was now living in a full-colour universe. In fact, that description is an understatement; I do not have words that are adequate to describe the abundance that entered into my life.

Engineering a scientist

For somebody who would later be credited with starting a new scientific field, my early exposure to science did not start auspiciously. My earliest memories were of getting sent out in the hallway for talking in science class, trying to survive boredom.

I struggled to read dry texts. When I finally got to high school where we were able to dissect animals and conduct chemistry experiments, I was hopeful. However, I hated the smell of formaldehyde and the dead critters with cold grey flesh were unappealing, to say the least. In chemistry something always blew up or went wrong. We accidentally knocked over Bunsen burners and caught the cupboards on fire. Our carefully followed experimental procedures resulted in black stinky powder and shattered flasks. I wondered if they had been purchased from a low-budget fake Pyrex-labelling business. I had one happy memory when my teacher's demonstration exploded and methyl violet indicator went all over the ceiling, fluorescent lights, her lab coat, and everybody sitting in the front row. Years later when I returned to the classroom the lights were still covered in what I affectionately called the "purple haze". Praise of Jimi Hendrix could be found engraved in our wooden desktops, along with couplings of students' initials inside etched hearts.

I was moved into a "gifted class" where I was permitted to get out of school two afternoons a week to study at Fernbank science centre across town. This was an opportunity to skip school without getting expelled, so what could be cooler? At Fernbank I met a PhD student with a sense of fun for learning. He taught us to make electrical circuits. He owned a laser and when I asked him how holograms were made he lent it to me, with everything I needed to make my own! There I was, a teenager driving across town with a laser in the seat next to me – it was much more exciting than school, and my curiosity was kindled.

After high school I earned a bachelor's in electrical engineering at the Georgia Institute of Technology, a minor in computer engineering, and took all my electives in physics. I then went to work as a member of the technical staff at AT&T Bell Labs while taking a master in electrical engineering and computer science and a doctorate in science at the Massachusetts Institute of Technology (MIT). I loved my work and poured myself into discovery after discovery, developing mathematics to describe the complexity I found in signals, images, and digital videos. I modified equations from signal processing, statistical physics, and stochastic processes, building models that could represent anything that could be digitized. And what couldn't be? Our mathematics could represent anything.

In fact, I wasn't content to just represent everything mathematically – I wanted to come up with the kinds of maths and models that could be used to interact *semantically* with everything. I wanted to create the first models that were smart and could reveal understanding of the data they represented. I was working at the new intersection of artificial intelligence, mathematics, digital image/video processing, and human–computer interaction, and was co-creating a novel field – content-based image and video retrieval.

As I was getting to the finishing stage of my doctorate the MIT Media Lab invited me to join their faculty. The Media Lab prided itself on a style not unlike the Salon de Refusés, a collection of mavericks outside of conventional disciplines. The lab was and still is focused on inventing the future – especially on the creation of new technologies to advance human learning, expression, and invention. I focused on "vision and modelling", teaching computers to see and interpret the information coming in through cameras. It was exciting figuring out how to teach computers to "see".

A group of us collaborated with Harvard's leading experts on human vision, trying to discover what goes on in our brains. How does our visual system figure out what incoming patterns of light really mean? Why do visual illusions fool us? How does all this processing fit into our tiny skull? How can we build a computer that does what our brains do in real time? The more we learned, the more new questions arose. Each answered question was immediately replaced by multiple new unanswered questions.

Through this experience I grew in awe of how the brain works. Our group of collaborators represented the top institutions in the world with access to the most powerful resources. And yet, with all the brightest ideas and fastest computers, we couldn't make a machine see as well as a toddler. Trying to build a brain makes concrete what you do and don't know about it. We humbly realized that the more we began to know, the more we saw there was to know. It was like a new kind of infinity.

As I learned more about the brain I bumped into something I wanted to avoid. I read about how emotion was at work deep in the brain, influencing perceptual processes, including how we see and hear. I was a woman trying to prove myself in science, and did not want to be associated with emotion, the topic connected with being irrational.

Like my colleagues, I believed emotion was only present when people "get emotional", or unbalanced. Certainly we did not want to build this kind of emotion into computers. But again, in trying to be open-minded and read in fields beyond mine, I discovered that the latest neuroscience findings indicated that emotion was always present, contributing to rational behaviours: perception, memory, language, decision-making, and other vital aspects of intelligent life. Emotion was contributing to intelligence even when a person did not appear to be emotional. As I saw this and thought about what we were trying to create machines to do, I realized that computers were going to need something like emotion if they were ever going to be truly intelligent.

I didn't want to deal with emotion; nonetheless, I recognized that it was important for what we needed to build. I tried to convince male engineers to work on it. Several told me that they didn't know what emotion was, or that at best it was "noise". They wouldn't take it seriously. I imagined my hard-earned reputation as a scientist and engineer being ruined if I started to do "work on emotion", the kiss of death for a female. But it turned out to be even more surprising.

One place where my faith has helped me with my science is that it has made me relatively fearless in learning. This is a real force: I was a very shy child, and quite afraid to stand up in front of a group of people. In fact, I flunked fourth-grade "Show and Tell" because it required me to get up in front of my classmates and talk. I refused to participate. But later I handed over the reins to God, and embraced the instruction, "Fear only God." I realized I could pursue knowledge and truth without fear of what others would think of me. Under God, all of the most intimidating or accomplished scientists have the same height. Emboldened to pursue something that seemed important, even if it wrecked my career, I began to learn all I could about a topic I named "affective computing". People did snigger behind my back and say, "Can you believe what she's working on?" My skin conductance was its highest the first times I presented on affect to groups of scientists and engineers, who were baffled why I would think this topic mattered. But the Media Lab embraces crazy new ideas and, while some people shook their heads, I pursued solid work in what was to become a new field.

Affective computing

The field of affective computing includes the development of technology to detect and respond respectfully to human emotions, and to help people to better communicate, understand, and self-regulate emotions. It includes creating computational mechanisms of emotion that contribute to intelligent decision-making, perception, action selection, and more. Within these goals there are abundant opportunities to build technology that is smarter than what there was before, and that genuinely helps people in new ways.

One problem is that most of us who recognize an emotion do so without realizing how we do it. We just open our eyes and see: "Somebody is angry." We don't actually understand how our facial expressions suddenly mirror another's, or how empathy is elicited, or how 10,000 possible facial expression combinations, flying by in milliseconds, get interpreted as "curious" or "thinking" or "annoyed". I decided it would be great to use our technology to understand and teach such non-verbal skills to a person who is unable to intuit this communication, and began to partner with people who have trouble reading emotion, especially many people on the autism spectrum. However, to accomplish this, we have to figure out how emotion recognition works. It turns out that reading and interpreting all the emotion games that zip across people's faces in a conversation turns out to be more complex than teaching a computer to play chess. And that's just the face; we also needed to understand vocal expression, prosody, gesture, posture, and other contextual information.

I invent technology in order to make the world a better place. I find it important to collaborate with and listen to artists, critics, and people who are much more human-oriented than technology-oriented. We rub against each other, sometimes making sparks, but more often making a deeper sense out of things. We join in asking, "What could make the world better?" And for each idea or design, "What's the worst thing that this could be used for and how can we avoid that use?" In designing technology that actually helps people who are marginalized by society we've got to watch out for places where they could be harmed or abused. We're trying to work with individuals who are diagnosed with autism and hear what harms they've suffered, what successes they've enjoyed, and how to help them have less of the former and more of the latter. In so doing, we change the way we build the technology, so that it serves their needs while also advancing science.

In all aspects of my life as a Christian, I attempt to listen for God's guidance and calling. I have been, and continue to try to be open to being led by God, to take on challenges even in places that are unpopular or unattractive. A priest once said, "The church is here to comfort the afflicted and to afflict the comfortable." I've felt repeatedly nudged in directions that were uncomfortable and that have led to important successes that I would never have chosen on my own. Sometimes I was sent into directions that I did not want to take at the time, but I took them because they were more in line with what the Bible said to do than with what I wanted to do. Today I see that greater gifts were provided because of those choices. I am reminded how in this life we see only in part.

Day-to-day difference

My natural tendency, my starting point as an atheist, was to be mostly alone, pouring myself into work, spending time with family and a few close friends, but otherwise disinterested about people unless they helped me pursue my self-interests. The academic community rewards natural tendencies to put self first: do great work in your own name, promote yourself, promote your work, maximize your status – build your career. But because of the powerful words of the Bible to consider others better than self, to look out for others' interests and not just our own, and most of all because of the example of Jesus, I was and remain challenged to turn from my selfishness. I try to serve others. This is not easy, and I cannot brag about this space. God does not need us, or our service, and serving others usually bounces back to help me more than I deserve or seek. What I have learned, however, is that no matter how little time I have, no matter how uncomfortable I am, no matter how paltry the value of my service, it is undeservedly blessed and turned to good. In this mystery, there is greatness beyond human reason.

Some people are really happy to see a scientist admitting their Christian faith publicly. I've walked in on a group discussing with incredulity that the visiting Colloquium speaker (me) could possibly believe in "that stuff on her web page". I smile because I used to be of the same mind – I used to think that people of faith had to be either idiots, or that they were not questioning their upbringing. I know some people will assume these false things about me. Some will (without evidence) think that I believe something just because I was raised to believe it (I wasn't). Some will try to describe broken processes or evolutionary processes in my brain that explain religious experience (they don't explain the historical evidence of Jesus). The kinder ones will think themselves generous for "tolerating diversity" by putting up with my different (wrong in their minds) thinking. I have walked in the smug shoes of all these thinkers. We need to encourage sceptics to get facts.

I have hope that today's learners are ready to ask hard questions. Why does our world exist? Do we exist for a purpose? Why do people, even the anti-religious who don't want to think there is any purpose or meaning, see purposeful forces, including design, in the universe? Why do we seek meaning in life? What is the evidence for a "first cause" that transcends space and time? What is the evidence for and against the God of the Bible, and the events and messages (recorded in the Bible) that are reported to be for all nations? Who was the historical Jesus; what did he say and do, what evidence supports following him today? Why are we not maximizing the number of children we have? Why does giving unselfishly feel better than receiving?

Many atheists fall into a trap. They assume that science is the ultimate measure of truth. Some assume that the only things that are true are things science shows, and that only the topics science can address are valid topics. Ironically, what they are doing is claiming – myopically, based on faith – that they have the only tools for truth. Meanwhile, there are many great questions and answers that are beyond the tools of science. Science cannot prove or disprove most events of history; science cannot answer ultimate questions about meaning and purpose; science does not explain the beauty and the order found in mathematics.

Science provides us with amazing tools; but it is part of the domain of a Mind outside of our comprehension, not the other way around. The God revealed to us in the Bible is outside of space and time, outside of the natural world, and the very Author of all intellectual tools, including our very ability to comprehend.

I continue the pursuit of knowledge, but no longer for myself. No longer do I call the shots. I have learned that it is in submission to and in relationship with the one Lord of the universe that I find life, meaning, and purpose in abundance. I walk in awe of the sacrifice and example of Jesus. I meet and hear stories of Jews, Hindus, Buddhists, Muslims, some who are not in a safe place to admit their receipt of God's grace and love – but who have embraced the gift of Jesus and whose lives have been changed in profoundly positive ways. I continue to be inspired by Christ's love for all people – regardless of ability or disability, culture, age, gender, religion or behavioural past. We all have infinite value and the offer of abundant life because of God's choice. What should we do with so great a gift?

Chapter 20

Science and Christian Faith Today

Professor Donald M. MacKay, BSc, PhD, F Inst Phys, FKC, member of the Physiological Society. Born 1922, died 1987. Educated at Wick High School, St Andrew's University and King's College, London. Professor of Communication and Neuroscience, University of Keele, 1960–82. Foreign Member, Royal Netherlands Academy of Arts and Science, 1983. Herman von Helmholtz Prize for Distinguished Research in the Cognitive Neurosciences, 1985. Eddington Lecturer, University of Cambridge, 1967. Foerster Lecturer, University of California, Berkeley, 1973. Gifford Lecturer, University of Glasgow, 1986.

A century ago it looked to many people as if science and Christian faith were heading for a fight to the death. Today the echoes of the conflict have almost died away. Is this "peace with honour", or is it a dishonourable truce? I believe the dispute deserved to die, because it was not really between science and Christianity at all but between mistaken views of each; and I would maintain that the true scientific spirit in fact expresses something which is a necessary ingredient of a truly Christian faith. Faith is not credulity; like scientific belief, it entails trust based on experience and on reliable testimony. It differs from scientific belief not in its standard of truth but in its mode of origin.

Both Christians and scientists have learned something since the debates of the last century. Christians have come to realize that true reverence for the Bible requires a positive effort to avoid misinterpreting it; and that scientific discoveries may sometimes be God's way of warning us off a too-literal approach. Scientists have been taught by science itself to distinguish more carefully between fact and interpretation, and have recovered some of their professional humility.

It would be mistaken, however, to use any *technical* changes in science (e.g., physical indeterminacy) as an argument for Christian faith. The Bible represents God as "upholding" the whole going universe – not merely the physically puzzling bits. While, to our finite minds, the idea of "upholding" or "holding in being" can convey only a hint of the truth, it serves at least to guard us against the image of a mechanic tending a machine.

It would be equally fallacious to argue from the present regularities that miraculous events, such as the resurrection of Christ, were "scientifically impossible". Just as a scene on a television screen, however "regular" it seems, could be unimaginably changed by merely turning a switch, so God's world is open to change at his will. The big difference is that no change in God's world could ever be capricious. God's actions may sometimes be astonishing to *us*; but they can never be inconsistent with *his* unchanging purposes. This is what distinguishes miracle (in the biblical sense) from mere magic. It is here, indeed, that I see the deepest harmony between Christian faith and the scientific attitude. The best basis for our scientific expectations is the rationality and faithfulness of the God who holds our world in being.

The basic issue

Three centuries ago, the founders of the Royal Society saw nothing incongruous in dedicating their scientific work "to the glory of God".

Two centuries ago, the new discoveries of science were being eagerly harnessed to "arguments from design" intended to support the Christian faith.

A century later, the climate of thought had changed; theologians and scientists were eyeing one another with mutual distrust, and before long men were speaking and writing as though science and Christianity were in for a fight to the death.

Today, the echoes of the great nineteenth-century conflict have almost died away, and theologians and scientists once more pursue their callings side by side in peace.

The true scientific spirit expresses something which is not only a possible but a necessary ingredient of a fully Christian faith. Christian faith is not credulity; like scientific belief, in one respect at least, it is *trust based on experience and on testimony judged reliable*. (This is not of course meant as a complete definition of faith!)

As everyone knows, the ostensible cause of battle in the past century was the Darwinian theory of evolution; but I have no qualifications to discuss the technicalities then in dispute, and in any case I believe that the basic dispute concerned a much more general question, which evolutionary biology just happened to raise in an acute form.

The Christian God is declared throughout the Bible to be a God of *action*. He not only *is*; he *does*. Science, however, is concerned to account for everything that happens in terms of other happenings ("causes") in the physical world. The chain-mesh of cause-and-effect is far from complete; but missing links are continually being found, and most nineteenth-century scientists saw no obstacle to its eventual completion.

What then of the God of action? This was the real question underlying the great debate. Did science, in its ever-filling picture, leave any room for God to act? To many scientists the idea of God seemed obviously a mere stopgap for want of scientific knowledge of what they would call the "real causes" of events. Some of the ablest theologians encouraged this belief by desperately searching for weakness in the scientific theories they regarded as competitive – performing in the process a valuable service to science, but fated to be squeezed from one untenable position to another under the pressure of accumulating fact. The very momentum of their retreat contributed to the general impression that the Christian faith was no longer credible for an honest and well-informed Victorian.

Changes – relevant and otherwise

What has happened between then and now to account for the different outlook today? Changes there have been in plenty. First, and most spectacular, has come the complete revision of our scientific notion of the physical world, culminating in Heisenberg's notorious *Principle of Uncertainty*. According to this, the "elementary particles" of the universe (electrons and the like) are fundamentally unpredictable in their motions. Either the speed or the position of an electron may be determined as exactly as we please – but not both exactly at the same time. At any one time we have to make a compromise, accepting less precision in the one specification if we demand more in the other. The average behaviour of large enough numbers of particles, like the average numbers of births or deaths in a large community, can, of course, be predicted more accurately, so that the dynamics of objects as large as billiard balls or planets are unaffected; but the Victorian dream of a "clockwork universe" of fully-predictable processes has been shattered.

I have begun with this particular change, not because I think it is crucial to the Christian position, but because I think it is not; and I fear that some – though by no means all – apologists have been tempted to make more of it than they should. Heisenberg's principle does establish a certain kind of incompleteness in the scientific picture which we are far from understanding; but the "gaps" it indicates are not at all of the kind for which nineteenth-century theologians were looking; and in any case I hope to show that a fully biblical doctrine of God's activity is made logically neither more nor less credible by such developments.

The second big change – in part a consequence of the first – is in the *mood* of scientists. By contrast with the jaunty confidence of the last century, it could, I think, be fairly described as "chastened". Particularly in the physical sciences, cocksure dogmatism has given place to a much more cautious and tentative way of presenting conclusions. Arrogant postures may occasionally be struck by a few exponents of the newer sciences, such as molecular biology and anthropology; but these attitudes are widely deplored by fellow scientists as atypical. It is sometimes said that the bankruptcy of classical physics, revealed by the discoveries of atomic phenomena, discredited Victorian materialism. For its logical implications I believe this makes too strong a claim; but at the psychological level I think it is profoundly true. These discoveries, from within science itself, have done much to recall us in science to a proper professional humility.

There have been changes, too, on the other side. I am not thinking now of the various attempts to compromise, in the name of "modernism", by abandoning unpalatable biblical doctrines and biblical authority. I believe such a compromise to be neither necessary, nor, in the long run, self-consistent. The lesson that all Christians have learned, however, is that what may seem the "obvious" way to interpret biblical material is not always the most reverent; that true reverence for the Bible requires a positive effort to avoid misinterpreting it. Sometimes it may even be scientific observations that God uses to warn us when we are pressing a literal scientific interpretation on a non-scientific idiom (as when Copernican astronomy came up against the official geocentric interpretation of passages such as Psalm 104:5). It has never been doubted by orthodox Christians that the same God was the Author of true discoveries in the book of nature as well as in the book of Scripture. But instead of arguing, as some did a hundred years ago, that this rendered scientific enquiry superfluous on matters dealt with in Scripture, Christians today are more alive both to the dangers of trying to use Scripture for purposes which it is not intended to serve, and to their responsibility, in God's sight, for following up the full implications of the knowledge he gives in these other ways.

The second big change – or rather, reformation – on the Christian side, has been in the understanding of what is meant by God's activity in relation to our world. Like all true religious reformations, this has been marked by a revival of emphasis on what the Bible actually has to say, as opposed to what it was thought to say or expected to say. In forcing this re-examination of thought-models, the nineteenth-century conflict has been an undoubted blessing. The trouble was that both Christians and non-Christians at that time had slipped into thinking of God as a kind of *machine-tender*. Partly under the influence of deistic notions, and of such stock works of apologetic as Paley's *Evidences*, they were tacitly agreed in adopting a mental picture of the world as a great machine, with God (if he existed) supervising its workings from outside. Divine activity in the world (if any) would then be possible only if parts of the machine were open to non-mechanical influence. Hence the importance attached to "gaps" in the chain-mesh of physical cause-and-effect, to enable God to intervene without wrenching a part of the (presumably perfect) machinery.

Undoubtedly, there are various biblical idioms which could be taken in isolation to justify this mental picture (e.g., Genesis 2:2; Psalm 102:25); and indeed, for practical purposes, it embodies an important truth, that God's normal pattern for his world is regular and reliable as clockwork. No single image need be expected to do justice to all aspects of his relationship to the universe, and it may well be asked why such a time-honoured (if relatively recent) thought-model should be set aside. An image has had its day, however, when its power to illuminate is exceeded by its power to mislead; and in our time this would seem to be abundantly true of the picture of God as a machine-tender. It is not that it cannot be stretched *ad hoc* to fit the biblical data it purports to embody, but rather that the *expectations* it evokes are radically out of key with much of what the Bible has to say about God's activity. Instead of finding a ready place within its framework, concepts such as creation or miracle appear as disconcerting "difficulties", felt by non-Christians at least to be vaguely incoherent with the rest of the picture they are offered. Worst of all, the whole facet of biblical teaching that deals with God as immanent in the events of nature is made to seem quite unintelligible.

For when we look at it more closely, the Bible as a whole represents God in far too intimate and active a relationship to daily events to be represented in these mechanical terms. He does not come in only at the beginning of time to "wind up the works"; he continually "upholds all things by the word of his power" (Hebrews 1:3, NASB). "In him [i.e., Christ] all things hold together" (Colossians 1:17). Here is an idea radically different from that of tending or interfering with a machine. It is not only the physically inexplicable happenings (if any), but the whole going concern that the Bible associates with the constant activity of God. God is the primary agent in feeding the ravens, or clothing the lilies (Luke 12:22–28, NASB); it is he who is active in the "natural" processes of rainfall and of growth; and even wicked men depend on him for their existence (Matthew 5:45) and serve his purposes (Acts 2:23). The whole multi-patterned drama of our universe is declared to be continually "held in being" and governed by him.

Divine upholding

What sense can we make of this unfamiliar idea of "holding in being"? Obviously it describes a mystery that we need not expect to understand at all fully; yet unless we can make something of it we cannot come to grips with its relation to our scientific and everyday ways of thinking about the world, which is our present concern.

To start with a negative, it is clearly meant to warn us against precisely the error we have been discussing, of reducing God to the status of a machine-tender. While insisting on the genuine distinction between God and his creation, the Bible throughout regards his activity as essential to, and visible in, all its continuing processes. Can we find a mental image that will do more justice to this relationship? We need not expect to invent a perfect analogy; and if I venture to suggest a possible thought-model it is only because I have found that it helps to tie together a range of biblical and scientific ideas somewhat wider than those covered by the earlier image, though still inevitably limited.

An imaginative artist brings into being a world of his own invention. He does it normally by laying down patches of paint on canvas, in a certain spatial order (or disorder!). The *order* which he gives the paint determines the *form* of the world he invents. Imagine now an artist able to bring his world into being, not by laying down paint on canvas, but by producing an extremely rapid succession of sparks of light on the screen of a television tube. (This is in fact the way in which a normal television picture is held in being.) The world he invents is now not static but dynamic, able to change and evolve at his will. Both its form and its laws of change (if any) depend on the way in which he orders the sparks of light in space and time. With one sequence he produces a calm landscape with quietly rolling clouds; with another, we are looking at a vigorous cricket match on a village green or a baseball match in a great stadium. The scene is steady and unchanging just for as long as he wills it so; but if he were to cease his activity, his invented world would not become chaotic; it would simply cease to be.

I do not in fact know anyone with sufficient dexterity to perform such feats at the required speed; but that is beside the point. I have sketched our hypothetical artist at work because I find this process quite a helpful illustration of some of the ways in which the Bible talks about God's activity in physical events.

Suppose, for example, that we are watching a cricket match "brought into being" and "held in being" by such an artist. We see the ball hit the wicket and the stumps go flying. The "cause" of the motion of the stumps, in the ordinary sense, is the impact of the ball. Indeed, for any happening in and of the invented scene, we would normally look for – and expect to find – the "cause" in some other happenings in and of that scene. Given a sufficiently long and self-consistent sample, we might in fact imagine ourselves developing a complete predictive *science* of the cricket world displayed before us, abstracting "laws of motion" sufficient to explain satisfactorily (in a scientific sense) every happening we witness – so long as the artist keeps to the same regular principles in maintaining the cricket scene in being.

Suppose, however, that someone suggests that our scientific explanation of these happenings is "not the only one", and that all our experience of them owes its existence to the continuing stability of the will of the artist who shapes and "holds in being" the whole going concern. However odd this may sound at first, it is obvious that in fact he is not advancing a *rival* explanation to the one we have discovered in our "science" of the cricket field; he has no need to cast doubt on ours in order to make room for his own, since the two are not explanations *in the same sense*. They are answers to different questions, and both may, in fact, be entirely valid.

The parallel I think is clear as far as it goes. The God in whom the Bible invites belief is no "cosmic mechanic". Rather is he the Cosmic Artist, the creative Upholder, without whose continual activity there would be not even chaos, but just nothing. What we call physical laws are expressions of the regularity that we find in the pattern of created events that we study as the physical world. Physically, they express the nature of the entities "held in being" in the pattern. Theologically, they express the stability of the great Artist's creative will. Explanations in terms of scientific laws and in terms of divine activity are thus not rival answers to the same question; yet they are not talking about happenings. They are (or at any rate purport to be) complementary accounts of different aspects of the same happening, which in its full nature cannot be adequately described by either alone.

Before we turn to work out some of the implications of our illustrations in more detail, it may be well to make clear what is *not* implied by it in this inadequate form. The human artist's invented world is unreal; but what God does is the only ultimate reality there is. The human artist's world is presented to us on a screen, of which we are merely powerless spectators. In God's world, however, we are part of the scene, brought into being as active participants as well as observers. Nor are we mere puppets. We contribute by our own decisions and actions to the total drama, and God rightly holds us responsible for the part we play, even while our existence in it is wholly dependent upon him.

In these and doubtless other respects, then, the illustration is deficient and could be misleading in its turn; but while some of the deficiencies can, I think, be remedied, there is no need for our present purpose to complicate the thought-model. Its function is not (heaven forbid!) to explain the mystery of God's activity, but only to bring out some of the features of the biblical idea of it which seem to have been neglected in disputes where God was presumed to be a "machine-tender".

Prior to an enquiry into the truth or falsehood of the Bible's claim, there is a real need in our day to get clearer in mind what is, and what is not, being claimed. If the biblical notion of "holding in being" is at all akin to that which we have been considering, then the whole relationship between scientific and biblical analysis of "causation" has to be reappraised. To argue hotly, for example, as some of our fathers did, whether something "came about by natural causes *or* required an act of God", is simply not to take seriously the depth and range of the doctrine the Bible is asking us to consider. To invoke "blind chance" as if it were an *alternative* to the action of God in creating us, as Professor Jacques Monod does in his book *Chance and Necessity*, similarly misconceives the Christian doctrine of creation and providence. For what in science we term "chance events" are recognized in biblical theism as no more and no less dependent upon the sovereign creative power of God than the most law-abiding and predictable of happenings (Proverbs 16:33). It may be fair enough to express personal hostility to this doctrine; but it is theologically inept to pretend that science as such has any quarrel with it. The trouble here (to quote J. B. Phillips) is that our ideas of God have not been too big, but too small. Admittedly, the revision of our conception of "reality" which the Bible calls for is far-reaching; but it is half-measures here that in the recent past have proved theologically disastrous. In the remainder of this paper I hope to bring out, with the help of a few key illustrations, the remarkable harmony of scientific and Christian belief which reappears when the nineteenth-century misunderstanding is replaced by a more thorough-going biblical emphasis.

Origins

Our first example may appropriately be the classical question of origins. As soon as we absorb the force of the biblical doctrine of God, it becomes clear that there is not just one question of origins, but two: one "internal", the other "external".

To enquire into the "origin" of the cricket match on our artist's screen, for example, may be to ask *either* about the earlier pattern of happenings in the world of the cricket field that must presumably have led up to the scene we are now witnessing, *or* about the artist's originative activity, without which there would be no happenings at all. The first kind of "origin" we might be able to infer in principle from scientific or commonsense observation of the happenings in the scene, the state of the scoreboard, and so forth, extrapolating backwards from as many clues as we could pick up. The second, however, we should never expect to determine in this way. It is, of course, concerned in a sense with the past; but it is concerned to account for the past (and the present) of the scene as a whole – as a phenomenon, so to speak – rather than with a unique moment in it. Only if the created scene contained some clues relating to the artist who is shaping and holding it in being could his existence, and the origin of the scene in this sense, even be discussed within *its* own framework. If it were so discussed, the appropriate term for its creation would certainly be the biblical *ex nihilo*.

In relation to our own world as God's creation, much debate in the past seems to have arisen from a confusion of these two questions of origin. Cosmology, on the one hand, is concerned to extrapolate backwards in time on the presumption of continuity, and to picture the initial situation (if any) to which the present state of affairs would form a "natural" sequel. The Bible, on the other hand, claims to be the clue to the origin of the world in our second, quite different, sense; not to its origin in time, but to its origin in eternity. Its basic concern is to reveal the nature and purposes of the Giver of the pattern we encounter as the physical world.

Even the first chapter of Genesis, despite its narrative form, makes clear, I think, that scientific "history" is not what it means to convey. Its pictures – especially if their details are studied in contrast to pagan myths of the time – teach something quite other, and deeper, than cosmology. They tell us "who" and "why", and the metaphysical order of priorities, rather than "how" in the physicist's sense. It may be worth while to substantiate this point in some detail, for too many people, including some "modernist" Christians, have been apt to speak of Genesis 1 as a "primitive attempt" by its writer to guess at what science has now revealed. In point of fact, the very structure of the Genesis narrative should have precluded this interpretation, since the story ends its creative period of six "days" with a complete, going universe, in which the writer clearly intended us to picture trees and animals, for example, more than six days old. Logically, then, the Genesis narrative resembles an account of the way in which an artist brings his scene into being; it leaves entirely *open* the field of investigation we call "cosmological origins", which must be determined by empirical examination of the scene – God's universe as created. Nor is there any suggestion that the past so determined – still less the present – is only "apparent" or "illusory": it is *the only past there is,* in the sense that science gives to the term. As Augustine put it long ago, God's creation is not *in tempore* but *cum tempore*: our scientific scale of time, extending backwards into the inferable past, is one of the intrinsic properties of the created order, and the biblical notion of creation as imaged in Genesis 1 is grossly distorted and diminished if it is restricted to a happening locatable at a point on the timescale, as if this were the point behind which scientific extrapolation must be impossible. The relationship of the divine Creator to our world is still more comprehensive, and the Bible's claim is in fact a bolder one. To draw a crude metaphor from our earlier illustration, Genesis 1, read at its face value, appears to narrate not just the inferable past of the "cricket match", but rather the artist's decisions as to the kind of match it should be. I do not pretend that this is at all a clear notion, except insofar as our own experience of "creative activity" (e.g., in writing) may afford some dim analogy.[1] But I see no reason to make any more complicated claim for the narrative such as (by reading the "days" as aeons of geological time) that it represents a disguised version of the past that the scientist can discover. The intention of such speculations is often the excellent one of harmonizing scientific discovery and inspired Scripture; our suggestion is only that the Scripture here *is not answering the same question,* so that to try to make it do so is to do it violence. It needs to be defended not against "science" but against well-meaning (or any other) attempts to make it into "science".

By the same token, it would seem that any attempt to find support for the Christian doctrine of creation in "explosive" theories of cosmology (which trace things back to a "big bang") and to oppose the "steady state" theories of Hoyle and others on *religious* grounds, would be misguided. The internal cosmological past of God's world is presumably "implicit in" its present structure by him, and he will expect us to look for it there with unprejudiced eyes, since we cannot specify in advance which kind he should have "written". The most we can say *a priori* is that nothing can happen or have happened in our world that is inconsistent with the character of its Author.[2] Steady-state cosmologies may have some objections to face on scientific grounds, but they would seem to have none *a priori* in the Christian doctrine of creation.[3]

My contention then is not that the narrative here should be read literally (since I do not know what it could mean if one tried to), but that it should be read for what it is – a revelation of the *metaphysical* origins of our world – and not as either a "primitive guess" or an inspired cryptogram on the *scientific* question of the cosmological past. Only in this way can we clear our minds for the depths of meaning that in faith we believe it to hold, for us just as much as for our less "scientific" forebears.

Obviously this leaves a problem of identifying the transition in the biblical record from the "divine history" of origins, to the "natural history" of our created order. I have no intention of suggesting a clear-cut solution, for I do not believe that the transition itself is clear-cut. I want only to contend for the reality and necessity of the distinction.

What has been said about physical origins would seem to apply equally to questions of the origin of man's sense of moral values. Conflict can surely arise here only if our two questions of origin are confused. On the one hand there is the technical scientific question of the inferable past history of man's moral ideas; on the other, the theological question of their divine givenness or otherwise. Data are so sparse that present "evolutionary" answers to the first question may be far wrong; but if they are wrong, there would seem to be no biblical reason to doubt that there is *some* answer to it in terms of mechanism which is right. I have already suggested that on closer examination the narrative in Genesis is not logically framed to supply us with an answer of this sort; its concern is within the second question. From the biblical viewpoint, to argue whether a sense of values developed naturally or was divinely given is to accept a false antithesis. To invoke "natural processes" is not to escape from divine activity, but only to make hypotheses about its regularity; and the historical development of a perceptual mechanism, whether in the single individual or in the race, is quite a different matter from the origin and validity of what is perceived. (For example, we cannot settle the validity of our ideas on geometry by discussing the embryological origin of the brain!)

Undoubtedly there have been some anti-Christian biologists who thought – and claimed – otherwise; but the biblical answer to such men would seem to be to question, not their science (unless for scientific reasons!), but their confounding of the metaphysical origin of ethics with the physical or psychological origin of man's "ethical mechanisms". Space does not allow a full discussion of the biblical doctrine of man; but inasmuch as the Bible regards man as a psychophysical unity, it implies that *some* physical account of the development of each of his faculties in their mechanical aspects is necessarily required, as the complement to the revealed facts of their divine origin. Even complete continuity of physical development would not, of course, preclude discontinuity of spiritual nature between man and other animals. To use a simple analogy, the proportion of gas to air in a burner may be increased continuously until the mixture suddenly sustains a flame. But when this happens we have a qualitatively new entity, the flame with a dynamics of its own, and with nothing to correspond to it in the earlier stages. Similarly, even in a continuous theory of human evolution (if anyone wants to speculate along these lines) one would have to reckon with the likelihood that the growth of a truly "human" pattern of organization, in the brain of the first true man, would be a self-catalysing process, raising him at one bound to a qualitatively new spiritual capacity inconceivable to his predecessors. My aim is not to recommend such speculations, but simply to emphasize the appropriateness of "reverent agnosticism", here as elsewhere, admitting our ignorance when conclusive evidence is not supplied either by revelation or observation.

Natural laws

A second example of the biblical approach illustrated here concerns the notion of the "natural law". As long as the world is thought of as a kind of machine, natural laws are bound to have something of the character of invisible cogwheels and levers. As soon as we move to the more dynamic thought-model illustrated by our artist and his screen, however, the notion of law takes on quite a new aspect.

In the cricket field on the screen it is possible to discover numerous examples of orderly behaviour that could be subsumed under general "laws". Quite possibly, as already mentioned, we might develop a successful deterministic science of the behaviour we are watching. As long – but only as long – as the artist's activity maintains the required regularities, our predictions should succeed. If his pattern were to change, or to fluctuate irregularly, our predictions might be upset, to a greater or lesser degree. But – and this is the point – the presence of such unpredictable happenings is not in the least *essential* to our belief that the whole scene of activity is held in being by the artist. In particular, whether the "natural laws" we discover in the scene are deterministic or indeterministic (i.e. statistical) *makes no difference* to our belief that it has a Creator who is in control of it. This belief does not rest on that kind of evidence.

Perhaps you see now why I insisted earlier that it is a mistake to harness Heisenberg's principle to Christian apologetic. For here, too, the question whether physical laws are deterministic or indeterministic in the scientific sense is irrelevant to the Bible's claim that they betoken the continuance of God's maintaining "programme". Thus whereas some have argued that only an indeterministic physics leaves *room* for God to act in our world, while others, like Monod, see the element of randomness as *eliminating* the possibility of divine control, biblical theism, if I understand it correctly, accepts neither of these mutually cancelling arguments. For the Christian, as we have noted, the events we classify scientifically as "chance" are as much divinely given as any others; and natural law is primarily an expression of God's faithfulness in giving a succession of experience that is coherent and predictable. "While the earth remains, seedtime and harvest, cold and heat, summer and winter, day and night shall not cease" (Genesis 8:22, esv). Thus the common saying that God can "use" natural means to achieve his ends, while undoubtedly true in its intended sense, suggests by its wording quite the wrong relationship of God to natural law. It would seem more correct to say that God sometimes achieves his ends in *"natural" ways* (i.e., in ways that do not upset precedent from a scientific point of view). God is not like a man, *using* his laws as tools that would exist independently of him; it is he who brings into being and holds in being the activities, whether scientifically "lawful" or otherwise, that we may recognize to be serving his ends.

Once his programme has reached its final consummation, moreover, we are told that the whole of the present world shall be "rolled up like a scroll", to give place to something unimaginably better (Isaiah 34:4; 2 Peter 3:13).

Miracle

Discussion of natural law leads directly to the problem of miracle. The old objection to miracles was that they involved God in tampering with his own mechanism – an intervention which was pronounced either scientifically impossible or theologically improper, according to taste. Against the full biblical doctrine of the natural world, however, the objection loses any force it had. In the first place, while the biblical concept of natural law, as we have seen, supplies the highest reasons for normally relying on our scientific expectations, it renders meaningless any notion of "scientific impossibility" where God is concerned. Just as even an ordinary television picture may be unimaginably altered at the turn of a switch, so God's world is entirely open to change at his will.

The last phrase, however, which might seem a gateway to all irrationality, embodies, of course, the most vitally important safeguard. Since the stability of God's will is declared to be the origin and foundation and standard of all rationality, no change that he sees fit to make in his "programme" could ever be *capricious*. He it is who makes and maintains the whole of his creation "a cosmos, not a chaos". Some of his actions at special turning-points in history may have been astonishing to us, and his sovereign will does abide our question; but we are never encouraged to regard them as irrational. This forms a crucial distinction in principle between biblical miracle and magic.

The Bible always presents a miracle, however physically surprising, as the *self-consistent* expression, at that particular point in history, of God's unchanging faithfulness to the purpose (however inscrutable) for which he has brought the whole pattern of events into being. Even of the central miracle of Christ's resurrection, Peter says that it was *impossible* that death should hold him (Acts 2:24). Appropriateness and rationality (as seen from the standpoint of eternity, though not necessarily manifest to us) are declared to be of the essence of the biblical concept of miracle. The Christian has no warrant to believe in a God of caprice.

It follows from all this that a biblical miracle is made neither more nor less credible by attempts (however well-intentioned) to find a "natural" process to account for its physical manifestations. What makes a miracle is not primarily its violation of scientific expectations (though this might be one result), but rather its function as an outstanding sign of God's power and purpose in the situation to which it comes. In some cases this might require nothing that need have shocked a scientist as such, the significance being in the timing rather than the manner of events; in others, if the record is to be read at its face value, it seems hard to deny that the normal *pattern* of events was radically altered. In every case it is clear that the event could not have fulfilled its communicative purpose unless it had been out of the ordinary in some sense for those concerned. My point is simply that the God of biblical doctrine would have no difficulty in bringing about the one kind of event any more than the other; but that the biblical doctrine nevertheless provides a more stable, rather than a less stable, foundation of our normal scientific expectations, in the stability of the will of a God who is always faithful.

The ground of faith

All I have said thus far is in one sense merely permissive. I have shown, I hope, that the biblical doctrine of divine activity is not only compatible with our scientific knowledge, but also positively encouraging to the attitude towards natural events that we call scientific. At most, however, all such demonstrations can make

Christianity only plausible. They are bound to leave us still with the question whether it is true, and how we can be convinced that it is.

Before concluding, then, we must return briefly to the point made at the start: that faith, like scientific belief, is a kind of trust that is based on personal experience as well as on testimony judged reliable. Christian faith is not just a body of second-hand beliefs, however self-consistent – not even if acquired from the Bible itself. Its essence is an active, day-to-day relationship of personal dependence on and obedience to the Giver of our daily round as he has revealed himself and his will in Christ and Scripture, in fellowship with other Christians – a relationship which both illuminates, and is illuminated by, the doctrines from which it is inseparable.

Neither personal experience divorced from biblical doctrine, nor intellectual acceptance of doctrine divorced from experience and practice, can sustain faith in the biblical sense. It is the day-to-day personal confirmation that God is as good as his word given in the Bible, together with the intellectual outworking of the implications of God's acts and purposes revealed there, that combine and interact cumulatively to grip the heart and mind and will with the authoritative conviction we refer to as faith.

I should perhaps emphasize that by "experience" here I am not referring to the esoteric feelings of the mystic, which are often taken as the paradigm of the "religious experience". I mean rather something which at the psychological level may be quite prosaic and ordinary, though different from sensory experience of the external world: namely, the whole realm of our moral experience, at the level of willing and choosing. "Whoever is willing to do the will of my Father," said Jesus, "shall come to know of my teaching whether it is from God" (John 7:17). To know the authoritative grip of God's will on one's conscience need involve no abnormal psychological phenomena; but it is the kind of experience that gives empirical content to otherwise theoretical talk of a personal relationship with him. It is not, of course, a matter of uncritically renaming in pious terms all that everyone experiences at this level. This would be mere superstition, akin to the reading of "messages" in an undisciplined sequence of words from a dictionary. In Christian doctrine God's promise to make himself known to us in personal experience is conditional on our approaching him by the way and in the spirit that the Bible indicates – ready for any consequence of discovering and following the purpose for which he has brought us and our whole world into being. This is no "nodding acquaintance", for there are deep things to be settled between each of us and God. By nature we prefer purposes of our own quite at variance with his; and for anyone who takes God at his word such unfamiliar concepts as repentance, atonement, forgiveness and grace turn out to have a definite operational significance that may hurt even as it heals.

But my purpose now is not to expound the Christian gospel. It has rather been to bring out something of what I meant by saying at the beginning that faith differs from scientific belief, not in its standards of truth but in its mode of origin. Essential checks against undisciplined subjectivism exist in the biblical revelation itself and in the testimony of fellow Christians past and present; hence in part the importance that has always been attached to intelligent study of the Bible, and to the fellowship of Christians in the church. It is only within this objective framework that the Christian's experience in stumbling obedience can validly grow into the astonished conviction that his faith is the sober truth.

Conclusion

We are emerging from a period of confused conflict during which the biblical doctrine of divine activity seems to have become largely distorted or forgotten. It is in this doctrine, untrimmed by any concessions to the spirit of our age, that I see the basis of the deepest harmony between Christian faith and the scientific attitude. There could be no better basis for our scientific expectations than the rationality and faithfulness of the One who holds in being the stuff and pattern of our world.

Notes

1. For a brilliant essay on this theme see Dorothy Sayers' *The Mind of the Maker* (Methuen, 1941)

2. This does not of course imply that we can deduce the character of its Author solely from what we are able to see in his world. The doctrine of the fall indicates that the whole present "programme" as we encounter it bears the marks of our chosen relationship of rebelliousness towards its Giver, so that apart from Christ's revelation of God's "eternal purpose" we could go hopelessly astray to his nature.

3. In justice it should be said that the essence of this point seems to have been appreciated by the much-ridiculed Philip Henry Gosse, FRS, who is best remembered for suggesting that God created the rocks with the fossils *in situ*. Certainly Gosse seems to have given his contemporaries the impression that "the creation" was a datable event a few thousand years ago on our timescale; and in this I have no wish to defend him. But, with all his faults, I think he showed more insight into the logic of the Genesis narrative than opponents such as Charles Kingsley, who held that on Gosse's theory the Creator had perpetrated a deliberate falsehood by creating rocks complete with fossils. For whatever the peculiarities of Gosse's view, the point apparently missed by Kingsley is that some kind of inferable past is inevitably implicit in any system, whether with fossils or without, so that to speak of "falsehood" here is to suggest a non-existent option. Creation in the biblical sense is the "willing into reality" of the whole of our space-time; future, present and past. If the Creator in the Genesis narrative were supposed to have made the rocks without fossils, this would not have helped, for nothing could have prevented the rocks from having some physically inferable past: their past would simply have been different, and moreover inconsistent with the rest of the created natural history. On Kingsley's argument, pressed to its logical conclusion, God ought not to have created any matter at all, since even molecules cannot help having some inferable past history!

Suggestions for Further Reading

There are many books about the relationship between science and faith. A number of the contributors herein acknowledge their debt to C. S. Lewis, particularly his *Mere Christianity* (most conveniently available in a 2012 reprint from William Collins). Other apologetic books are *Basic Christianity* by John Stott (IVP) and *Simply Christian* by Tom Wright (SPCK).

Classical books on the relationship between science and Christianity include:

Barbour, I. (1966), *Issues in Science and Religion*, SCM

Berry, R. J. (ed.) (2012), *Lion Handbook on Science and Christianity*, Lion

Coulson, C. A. (1955), *Science and Christian Belief*, Oxford University Press

Henry, C. F. H. (ed.) (1978), *Horizons of Science*, Harper & Row

MacKay, D. M. (reprinted 1997), *The Clockwork Image*, IVP

Ramm, B. (1954), *The Christian View of Science and Scripture*, Eerdmans

There are very many more books on the subject. For starters:

Alexander, D. (2001), *Re-Building the Matrix*, Lion

Alexander, D. (rev. ed., 2014), *Creation or Evolution: Do We Have to Choose?*, Lion

Alexander, D. & White, R. S. (2004), *Beyond Belief*, Lion

Berry, R. J. (2003), *God's Book of Works*, T&T Clark

Collins, F. (2006), *The Language of God*, Free Press

Falk, D. (2004), *Coming to Peace with Science*, IVP

Haarsma, D. & Haarsma, L. D. (2011), *Origins*, Faith Alive

Houghton, J. T. (rev. ed., 2007), *The Search for God: Can Science Help?*, Regent College Publishing

Hummel, C. E. (1986), *The Galileo Connection*, IVP

Jeeves, M. A. & Berry, R. J. (1998), *Science, Life and Christian Belief*, Apollos

McGrath, A. E. (rev. ed., 2009), *Science & Religion: An Introduction*, Blackwell

McLeish, T. (2014), *Faith and Wisdom in Science*, Oxford University Press

Miller, K. R. (2007), *Finding Darwin's God*, Harper Perennial

Montgomery, D. R. (2013), *The Rocks Don't Lie*, W. W. Norton

Polkinghorne, J. C. (1998), *Science & Theology: An Introduction*, SPCK

Poole, M. W. (3rd ed., 2007), *User's Guide to Science and Belief*, Lion

Southgate, C. et al. (eds.) (2nd ed., 2005), *God, Humanity and the Cosmos*, T&T Clark

Ward, J. F. K. (2008), *The Big Questions in Science and Religion*, Templeton

White, R. S. (2014), *Who is to Blame? Disasters, Nature and Acts of God*, Lion

Histories of the relationship between science and faith:

Brooke, J. H. (1991), *Science and Religion: Some Historical Perspectives*, Cambridge University Press

Harrison, P. (1998), *The Bible, Protestantism and the Rise of Natural Science*, Cambridge University Press

Hookyaas, R. (1972), *Religion and the Rise of Modern Science*, Scottish Academic Press

Rios, C. M. (2014), *After the Monkey Trial*, Fordham University Press

Russell, C. A. (1985), *Cross-Currents: Interactions between Science and Faith*, IVP

Of the making of books there is no end: there are many other studies of particular topics, many of them concerned with the ethical implications of scientific advances – evolution, environment, determinism, energy, medical dilemmas (particularly the beginning or end of life). But the above list is a starting point for anyone wanting to read further.

Index of Bible References

Gen 1 35, 214, 220,
    248, 253, 284, 333,
    334
Gen 1:26-27 214
Gen 1:26-31 248
Gen 1:28 220
Gen 2:2 327
Gen 2:15 143
Gen 3:17 94
Gen 8:22 73, 338
Gen 9:3 283
Gen 9:8–17 97

Ex 3:2 75
Ex 20:11 214
Ex 23:10–11 146

Lv 25:1–13 146
Lv 25:23 94

Dt 10:17–18 234

Jos 3:15–16 73–74

1 Kg 3:9–12 222

Jb 38 283

Ps 8 153, 230
Ps 8:4 153
Ps 24:1–2 94
Ps 34 201
Ps 54:4 201
Ps 102:25 327
Ps 104 98, 143, 326
Ps 104:5 326

Ps 104: 24–30 98
Ps 111:2 219
Ps 121:4 214

Pr 3:13 222
Pr 16:33 332

Is 6:1 82
Is 55:8–13 102
Is 65:18–20 238

Jer 12:4 94

Ez 34:17–19 99

Hos 4:3 99

Mt 5:45 328
Mt 6:33 299
Mt 10:29 32
Mt 11:28 119
Mt 16:3 32
Mt 22:35 122
Mt 28:19–20 220

Lk 3:1 82
Lk 8:17–18 240
Lk 12:13–48 220
Lk 12:22–28 328
Lk 12:48 290
Lk 19:12–27 220
Lk 20:9–18 220

Jn 3:16 143, 206
Jn 7:17 341
Jn 14:6 161

Acts 2:23 328
Acts 2:24 77, 340
Acts 17:23 47
Acts 17:25–28 72

Rom 1:18–20 95
Rom 7:19 154
Rom 8:19–22 94
Rom 8:19–23 99
Rom 12:4–7 138

1 Cor 8:13 140

2 Cor 5:17 95

Phil 2:1–11 252
Phil 2:3–4 241
Phil 2:6–8 52

Col 1:15–20 99
Col 1:16 68
Col 1:16–17 72
Col 1:17 328
Col 1:19–20 94
Col 3:17 201

1 Thes 5:17 34, 95

Heb 1:3 206
Heb 11:3 11, 214
Heb 13:8 73

2 Pet 3:13 339

Rev 3:20 211
Rev 5:13 95
Rev 11:18 99

Index

Abortion 233, 304–305
Adam 79–80, 228, 247–48, 283–84
     place 74–75
Adam and the Ape 214
Adaptation 193, 264–65, 274, 280, 287
Addison, Joseph 50
Affective computing 308, 317
Agnosticism 46–47, 106–107, 115, 118, 179, 278, 337
Alexander, Denis 104, 239, 250, 253, 288, 288, 344
Altruism 113
Amphibia 86, 88, 91, 93, 95–97, 103
Ancient repetitive elements (AREs) 130–31
Animism 143–44
Anthropic Principle/phenomenon 26
Antidepressants 148, 152
Apes 214, 228, 266
Artificial intelligence 315
A Rocha 86, 94, 145
Astronomy 14, 30, 51, 54, 65, 83–85, 133, 196, 198–203, 207–209, 243, 326
Astrophysics 54, 58
Atheism 9, 12–15, 17–20, 45–48, 54–56, 59–60, 107, 110, 114–115, 118, 133, 141, 157, 178–79, 182–85, 190–92, 194, 246, 248, 250, 256, 270, 272, 276–77, 279, 284, 292–93, 308, 319–20
Atheism, new 9, 277
Augustine, Saint 24–25, 249, 334

Bancewicz, Ruth 174
Barker, Monty 148, 161
Barfield, Owen 269
Battle for the Mind 148, 293

Bauckham, Richard 224
Believing in God 185
Berry, R.J. (Sam) 103, 194–95, 210, 216, 224
Beyond Science 288, 298
Bible and Ecology 224
Biodiversity 86, 93, 96, 103, 195, 276
Black holes 30, 54, 58, 60, 62, 198
Blind Watchmaker, The 180
Bohr, Niels 106
Bonhoeffer, Dietrich 167
Botany 136–38, 140, 142, 144
Boyle, Robert 46
Brainwashing 293
Briggs, Andrew 39
Briggs, George Wallace 51
Brosius, Jürgen 256–58, 271, 274
Burgess Shale 255, 259–63, 275
Burning bush 75

Cambrian "explosion" 255, 259–61, 263, 268, 274–75
Camera-eyes 263–64
Cancer 18, 35–36, 124, 185, 259, 306
Carlyle, Thomas 258
Christian Ecology Link 145
Christians in Science 136, 209–210
Cavendish Laboratory 39–40, 49, 219
Causes 10, 168–69, 246, 324, 331
Chaos 29, 38, 82, 187, 194, 305, 330, 339
Clerk Maxwell, James 39
Climate change 28–29, 35, 94, 96–97, 145, 182, 219, 240, 251–53, 276
Clockwork 72, 325, 327, 344
Clockwork universe 325
Code of Environmental Practice 220
Cognition 266
Cognoscere 164, 168

Collins, Francis 49, 104
Computer model/analogy 28, 37
Contingency 181–82, 186, 190, 192, 228, 230, 256, 274
Conway Morris, Simon 48, 255–56, 274–75
Conservation 86–87, 89–97, 99–103, 140–41, 176, 181–82, 185–86, 190, 196, 219–20, 285, 292
Convergence 48, 255, 263–66, 268
Copernicus, Nicholas 133
Coral reefs 96
Cosmic artist 330
Cosmic Designer 46
Coulson, Charles 22, 27, 49, 53, 344
Counter-culture 252, 311
Creation, Book of 10
Creationism 47, 78¬–80, 128–30, 215, 223, 248, 256–57, 289, 293
Creationism, Young Earth 248
Credulity 131, 217, 223, 262, 320, 322, 324
Creed, Nicene 174
Crucifixion 56–57, 82–84, 120–21, 192, 213
Cystic fibrosis 104, 123–24

Darwin, Charles 9, 13, 53, 112, 128, 131–32, 139, 179–80, 194, 211, 215, 222, 256, 259, 261–62 265, 274, 289, 324
    funeral 222
Darwinism 13, 128, 132, 256, 274
Dawkins, Richard 12–13, 18–20, 27, 56, 180, 182–83, 193, 195, 250, 262, 272, 275, 281, 293
Days (in Genesis) 69, 146, 214–215, 223, 249, 282–83, 334
Deism 17, 45–47, 118, 327
Designer, Cosmic 46, 48, 130
Determinism 28–30, 150, 217, 337–38, 346
Diamond, Jared 262–62, 275
Dictamnus albus 75
Dirac, Paul 106
Disasters, natural 251–54

DNA 104, 107–108, 122–25, 127–28, 130–31, 187, 228, 232, 242, 290, 294
Dobzhansky, Theodosius 131, 134
Dominian, Jack 153
Done, Christine 10, 54
Dualism 155, 158, 230–31

Earth, age of 78–80, 247–50
Earthquakes 74–75, 208, 239, 241, 243, 245, 247, 249, 251–53
Ecology 90, 94, 137, 142–43, 145–47, 180–82, 184, 187–89, 191, 193, 195, 210, 215, 222, 224, 276–77, 280, 283, 285
Ecosystem 10, 86–87, 96, 277, 285
Ecclesiastes 153, 160
Einstein, Albert 22, 106–107, 114, 132
Embryos 111, 212, 230–32, 264, 305, 336
Emergence 19, 24, 41, 80–82, 121, 154, 165, 184, 249, 257, 261–63, 266–68, 278, 282, 284
Evidences for Christianity 327
Evolution 18–19, 21, 24, 47–48, 65–66, 69, 78, 81–82, 109, 113, 118, 127–29, 131–32, 134, 137, 139, 141, 159, 176, 179–82, 184, 188, 192–94, 204, 213–215, 219, 221–23, 229, 248–50, 255–57 259–69, 271, 273–75, 280–84, 288–89, 293, 308–309, 312, 320, 324, 329, 336–37, 344, 346
Exoplanets 207
Extinction 86–87, 92–93, 96–97, 103, 181–82
Eyes, camera see Camera-eyes

Fall 94, 269, 283, 343
Faraday Institute for Science and Religion 174, 239, 250–51, 253, 288, 306
Flood 252, 283
Fossils 29, 35, 80–81, 128, 247, 259–62, 343
Fossil fuels 29, 35

Fossil record 128
Four Loves, The 113
Freud, Sigmund 156, 159, 297
Fuels, fossil see Fossil fuels

Gaia 190, 195
Galactosemia 108
Galton, Francis 222
Gaps, God of the 22
Gaps, explanation of 22, 325¬–27
Genesis, Book of 35, 49, 69, 73, 79,
     81, 94, 97, 143, 180, 185, 192, 204,
     210–211, 213–215, 217, 219–20,
     221, 223, 248–49, 253, 282–84,
     327, 333–34, 336, 338, 343
Genetics 37, 104, 107–108, 122–24,
     130–31, 141, 148, 150, 158, 193–
     94, 210, 212, 214–215, 222, 228,
     230, 248, 288, 294, 303–306
Genome 49, 104, 108, 122–31, 228,
     274
Geology 80, 213, 239, 243–44, 246–
     47, 259, 261, 275, 334
Geophysics 74, 239, 243–44, 307
God and Evolution 214, 223
God Delusion, The 12, 195, 275
God of Surprises 190
God of the Gaps see Gaps, God of the
God's image 35, 214, 220, 227–228,
     241, 248
Gore, Al 135, 276
Gosler, Andrew 176
Gosse, Philip Henry 80, 343
Gould, Stephen Jay 18, 27, 261–63,
     275, 287
Gray, Patricia 267

Hacking, Philip 10
Healthcare 253
Heisenberg, Werner 106, 325, 338
Holloway, Richard 150–51
Hominids 248
Homo sapiens 111, 192, 247
Houghton, John 28, 38, 195, 275, 345
Human Genome Project 49, 104,

108, 124–27, 130, 228
Human evolution 127, 131, 283, 309,
     337
Humphreys, Colin 64, 172
Huxley, Thomas Henry 9, 46–47,
     106, 180, 211–22

Image, of God see God's Image
Immanence 190, 215, 221, 328
Immune system 265–66, 275, 306
Inconvenient Truth, An 276–77,
     279–87
Information theory 187
Insurance policy 9
Intelligent Design 47–48
International Council for Bird
     Preservation (ICBP) 90, 103
International Union for the
     Conservation of Nature (IUCN)
     219
Interventionism 46. 48, 75, 78, 116,
     211, 217–218, 305, 339
Islam[ist] 300, 302, 311

James, William 22
Johnson, Phillip 47
Jordan, River 73–75
Joshua 73–75

Kerr, Warwick 141
Kepler, Johannes 11, 73
Kingsley, Charles 343

Language 111, 268–69, 275, 316
Language of God, The 49, 104, 125,
     345
Law, moral 111–112, 114–115, 118,
     131
Law, natural 132, 337–39
Law, physical 30, 330, 338
Lewis, C.S. 21, 53, 110–113, 120–22,
     134, 190, 237, 269, 271, 281–82,
     344
Limits of Science, The 9, 17, 68, 184
Limits to science 9, 16–17, 29, 68
Logos 52, 269

Lorenz, Edward 29
Lovelock, James 195

McGrath, Alister 12, 193–94, 345
MacKay, Donald 10, 195, 217, 291–92, 197, 322, 344
Mace, Georgina 92, 103
Marsupials 263–64
Marx, Karl 12, 301
Medawar, Peter 17, 184–85
Mere Christianity 110, 134, 281, 344
Metaphysical Society 47
Metaphysics 10, 17–18, 47, 177, 186, 190, 256, 270, 273–74, 333, 335–36
Meteorology 28–29, 32
Methuselah 284
Milky Way 30, 207–208, 229
Miller, Jonathan 72
Miracles 53, 59–60, 71, 73–76, 78, 215–218, 222–24, 272, 279, 323, 328, 339–40
Miracles of Exodus, The 76
Missionary earthkeeping 144
Modernism 112, 181, 194, 246 326, 333
Moore, Aubrey 135
Moore, Gareth 185
Moral law *see* Law, Moral
Monod, Jacques 81, 332, 338
Moses 75–76
Music, animal 267
Music of Life, The 18, 27, 193–94
Mystery of the Last Supper, The 84

Nanotechnology 40–41, 162–65, 167, 168, 171–73, 175
NASA 54, 60
Natural disasters 252–53
Natural law *see* Law, Natural
Natural theology 23, 46
Nebelsick, Harold 217
New Age 143, 146, 220, 272
New atheism *see* Atheism, new
Newton, Isaac 73

Newton, John 165, 175
Nicene Creed 174
Noble, Denis 18–20, 27, 193–94
Neonatology 225–27

Ohm's law 70–71
Oldroyd, David 256–57, 274
Ollason, John 280, 287
Omphalos 80
Optimality 193, 280, 287
Origen 249
Origins 47, 132, 150, 264, 332, 334–35, 345
Origin of Species, The 139, 180, 211
Ornithology 86, 90–91, 176, 179, 183, 188
Out-of-body experiences 270
Ovid 154

Packer, J.I. 159
Paediatrics 108, 225, 303
Paley, William 327
Peacocke, Arthur 131, 134, 290, 297
Pentecost 77
Personhood 232, 236
Physics 15, 28–29, 31, 39–40, 43, 53, 58, 60, 62, 65, 106, 196–97, 199–200, 225, 235, 242–43, 267, 278, 281, 314–315, 326, 338
Picard, Rosalind 8, 10, 308
Pikaia 263
Pippard, Brian 39
Plato(nism) 26, 52, 112, 267
Polanyi, Michael 22
Polkinghorne, John 133, 135, 194, 345
Pollution 28, 95, 145, 182, 198, 219, 221
Population 97, 129, 132, 215, 219, 252, 256, 258, 261, 277, 285, 300
Poverty 113, 168, 192, 219
Prance, Ghillean 136, 140
Prayer 28, 30, 32–37, 47, 57, 93, 116, 119, 137, 144, 164, 178, 197, 200–203, 243, 297

Preimplantation diagnosis
Problems of Evolution, The 184
Proverbs 222, 309, 313, 332
Psychiatry 148–61, 288, 294–97

Quantum computing 41–45

Radda, George 21
Radioisotope dating 300
Raffaelli, David 10, 276
Ramsey, Ian 23
Rebuilding the Matrix 288
Reductionism 43, 113, 156–57, 248, 293, 296–97
Relativism 151, 246
Rendall, Robert 222
Resurrection 36–37, 53, 56, 66, 71, 76–77, 120–21, 161, 192, 206, 216–217, 271–73, 275, 323, 340
Russell, Bertrand 14, 56
Russell, Colin 190
Rutherford, Ernest 40, 219

Sabbath 136, 145
Sanctity of life 59, 111, 192
Sargant, William 148, 156, 293
Sayers, Dorothy 64, 271, 343
Schaeffer, Francis 168–69, 174, 292
Science, limits to *see* Limits to science
Scientism 148, 160, 262, 273–74
Secularism 257, 301–302
Selection [Darwinian, natural] 112, 128, 131, 194, 215, 280–81, 283
Selfish Gene, The 18, 27, 182–86
Shannon, Claude 41–42, 187–88, 195
Simpson, George Gaylord 261–62, 275
Singer, Peter 233
Species, rare 88
Star of Bethlehem 83
Stewardship 141, 145, 219–21, 286
Sticklebacks 129
Stratigraphy 256

Stuart, Simon 86, 100, 103
Surprised by Hope 190
Surprised by Joy 190
Swinburne, Richard 26

Temple, William 190
Tennyson, Alfred 15
Test of Faith, The 174
Theism 26, 46, 49, 151, 256, 332, 338
Thermodynamics 42, 107, 168–69, 290
Transcendence 17, 187, 215, 221, 228–29, 269–70
Tree of life 69, 128
Tsunami 252
Turing, Alan 42
Turkey 298–302, 305
TV, as analogy

Uncertainty Principle 325
Ussher, Bishop 79

Value, contingent 186, 190
Value, intrinsic 182, 186, 189–90
Value of life 184, 186, 237
Vanauken, Sheldon 115
Volcanic eruptions 198, 252

Watchmaker, Divine 215, 218
Watson, Jim 125, 127
Westminster Catechism 212
White, Lynn 146
Weather 28–29, 32, 245, 306
White, Robert 253, 306–307, 344
Williams, Harry 155, 161, 271
Wiseman, Jennifer 10, 196, 199
Wonderful Life 261–62, 275
Wood, John 10, 162–63
World Conservation Strategy 219–20
Wright, Tom 190, 271, 344
Wyatt, John 225

Young Earth Creationism *see* Creationism, Young Earth